New World, New Church?

New World, New Church?

The Theology of the Emerging Church Movement

Hannah Steele

scm press

© Hannah Steele, 2017

Published in 2017 by SCM Press
Editorial office
3rd Floor
Invicta House
108–114 Golden Lane,
London
EC1Y 0TG

SCM Press is an imprint of Hymns Ancient & Modern Ltd
(a registered charity)
13A Hellesdon Park Road
Norwich NR6 5DR, UK

www.scmpress.co.uk

British Library Cataloguing in Publication data

A catalogue record for this book is available
from the British Library

978 0 334 05490 0

Typeset by Manila Typesetting Company
Printed and bound by
Ashford Colour Press Ltd.

Contents

*This book is dedicated to my Dad who
taught me more about
love for Christ and his church than I could
ever learn from books.*

I

What is the Emerging Church?

Introduction

Christians throughout the ages have been faced with the issue of how the church is to relate to its surrounding cultural context and what its message and role should be in challenging times. The decline of institutional Christianity in the West at the start of the twenty-first century has propelled many within the church to attend to that task with renewed urgency.

I first became interested in this subject through my own involvement in mission activity in a church experiencing growth and change in South East London. While my own personal engagement was more associated with the mission-shaped church, or 'Fresh Expressions' movement as it later came to be called, it was the frequent appearance of the phrase 'emerging church' that most captured my imagination. This term 'emerging church' seemed to gain rapid momentum over a very short period of time through its blogs and conferences, but at the same time it has been anathematized and even, more latterly, declared redundant by some.

Of all the approaches being offered about how the church could and should relate to postmodern culture, the one being presented by the emerging church, and primarily American voices such as Brian McLaren and Tony Jones, seemed to be calling for the most radical change. It was this group, described in this book as 'the emerging radicals', who, of all the writers engaging with the relationship between church and culture, seemed unafraid to challenge the settled assumptions of evangelicalism in order to explore the possibility of creative and alternative ways of being and doing church. However, the speed with which this conversation was taking place, and the rapidity with which publications were produced and absorbed, raised serious questions for me about the nature of its cultural engagement and how much theological critique was taking place. While this book seeks to chart the emerging church's remarkable journey from a conversation of like-minded innovators to its current widespread popularity and represents my own intrigue and interest in this movement, it also endeavours to contribute something to this ongoing conversation.

As time progressed and the emerging church was gaining popularity, I also became aware of the lack of published evangelical responses to the movement. Although there had been articles and collections of essays, no comprehensive theological response had been offered. Donald Carson was the exception to this rule, although his response focuses on the emerging church's epistemology, which is arguably only one aspect of its contribution, and does not reflect the impact of the emerging church on the future shape of the church. My exploration of the theology of the emerging church seeks to offer an appraisal of both the strengths and the weaknesses of its cultural and theological engagement, drawing out what is to be learned from its approach while also questioning its broader theological engagement.

My conviction is that the emerging church finds its origin as a protest movement within evangelicalism, with its protest oriented against the perceived assimilation of modern values into its theological and ecclesiological expression. While protest movements can often symbolize *Kairos* moments for change within our ecclesiastical patterns and structures, leading to renewal and even revival, such movements can also tend towards the establishment of a reactionary theology that is in danger of throwing the proverbial baby out with the bathwater.

While protest movements can deliver prophetic and timely challenges to institutions resistant to change, it is not always clear how they then relate to the very tradition from which they have emerged and in which they are calling for change. Such movements can also be difficult to classify since it is often clearer what they are against rather than what they are for.

This provocative phrase from Brian McLaren seems to go to the heart of what this movement is all about.

'You see, if we have a new world, we will need a new church.'[1]

This statement raised questions for me: are we really in a new world? If we are, does the church need to reimagine itself entirely? And what might a theology for that new church look like? As I continued exploring the emerging church I discovered that its protest was mainly against three areas of theology: eschatology, missiology and ecclesiology, and that it offered revision of its theology within these categories. These three disciplines seem to be most crucial in establishing the shape and future of the church in the world today. Furthermore, these three areas cannot be viewed in separate silos; it is their interrelation that enables us to imagine and grasp both what the church is and what the church could be in the world today. The majority of this book will therefore deal with these three critical theological themes, exploring both that which is gained and that which is lost in the emerging protest and revision of each of these areas.

The issues that the emerging church raises are of great significance to the future of evangelicalism – if not to the future of Christianity in the West. The need to address the role of the church has perhaps never been more urgent or challenging a task than in the current cultural climate. The plethora of books and publications seeking to address this very subject make that undertaking all the more challenging as, increasingly, we are pulled in different directions. The emerging church's contribution to the debate is a hugely important one. The rising popularity of its publications and the sell-out tours of its protagonists are evidence of a movement that is raising questions that resonate with many, both within and outside evangelicalism. Evangelicalism cannot dismiss the emerging church as merely another model of how to do church, as the nature of the revolution it offers is far more serious than that. While some question whether the emerging church as a movement exists any more, nevertheless the ideas and conversation raised by its originators continue to gain momentum and acceptance.

It is my contention that evangelicalism must listen and respond to the theological protest and revision being offered by voices within the emerging church. The questions that it raises are too important to be ignored and some of the proposals that it offers have the potential to change the shape of western Christianity in the immediate future. Galvanizing a generous yet scrupulous critique of this movement is one of the most pressing responsibilities facing evangelicalism. My bold hope and prayer is that this book will play some small part in contributing to that most critical and urgent task.

The origin of the emerging church

While pinpointing the start of the emerging church is not easy, the protagonists within the movement refer to a seminal moment that took place in 1995 at the Leadership Network gathering in Colorado Springs. In a seminar on how to reach young people, Brad Cecil suggested that the postmodern writings of Derrida and others were critical to the missiological task of reaching Generation X.[2]

Tony Jones, who later became the first and only national co-ordinator of Emergent Village, described the impact this seminar had on Mark Driscoll, Doug Pagitt and others:

> (They) couldn't articulate it yet but they could feel it. It felt like the beginning of something new and the overthrow of something old. It felt to them like the burgeoning of a whole new way of understanding who they were as Christians. And they knew that they needed to do something about it. They began travelling the country looking for others who got it.[3]

The inception of the emerging church cannot be confined to this one single incident, any more than the Reformation can be confined merely to Luther's nailing of the 95 theses to the church at Wittenberg; nevertheless such events play an important role in deciphering what lies at the heart of these movements for renewal. The Colorado Springs incident indicates three significant factors in the inception of the emerging church conversation: the first is that it arose out of missiological concern; the second is the importance to the emerging church conversation of the shift from modernity to postmodernity; and the third is that it was catalysed by dissatisfaction with the current state of modern American evangelicalism. Tony Jones describes this initial group as 'a group of church misfits and cast offs', most of whom had 'cut their teeth in mega-church evangelicalism'.[4] This significant moment at Colorado Springs led to a burgeoning 'network' of shared ideas and conversation, and a corporate sense that if the church was to survive in the twenty-first century then radical change was required. The fact that this conversation progressed primarily through the social media of Facebook and blogs meant that anyone could 'write theology' for others to read and discuss. This represents a significant shift in how theology is communicated and adapted, also indicating the fast pace at which this movement has evolved.

While there remains conflict over what the term 'emerging church' actually represents, and some of its early protagonists have since disassociated themselves from it, I will continue to use the phrase and identify what I consider to be three strands of thought within it.

First, there are the 'emerging missioners'. These, I would argue, are represented by Dan Kimball and Scot McKnight who are missionally focused and whose primary concern is thinking comprehensively and intelligently about the culture of those 'outside' the church. They are looking at what creative and daring changes can be made to the way church is structured in order to reach out to those who would not darken the doors of traditional churches. Within Britain I believe that fresh expressions and the writings of Graham Cray and Michael Moynagh are examples of emerging mission that seek to look creatively at the way faith is expressed outside the traditional church format. The protagonists within the emerging missioners are church practitioners and evangelists.

The second strand of the emerging church that I have identified is the 'emerging ancients'. While this is perhaps the smallest of the strands, there would appear to be a shift by some groups within evangelicalism towards a discovery of the past. The emerging ancients seek to re-establish connection with the history and tradition of the church. The desire to link together imagination, contemporary culture and the Christian tradition is typical of the emerging ancients, and as an emerging strand it remains strongly ecclesiastical.

The third and final strand to be identified within the emerging church is what I have called the 'emerging radicals' and it is the impact of these writers that I am most interested in exploring here since they are the ones publishing most prolifically and proposing the most radical revision of eschatology, mission and church in our current context.[5] The emerging radical's assumption is that the pervasiveness of postmodernity calls for radical revision and not simply cosmetic adjustment. In many ways Tomlinson's publication *The Post-Evangelical* can be seen as a trailblazer for this more radical approach, particularly within the British context.

The individuals that I would consider of most influence within the emerging radicals are primarily Americans: Brian McLaren, Tony Jones, Doug Pagitt and Rob Bell. However, the British voices of Kester Brewin and Pete Rollins are, arguably, similarly influential. There are many other writers that I have consulted in gaining a full picture of what the emerging radicals believe, not least Phyllis Tickle, Nadia Bolz-Webber and others, yet the writings of these six men will be the primary focus of this book.

Important themes in the emerging church

Definitions of 'emerging church' are as varied as they are plentiful, and while some have rejected the use of the term 'emerging church' on account of its broadness, others have rejected it for its narrowness.[6] Pete Rollins refers to the nebulous nature of the emerging church and questions whether it can, or indeed should, be defined at all.[7] This diverse and fragmented nature, along with the resistance of its leaders towards 'labelling', makes the task of definition a challenging one.

The most comprehensive attempt to define the emerging church is the research of Eddie Gibbs and Ryan Bolger in *Emerging*

Churches: Creating Christian Communities in Postmodern Culture. Tony Jones himself suggests that there are three core characteristics of the movement: disappointment with modern American Christianity; a desire for inclusion; and hope-filled orientation.

From my engagement with the writings of these emerging radicals, I have identified three characteristics which provide insight into exploring what lies at the heart of this burgeoning movement: characteristics which express something of the context of the emerging church; the challenges in critiquing it; and the distinctive contribution that it offers to the wider church.

A movement of protest

The emerging church is a protest movement: a movement in reaction to many aspects of the perceived culture of evangelicalism, particularly the extent to which it is influenced and shaped by the values of modernity. In *The Church on the Other Side*, McLaren insists that one of the primary tasks of the emerging church is to rid the church of the 'vestiges of modernity'.[8] He lists the following ways that modernity has corrupted the church:

1 An emphasis on conquest and control.
2 Mechanistic ideas of faith and salvation.
3 Objective/reductionistic/analytical ways of studying the Bible.
4 Secularism.
5 Individualism.
6 Consumerism.

The language of protest is common currency in the emerging church, an attribute which has earned its advocates the appellation 'angry young white children of Evangelicalism'.[9] Gibbs and Bolger acknowledge that emerging leaders are often more clear about what they are emerging from than what they are emerging into.[10] The phrases 'redefining', 'reimagining' and 'rethinking' are common in emerging vocabulary. The desire to be distanced from modernistic evangelicalism is part of the emerging church's appeal. The statement on the Ikon website that 'D-O-C-T-R-I-N-E-is s-u-f-f-o-c-a-t-i-n-g- me' indicates the perception that modern Christianity is stifling and constrictive.[11] In addition, the following quote by McLaren illustrates the remorseful tone in which the emerging radicals refer to the church under modernity and the harshness with which they regard its failings:

> I often think that one of the greatest gifts we Christians could give to Jesus would be just to shut up about him for a few years, during which time we would try to come to terms with what a mess we have made of the simple path that he introduced to planet earth.[12]

The emerging radicals regard relevancy as the erroneous priority of the mega-church movement with its 'celebrity pastors' who sought to 'lure back' the 'seekers' of the baby boom generation.[13] The attempt by the seeker-sensitive movement to make church relevant and accessible is chided by emerging radicals as failing to make any impact on Generation X, the children of the baby boomers, among whom the emerging radicals count themselves. The emerging radicals believe that these approaches are evidence of evangelicalism's complicity with modernity:

> What we're trying to do is say, 'We've already over accommodated to modern culture. We've commodified our message; we've turned our churches into purveyors of religious goods and services.'[14]

The emerging radicals are not reticent in acknowledging the extent to which their own church backgrounds give rise to their current protest; the quantity of anecdotes that cite painful experiences at the hands of fellow believers is substantial.[15] Furthermore, the unpleasant responses some have received from others within the Christian media have further fuelled their protest.[16] By and large, the emerging radicals were brought up through the mega-churches and seminaries of American conservative evangelicalism.

Pete Rollins locates the error of the modern church in its alliance to reason.[17] He suggests that while the church rejected the anti-ecclesiastical slant of the Enlightenment, its high regard for reason was 'eagerly embraced' and the church ended up mirroring its 'underlying propositions'.[18] Rollins even suggests that the modern church is guilty of intellectual idolatry.[19]

At this point it is perhaps important to draw a preliminary distinction between the emerging church in the USA and its counterpart in the UK. What many emergers are protesting against is the concept of a Christian subculture which is epitomized in the pragmatism of the mega-church and its ability to create an entire consumer experience around the act of church attending. The emerging radicals dislike the mega-church's reliance upon the sacred/secular divide and its suspicion of anything that challenges that dichotomy. Within the UK, however, the disjunction between church culture and secular culture is arguably less and some would suggest that the church in the UK has been less suspicious of alternative approaches, perhaps particularly in terms of alternative worship which has co-existed with the mainstream church since its birth in the late 1980s.

The difference between these two contexts demonstrates that the emerging church scene in the USA is more protest oriented than its UK counterpart. While the outspoken comments of American evangelical leaders such as Pat Robertson or the late Jerry Falwell understandably create outrage among emerging radicals, one cannot imagine British evangelical figureheads having either the platform or the requisite sentiment for such polemic.[20]

Yet understanding the emerging church as a protest movement is of critical importance, since it cannot be evaluated without understanding the context from which it is emerging. Furthermore, the remonstrative nature of the movement fuels the rebel mentality upon which the emerging radicals thrive and through which they have gained popularity. Ikon's gathering on *Fundamentalism* at the Greenbelt festival was a case in point. The gathering was bombarded by fundamentalist protestors decrying Ikon: a protest which Rollins later revealed was deliberately staged to create effect. Several of the publications of the emerging radicals come with accompanying warnings about their radical and unorthodox nature, urging those of a delicate theological disposition to refrain from reading and citing stories of how their books have been outlawed by some conservative churches. The emerging radicals consider themselves to be orthodox heretics, uniquely aware of the cultural captivity of the modern church while the mainstream church remains blissfully ignorant.

It is in this way that the emerging church must be understood first and foremost as a protest movement, with the emerging radicals as rebels, pioneering a vision of a new and better future. It is my contention, and the heart of this book, that this protest is primarily against three particular aspects of evangelicalism: eschatology, missiology and ecclesiology. It is a protest against the eschatology of dispensationalism popularized in the *Left Behind* series, which promotes a negative outlook of the world and a limited view of evangelism. It is a protest against missiology that is limited by being defined in terms of evangelism and soul saving, where right belief is regarded as the criterion of acceptability. Finally, it is a protest against institutional ecclesiology, which is performance oriented, driven by a pragmatic and consumer attitude towards the shaping of church.

A fragmented movement

Second, attention must be given to the fragmented nature of the emerging church. The plethora of attempts to delineate the emerging church into various strands is evidence of its nebulous nature and its diversity. Its fragmentation is further evidenced by the multiplicity of labels used to define sub-groups within it, such as 'anglimergent', 'luthermergent', 'presbymergent' and 'queermergent'. The fact that such labels exist in a self-identified, post-denominational movement is an indication of the confusion surrounding this phenomenon. Stephen Hunt suggests that the fragmentary nature of the emerging church reflects the fragmentary nature of the postmodernity within which it is emerging. Hunt argues that there is no consistent typology of the emerging church and one must talk about tendencies rather than coherent characteristics.

In their book on the emerging church, Gibbs and Bolger make clear that the emerging church is not a homogenized movement and there is much that falls under the breadth of the emerging banner. However, the lack of synthesis across the movement, not least in terms of the differences between its US and UK contexts, does not mean that commonality cannot be found. I have already suggested that the emerging church in its US incarnation is arguably more protest oriented than its British equivalent, but the influence of US emerging writings upon the UK scene cannot be ignored. Rob Bell's 'Love Wins' tour of the UK in 2011 sold out in a number of major venues, clearly demonstrating the popularity in the UK of the issues raised by the emerging conversation. In terms of influence, it is fair to suggest that the emerging church figureheads within the USA are more influential upon the UK context than vice versa. Hatch argues that this pattern of transatlantic influence has been a constant factor in the development of evangelicalism and that, from Finney and Moody through to Billy Graham, it is Americans who have 'mastered the common touch on both sides of the Atlantic'.[21] It would appear that protagonists within the emerging church, such as McLaren and Bell, continue this trend.

Roger Olsen argues that the emerging church must be properly understood as a movement rather than an organization, as its lack of centre and boundaries indicate. Understanding the emerging church as a movement means that it can be slippery and difficult to define, primarily identified by its shared interests and ideas rather than communal practices. Olsen argues that there is more than reasonable historical precedent for the influence of movements within evangelicalism, as the charismatic movement of the 1960s and the Jesus movement of the 1970s indicate. Movements, by definition, are flexible, dynamic and changing and 'every movement has its adherents who refuse to be identified with it'.[22] Notwithstanding the inherent difficulties of defining a movement, Olsen suggests that by surveying the ideas of those who self-identify with the movement, along with the scholars who support or critique it, it is possible to discern what common threads lie at the heart of the movement, without ignoring its lack of homogeneity.

One further aspect which makes the classification of this fragmented movement problematic is its open-ended conversational bias which finds restrictive labelling objectionable. The emerging endeavour is more often referred to as a 'conversation', a highly ambiguous and anti-polemical term, making critical engagement difficult and which can possibly be perceived as an attempt to dodge the issues of definition, as the following comment from McLaren exemplifies:

> Take for example, a word like 'salvation'. I would love us to have some very important conversations about what that term means. I am not raising this because I disagree with the Bible, but when I look at the Bible, I realise that salvation in the Bible isn't just getting souls into heaven. The word's meaning is much richer than that.[23]

The uncertainty inherent in the choice of word 'conversation' raises the question of whether it is merely stylistic consideration or whether it masks a more serious commitment to the postmodern premise that one cannot be certain about anything. The title of Rollins' book, *The Idolatry of God: Breaking our Addiction to Certainty and Satisfaction* indicates that it is a choice based on more than linguistic preference.

A movement responding to cultural change

The third and final characteristic that must be taken into consideration at the outset is that the emerging church is deliberately and self-consciously a response to cultural change. Central to the emerging church's raison d'être is the conviction that times have changed and that radical action is required if the western church is to survive in the twenty-first century. In this way, the emerging church finds itself taking part in a broader conversation taking place between the academy and the church about the predicted decline of institutional Christianity in the West. However, what is most distinctive about the emerging church's contribution to this debate is the positivity with which this cultural change is embraced and its potency to shape Christian faith and theology for the twenty-first century. The emerging church's relationship to culture will be explored more thoroughly in the following chapter.

The title 'emerging church' raises the question of whether the church is primarily emerging *from* something or *into* something. Its strongly protest-oriented stance indicates an emergence from inherited patterns of church. However, its positivity towards culture indicates an emergence into a new expression of church for a new cultural world.

Webber defines post-war evangelicalism in terms of three distinct groups: 'traditional evangelicals' (1947–1980), typified by the bastions of modern evangelicalism such as Billy Graham and John Stott; 'pragmatic evangelicals' (1980–2000), typified by the church growth movement of Willow Creek; and the 'younger evangelicals' which he believes emerge as the first breath of evangelicalism in the new postmodern world.[24] Webber sees the emerging church or 'younger evangelicals' as having a unique opportunity to respond to the cultural change taking place:

> The emerging church has the potential to establish a new kind of evangelicalism that will relate to the current cultural crisis.[25]

Webber's comment raises the important issue of how we should understand the emerging church's relationship to evangelicalism. Is the emerging church one further strand in an already fragmented evangelical movement or is it a deliberate attempt to create something entirely different? One thing is clear: the emerging church has evolved from evangelicalism, and this background drives the new direction it seeks to take. However, before exploring this new direction, we must consider how its evangelical context has catalysed its emergence and how it influences its theology and praxis. One could argue that, in many ways, the emerging church does not represent anything new, since evangelicalism has often operated as a movement that has sought to respond to its changing cultural context. However, a key question remains as to whether the emerging church is simply another example of evangelical desire to resonate culturally, or whether a bolder move is being made; that of allowing culture to shape and redirect the Christian message. A brief exploration of the history of evangelicalism can provide us with some understanding of how, as a movement, it has related to changing cultural contexts while also enabling us to discern some of the features which give rise to the current emerging protest. It is through understanding the emerging church as a protest movement that we are compelled to question where it now sits within the vastly fluctuating landscape of contemporary evangelicalism. Can we regard it as a movement of renewal within evangelicalism or simply another example of the faddism towards which evangelicalism tends to gravitate? Or is it, as some of its critics suggest, a more radical rupturing from its evangelical roots and even a departure from orthodoxy itself? Discerning the features which give rise to the emerging church's protest will enable us to understand why this movement resonates so strongly with many evangelicals. It can also enable us to explore to what extent the emerging church can be considered a genuine and faithful expression of evangelicalism and to what extent it signifies a significant departure from it. Exploring the broader historical background of evangelicalism itself will enable us to understand the theological trajectory from which this movement emerges and which, at points, it pits itself against.

The start of the evangelical movement: 1730–1790

It was the best of times, it was the worst of times, it was the age of wisdom, it was the age of foolishness, it was the epoch of belief, it was the epoch of incredulity, it was the season of Light, it was the season of Darkness, it was the spring of hope, it was the winter of despair, we had everything before us, we had nothing before us, we were all going direct to Heaven, we were all going direct the other way.[26]

England in the 1730s was a place of contrasts. While society experienced relative economic and political stability, crime was rife and the church on the decline, increasingly ridiculed by those in the upper classes. In rural areas, resources were spread so thinly that the church achieved minimal impact. Some have argued that the church had lost its way, 'unspiritual, discredited, useless'.[27] In this milieu of religious antagonism and apathy the conversion of John Wesley at Aldersgate Street on 24 May 1738 was a significant milestone, and the subsequent revival and renewal within the church marked the beginning of what was later classed as evangelicalism. When George Whitfield returned from the States having had a similar conversion experience, along with an exposure to the US-style mass open-air preaching, he enlisted Wesley for a similar-style ministry in the UK. Bebbington suggests that this kind of revivalism was 'bound up with a whole new cultural mood'.[28] From its early origins, we can understand evangelicalism as a movement which has always sought to respond to its cultural context with creativity and opportunism. The mid 1700s saw Wesley and Whitfield engaged in ceaseless open-air ministry across the length and breadth of the country, with Wesley reportedly preaching every day for eight months without reprieve. The aim of this horseback crusade was to cover as much ground as was physically possible, gathering people together in whatever venue could be secured, preaching a message of deliverance from sin to which thousands responded. Yet this ministry was not without its opposition; they were driven out of some villages and the church authorities refused to endorse this unusual ministry. This early evangelical movement had several characteristic features, which proved significant in the momentum and establishment of its influence, demonstrating further how evangelicalism can be understood as a movement responding both consciously and subconsciously to its changing cultural environment.

Commitment to change and flexibility
Prior to Wesley's itinerant ministry, the role of an Anglican clergyman was defined strictly within parish boundaries which would only be exceeded with the resident incumbent's permission. However, both his Arminian conviction of the urgency of the salvation of every man and woman and the relatively poor state of the pastoral ministry in many churches prevented

him from behaving within the confines that his rites of ordina-
tion dictated. The issue of parochial boundaries was something
over which evangelicals disagreed and played a significant role
in the secession of the Methodists from the established church
after Wesley's death.

By means of follow-up to the open-air preaching, many mid-
week societies were established, where further discipleship and
teaching could take place. Though these were expressly orga-
nized in such a way as not to distract from the mainstream
church, their existence indicates that, for many, institutional
Christianity was no longer fulfilling its function. This tendency
to initiate external societies and groups when faced with either
opposition from the mainstream institution or low resources
became part of the modus operandi for evangelicals. Flexibility
became a hallmark of this burgeoning new era of evangelicalism. Bebbington comments that it is in this way that the evangelicals employed the cultural changes which surrounded them:

> The spirit of the age – flexible, tolerant and utilitarian –
> affected Evangelicals as much in practice as in thought. Field
> preaching, an activity that lay near the heart of the revival
> was an embodiment of the pragmatic temper. If people
> would not come to church, they must be won for Christ in
> the open air.[29]

The preaching of lay women was similarly advocated upon pragmatic justifications, though this was in stark contrast to the
domestic expectations.

This period demonstrates the important role that pragmatism
played in evangelical ecclesiology. However, Hilborn suggests
that the evangelical preference for pragmatism can frequently
distract from the importance of theological reflection upon its
cultural context. The early evangelicals were not primarily aca-
demics concerned with the intellectual debates on ecclesiology,
but pioneering evangelists convinced of their missiological duty
who also found themselves within the established church. Their
concerns about ecclesiology were driven by practical concerns
necessitated by their primary allegiance to mission. It is in this

context that the evangelicals sought to work out their understanding of the relationship between their commitment to mission and their commitment to the church. For example, which was to be primary: a minister's obligation to preach the word of God or obedience to canon law? Such issues were not theoretical debates but worked out at the coalface of daily ministry, and maintaining the balance between evangelism and ecclesiastical allegiance proved to be an 'agonising task'.[30] This struggle highlights a tension between separatists and those who believe they should stay within mainstream denominations, a tension which has often surfaced in the history of evangelicalism.

Welcoming lay initiatives

Despite the high clericalism of the established church and its subsequent opposition, the co-option of lay preachers was deemed prudent in the immense task of the evangelization of the nation and became a hallmark of evangelical mission. Thus the evangelicals became increasingly confident in operation outside the parameters set by the established church. The elevation of lay participation is in some part due to the evangelicals' ability to harness and use their changing cultural context in which individual empowerment was key. While individualism became a feature of modern thought, for the evangelicals the badge of conversion became one of its defining features. Personal conversion was the focus of evangelical literature and teaching and 'the line between those who had undergone the experience and those who had not was the sharpest in the world'.[31] Brown argues that by placing prominence upon conversion the evangelicals demonstrated their indebtedness to their cultural background and the elevation of individualism during the Enlightenment.

> The conversion came to be the most powerful and widely understood symbol of individual freedom in late eighteenth and nineteenth-century Britain. In a society where equality in political democracy had still a century to run, the equality of the conversion was a powerful notion. It mobilised those most affected by economic and social change, and evangelicalism became associated with 'improvement'.[32]

The journey of the evangelical party is not one of dramatic growth and success and at times it appears faltering and dispersed. Initially the evangelical party struggled to maintain any significant foothold within the institutional church.

Strategic leadership

When certain evangelicals began to adopt a more strategic approach to leadership secession, evangelicalism began to establish itself as a major presence within both the Church and society at large.[33] Charles Simeon (1759–1836), during his 54 years as curate at Holy Trinity Church, Cambridge, prioritized public preaching, doctrine classes and also training others as preachers, and thus a large proportion of the future generation of evangelical leaders were trained at the pulpit of this one curate.[34] He also implemented the purchase of the patronage of over 100 parishes under the foundation of the Simeon Trust, ensuring continuity of evangelical leadership in many parishes.

Renewed corporate worship

Within evangelicalism, periods of renewal and growth have often been accompanied by a new language of hymnody. This early period witnessed the introduction of hymn singing in the place of metric psalms, exchanging biblical paraphrase for a freer, more doctrinally explicit and experiential form of corporate worship.[35]

It is through this renewed corporate worship that the impact of Romanticism upon evangelicalism becomes apparent, again demonstrating the strong link between evangelicalism and the spirit of the age.[36] Romanticism emphasized 'the importance of nature as a manifestation of beauty and the source of inspiration' along with a strong affirmation of the individual and the place of emotion and human intuition.[37] Isaac Watts promoted English hymnody that exchanged biblical paraphrase for a freer and more experiential form of corporate worship. Newton and Cowper worked together in producing the Olney Hymn book, used for congregational singing in both England and America. The influence of John Wesley's preaching on the English revival is well documented, but the hymns written by his brother Charles were an equally enduring legacy. The influence of Romanticism changed the nature of corporate worship and ensured that evangelical doctrine was widely communicated through its memorable and expressive song-writing. The promulgation of the evangelical message was also enabled by the proliferation of evangelical literature. Tracts and leaflets containing pithy summaries of religious doctrine were published along with the wide circulation among the poor of Hannah More's moral tales.[38] Such literature, along with other Christian journals and magazines, found its inspiration in evangelicalism's rejection of much of the mainstream literature of the day on account of its perceived immoral content. The foundation, in 1799, of the Religious Tract society was arguably significant in promoting the evangelical cause.[39]

Commitment to mission and social engagement

A further hallmark of the early stages of evangelicalism was the foundation of several voluntary societies which enabled a more strategic approach to missionary engagement both at home and abroad. Such voluntary organizations have always been 'the peculiar glory of the evangelical party'.[40]

The foundation of the Church Mission Society in 1799, and other similar societies, provided the evangelicals with an increasing sense of corporate identity and the opportunity to devote themselves to their two-pronged missionary endeavour of work among the poor and needy, and Gospel proclamation. Evangelical commitment to mission on a local scale drove them to establish a number of organizations operating nationally which attempted to unite and resource mission in Britain. In the first instance, the foundation of the London Missionary Society in 1795 was an example of pan-evangelical partnership which was not the normal Evangelical modus operandi. The most influential organization was the Church Pastoral Aid Society, founded in 1836, which, observing the increasing urbanization of the Industrial Revolution, sought to resource the church in an increasingly challenging task. There was nothing radical in its aims other than supporting small-scale localized gospel ministry, which the evangelicals had been prioritizing since Wesley. While the early evangelicals may have been loyal to the church, their greater commitment to gospel ministry trumped bureaucracy and made them unafraid to operate insubordinately for the greater good.

The nature of mission has been a contentious debate within evangelicalism, but the evidence indicates that evangelicals in the early nineteenth century adhered to a two-fold commitment: preaching of the Gospel for conversion along with a commitment to alleviate the suffering and its causes in the society around them. At the forefront of the pursuit of humanitarian reform was a circle of individuals, later known as the Clapham Sect, whose influence cannot be neglected in any exploration of how evangelicalism responded to its cultural environment.[41] By the dawn of the nineteenth century, evangelical influence was gathering momentum and it became apparent that there were a considerable number of MPs with evangelical sympathies, such as William Wilberforce and Henry Thornton.[42] The persistent devotion of such individuals to their cause, by now a hallmark of the evangelicals, was catalytic in several parliamentary acts and appeals, in the first instance the abolition of the slave trade, followed by the abolition of slavery within the British Empire.[43] A holistic concept of missionary discipleship and its social and political outworking must arguably be one of the chief characteristics of the evangelicals of this period.[44]

Alongside a two-fold commitment to social reform and persistent preaching of the gospel, evangelicalism was also characterized by a strong emphasis on personal piety.[45] Wesley's habit of early rising for prayer had become a model that many evangelicals followed along with a determined dedication to the eradication of personal sin and wickedness. Often self-sacrificial in their time and resources, 'worldly' leisure activities such as dancing or card-playing were considered at best frivolous and at worst evil in the light of the massive task of evangelization that lay before them. However, while evangelicals were by and large committed to personal renunciation of 'the world', there was at times a rather arbitrary delineation of what constituted 'the world'.[46] Notwithstanding some of the arbitrariness of its ethical stance, evangelical commitment to personal piety demonstrates that evangelical relationship to culture was not simplistic but involved a level of spiritual discernment. In its early stages, it was often in acts of personal holiness that evangelicalism found itself most at odds with the world around it.

This exploration of the beginnings of evangelicalism demonstrates that, from the outset, evangelicalism has been concerned with responding to the cultural environment in which it finds itself. This relationship is a complex and nuanced one in which evangelicals sometimes operate in antithetical reaction to their cultural context and sometimes in co-operation, and even participate as creators of wider culture themselves. In many ways, this has been a defining feature of the evangelical modus operandi. However, the origins of evangelicalism have been explored primarily within a British context and thus, since the emerging church arises predominantly within an American context, some attention must be drawn to how evangelicalism has related to American culture. I shall do this by exploring the period during the Second Great Awakening which further demonstrates both the complexity and the importance of evangelicalism's ability to discern the times.

The Second Great Awakening

Revivals played a significant role in the expansion of evangelicalism within America in the early nineteenth century, especially the Second Great Awakening. From 1795 to about 1810 there was a broad rekindling of interest in Christianity throughout America. This renewed interest provided a pattern of revival behaviour which continued throughout America until after the Civil War.[47] Wolffe argues that the most significant outcome of the tent meetings that took place during this revival was not purely the numerical expansion of evangelicalism, but the way in which these revivals bridged the gap between the church and wider culture, acting as a catalyst for 'collective acceptance of profound changes in the social order'.[48] Boyd Hilton's *The Age of Atonement* argues that the ethos of evangelicalism was similarly dominant in shaping the attitudes of the upper and middle classes in Britain during the first half of the nineteenth century. This is perhaps seen most clearly in the proliferation of evangelical philanthropic societies which sought to minister to various disadvantaged groups within society. Wolffe argues that, in this regard, wider changes within society were reflected in how the evangelicals operated:

> The expansion of evangelicalism concurrently with the development of larger, more anonymous urban communities helped to stimulate more organized philanthropy.[49]

While one must always resist the tendency to overgeneralize, Wolffe makes clear the evidence from recent scholarship which confirms that evangelicalism played a significant role in transforming society during this period.[50] Balmer argues that characteristic to evangelicalism in America has been its adaptability and pliability and that the 'genius' of its approach is seen in the ability of its leaders to 'speak in the idiom of the culture'.[51]

Arguably the most influential figure during the Second Great Awakening was Charles Finney, whose innovative and creative preaching style was driven by his desire to 'win souls' and his conviction that 'any talent, method or institution' could be employed to that end.[52] Although evangelism was of primary importance to Finney, he was also a keen abolitionist and an advocate of temperance and benevolence.

Finney is significant in any discussion which seeks to explore how American evangelicalism has related to its cultural context. Finney pioneered a more audience-centred approach to preaching, which was applied through his spontaneous preaching style, his use of the 'anxious bench' to elicit a response, and his vocal denouncement of the formal study of theology because he believed it 'produced dull and ineffective communication'.[53] Finney was happy to use what he considered to be the populist persuasive methods of publicity used by politicians and suggested that preachers should do likewise in order to properly gain attention:

> He is a crucial figure in American religious history. A bridge between cultures, he conveyed the indigenous methods of

popular culture to the middle class. As a transitional figure he introduced democratic modifications into respectable institutions.[54]

Hatch maintains that understanding American evangelicalism within its cultural context helps to demonstrate the difference between it and its UK counterpart. In a post-revolution America, the democratic and populist orientation has shaped and defined its religious expression also. This democratic impulse led to a greater innovative approach than that afforded to its British equivalents who were more constrained by hierarchy, institutional conventions and high culture:

> Americans who espoused evangelical and egalitarian convictions, in whatever combination, were free to experiment with new forms of organization and belief.[55]

Hatch argues that one of the features of religious movements that arose in the early nineteenth century was the impact of democracy and individualism upon their identity. The power of such movements is demonstrated in their 'ability to communicate with people at culture's edge and to give them a sense of personal access to knowledge, truth and power'.[56]

Balmer suggests that the Second Great Awakening demonstrates American evangelicalism's ability to relate to its cultural context not only in its form and praxis but also in its theological development. He argues that the post-millennialist theology which emerged at this time fitted the 'temper of the times' well, since it 'gave people the assurance that since they had recently taken their political destiny into their own hands, they also controlled their religious destiny as well'.[57] Balmer also suggests that this cherishing of individualism, along with the belief that one can create his or her own destiny, has been a lasting legacy within American evangelicalism and one that features in emerging eschatology also.

Just as pragmatism was noted as a feature of UK evangelicalism during its early stages, so Balmer identifies it as a feature of American evangelicalism also. In many ways Finney's approach is that of an exemplary pragmatist whose innovative and often spell-binding approach was well suited for the zeitgeist and 'assured all Americans that they controlled the mechanism of salvation, and the evangelical tradition has never been the same'.[58] The era of Charles Finney demonstrates the fact that evangelicalism has often operated as a movement that has sought to respond to its cultural context in a reciprocal manner.

Missionary engagement and cultural change

It is often in the case of missionary engagement that evangelicalism can most clearly be identified as a movement responding to cultural change, as the examples of Wesley and his counterparts and, latterly, Finney demonstrate. Further evidence of this principle can be seen in the latter half of the nineteenth century in the ministry of both Spurgeon and Moody. While Moody sought to be innovative in his preaching, often preaching to crowds of 40,000 people a week, he despised sensationalism. Moody's approach was less direct than that of Finney, as his adoption of the inquiry room in place of Finney's anxious bench demonstrates. Moody's 'inquiry room' was a place where spiritual seekers could sit and receive gentle counsel and prayer, in contrast to having to sit beneath Finney's piercing gaze.

Bebbington offers both Spurgeon and Moody as classic examples of his four characteristics of evangelicalism: biblicism, conversionism, activism and crucicentrism. Both these individuals played significant roles in establishing evangelicalism as a formidable force by the mid nineteenth century, although Spurgeon was arguably the more provocative of the two. Unafraid of controversy, Spurgeon often spoke out against the established church and rejected social convention and etiquette. Bebbington comments that the vigour with which Spurgeon criticized social convention is 'an indication of the potency of the social tide he was trying to hold back'.[59] A keen follower of Spurgeon, Moody was, however, less controversial, emphasizing storytelling and the love of God in contrast to more reformed approaches, even being accused by some of downplaying the need for repentance. However, in both the style and content of his preaching,

Moody's ministry reached and resonated with the masses, even the working classes.

Bebbington also argues that the growth and establishment of evangelicalism during this period was largely due to the synchronicity between the message being preached and the intellectual ideas of the day and that its influence was made possible partly because of its cultural resonance.

> Evangelicals in general shared the confidence of progressive thought in reason, a sifting of the facts and fresh achievements in science. That same set of premises that underlay expectations of the advance of human knowledge apparently provided a strong foundation for Christian belief.[60]

By contrast Spurgeon's approach was often more confrontational towards the dominant intellectual ideas, not least the uncertainty being generated by Darwin and the new intellectual discourse. Tate suggests that Spurgeon's strong emphasis on the assurance of salvation was, for many, a reassurance against such intellectual developments:

> His call to conversion offered escape from the zeitgeist of doubt and a sense of integration with the sacred narrative of the Christian Faith.[61]

Mission at the end of the nineteenth century occurred largely through open-air preaching and large-scale missions in which both Spurgeon and Moody set the pace. Evangelicalism continued to hold a high regard for overseas mission and the Cambridge Seven acknowledged the mission of Moody in Cambridge as being decisive in their call overseas.[62] The foundation and development of the Cambridge Inter-Collegiate Christian Union in 1877 also owed much to the Moody Missions of the 1880s. However, despite conversions of many academically able individuals, more attention was given to preparation for overseas mission than to developing a robust evangelical theology, which meant that evangelicalism failed to have any significant impact upon academic institutions of the day. As the divide between conservative and liberal became accentuated, so the evangelicals became increasingly ghettoized. The social-justice conscience, which had been a dominant feature in the philanthropy of Wilberforce and Shaftesbury, became neglected for several reasons. The increasing polarity between conservative and liberal evangelicals meant that issues of social conscience had become associated with a liberal agenda. Where evangelicals did express concern for social reform was mainly through nondenominational or interdenominational organizations. The greatest evils in society were no longer the terrible conditions of the poor or the unequal distribution of wealth but the immorality, excessive drinking and gambling, and it was these which became the focus of evangelical anti-propaganda. This differing opinion on social engagement highlighted other theological divergences, as those conservatives of a pre-millenialist position regarded the social gospel's propensity towards a post-millenialist belief in the steady establishment of kingdom values on earth as an unrealistic and unbiblical eschatology, a conviction which was confirmed by the proceeding two world wars.

> A high proportion of those who came out of its horrors with any strong Christian convictions were people of a clear biblical faith, and the liberal optimism about human nature was made to seem very implausible.[63]

The instances of nineteenth-century mission offered here demonstrate the important and often complex relationship that evangelicalism had with its cultural surroundings. However, notwithstanding the complexities, the simple point that evangelicalism has always been a movement seeking to respond to cultural change is clearly demonstrated through these examples. Therefore, in order to explore the emerging church as an evangelical movement which is similarly responding to cultural change, we must first of all consider the more recent historical context that has given rise to the emerging church and has in many ways laid the foundation for the protest which it now seeks to make.

Post-war evangelicalism 1940s-1990s

While the inter-war period was characterized by division and decline of evangelicalism, the post-war optimism of the 1940s and 1950s proved to be fertile ground for a new breed of evangelicalism to emerge and take prominence. Finstuen captures the spirit of the age as one of 'anxiety' about the possibility of a third world war and the state of the post-war economy.[64] Within this anxious climate evangelicalism, and indeed Protestantism itself, flourished as people returned to church, seeking hope amid uncertainty. It is from this mainstream visible and vocal movement that the emerging church eventually emerged in the late 1990s. In order to understand some of the impetus behind this emergence, I will consider several factors that influenced the shape and development of post-war evangelicalism, each of which contributes in its own way to reasons for the later emergence of the emerging church.

The intellectual development of evangelicalism

The post-war period witnessed the conversion and subsequent ministry of significant individuals who were to contribute greatly to the future expansion and development of evangelicalism. Integral to evangelicalism's development at this time was the ministry of Revd E. J. H. Nash, or Bash as he was familiarly known, and the intelligent and articulate individuals discipled through his public school camps, not least John Stott, David Watson and Michael Green.[65] Warner argues that the 'rationalistic conservatism' of the 'Bash Camps' was a lasting legacy within post-war evangelicalism.[66] The growth of the Bash Camps arguably contributed to the emergence of a more intellectually respectable form of evangelicalism which regarded academic rigour as a pursuable goal and was not fearful of engagement with secular academic disciplines.

This desire to engage intellectually with cultural and academic changes occurring is in stark contrast to the fundamentalist approach that emerged in the USA during the 1920s, which sought to distance itself from academic theology, focusing instead on internal ecclesiastical disputes. This pre-occupation with defending 'their corner' meant that evangelicals failed to take heed of the changing social and cultural tides and engage with issues that were to have far more penetrating influence and consequence, not least Darwin's *On the Origin of Species*. This failure meant that evangelicals were ill-prepared for the challenges of science and biblical criticism in the early twentieth century. This resulted in a crisis in evangelical confidence intellectually; a crisis epitomized in the detrimental media coverage of the Scopes trial in 1925 where the intellectual sophistication of agnosticism triumphed over evangelical naivety.[67] Fundamentalism emerged at this time in America and became known for its anti-intellectualism, with the Pulitzer Prize-winning author Richard Hofstadter describing fundamentalism as the antithesis of intellectual life.[68] Bebbington argues that fundamentalism had three main features: belief in inerrancy; a pugnacious manner; and repudiation of the intellect. Bebbington also observes that fundamentalism did not emerge in Britain with the force and presence that it did in America, a fact that proves relevant when considering the emerging church as a protest movement against it.

However, evangelicalism in the 1950s became known as an intellectually respectable movement, aided by the ministry of the Inter Varsity Fellowship (IVF) among students. Though a medical student, Douglas Johnson was influential in the inception of the IVF and in the development of a more credible form of evangelicalism, aided by his friend and mentor Dr Lloyd Jones.[69] Though never an evangelical, the writings and radio talks of C. S. Lewis served as a great reproof to liberalism and further strengthened the intellectual appeal of orthodox Christianity.[70] This surge in confidence was aided greatly by the rising number of evangelical theological publications produced through Tyndale House and the IVF's publishing house and also by the provision of theological training – for example with the foundation of the London Bible College in 1943 – for those wishing to pursue ministry opportunities.

The new breed of intellectually credible evangelicals that emerged in the 1950s were better equipped than their predecessors to face the voices of criticism both from within the church and the university. Thus, the publication in 1977 of both the collection of essays entitled *The Myth of God Incarnate* and Barr's *Fundamentalism and the Word of God* did not deliver the devastating blow that they might have done 50 years previously. Within the USA, the foundation of the Fuller Theological Seminary in 1947 established evangelicals' intellectual credentials, as evangelical leaders began to realize that establishing evangelicalism's academic credibility would be one of the keys to its survival in the latter half of the twentieth century.

While belief in pre-millennial dispensationalism had accompanied the rise of fundamentalism at the turn of the century, as fundamentalism dwindled in the latter half of the twentieth century, popular dispensationalism became increasingly fashionable. Its influence within evangelicalism is evidenced in the fact that the bestselling book in the 1970s in the USA was Hal Lindsey's *The Late Great Planet Earth*.

Perhaps the most noteworthy individual in post-war evangelicalism in the UK who influenced its rise to intellectual credibility was John Stott.[71] Although he shunned promotion to the church hierarchy, his parish ministry, with its emphasis on guest services, international student hospitality and lay ministry and training, became a model for many clergy. Stott represents the tenor of evangelicalism that emerged in this period in both his commitment to 'thinking' Christianity and in his commitment to personal evangelism and appeal for conversion. Perhaps one of his most lasting legacies to evangelicalism was his development of the idea of 'double listening' which sought to move evangelicalism away from becoming so absorbed with the word of God that it escaped into it in retreat from engagement with the outside world. He encouraged ordinary believers to listen to both the voice of God in scripture and the voices of those around them in the world in order to be authentic contemporary Christians:

> These voices will often contradict one another, but our purpose in listening to them both is to discover how they relate to each other; double listening is indispensable to Christian discipleship and Christian mission.[72]

Stott's commitment to 'double listening' meant that he contributed both to the development of evangelical doctrine but also, and perhaps more significantly, to the development of an evangelical response to important social and ethical issues such as abortion, sexuality and poverty. I will later explore how the emerging radicals' understanding of the way in which scripture relates to contemporary culture shapes their identity as a movement.

The growth of large churches

The post-war period also witnessed the rise of large evangelical churches; the modern belief that bigger is better meant that success became judged by numerical growth, leading to competition between churches.[73] The growth of the mega-church became a dominant feature of evangelicalism, especially in the USA, with Willow Creek being the prototype of a church which consciously sought to utilize the tools of marketing strategy to facilitate church growth. In 1989, Guideposts magazine awarded Willow Creek the high accolade of 'Church of the Year' which was followed up by an article in the *LA Times* describing Willow Creek as:

> One of a very few churches in the nation shaped by a targeted 'customer' survey. It is also a huge success: From a modest gathering of 125 people who first met in a rented movie theatre 14 years ago, it has grown to its current position as the nation's No. 2 Protestant congregation in terms of weekend attendance, second only to an independent Baptist congregation in Indiana.[74]

In the 1970s Bill Hybels began Willow Creek with the intention of making church accessible for those deterred by the dull and irrelevant nature of church. The services were stripped of the trappings associated with formal religion; vestments, altars, choirs and organs made way for multimedia technology and Christian rock bands mimicking the contemporary style. While radical in the 1970s, this approach became commonplace in mainstream evangelicalism 20 years later.

However, in 2007, in response to research done at Willow Creek and other churches within the same network, Hybels magnanimously made public the recognition that this approach failed to adequately disciple new believers.[75]

Rick Warren's Saddleback Community Church in Los Angeles is similarly influential as a mega-church with its website claiming that its congregation has grown from 200 members in 1980 to one in nine people in the local community who call Saddleback their home.[76] Warren's 'purpose-driven' ethos has gained global appeal with over 200,000 leaders being trained in its philosophy, which encourages readers to produce a purpose statement for life.[77] The most obvious examples of mega-churches are in America, but similar growth can be found in the UK with churches such as St Michael-the-Belfry in New York and Holy Trinity Brompton and Kensington Temple in London all experiencing significant growth during the 1980s and 1990s. While varied in theological perspective to a degree, many of these churches were influenced by the practices of the Church Growth movement, espousing a pragmatic and pro-grammatic approach to church life as a means of growth. The teachings of Donald McGavran, a third-generation mission-ary in India, can be regarded as most influential in establish-ing the church growth principle as a prominent trend shaping twentieth-century missiology. This particular understanding of evangelism as necessarily involving 'converts in churches', along with the elevation of evangelism rather than social action as the driving force in mission, has arguably shaped many of the aforementioned churches. Expediency was key, with any available tools employed in the task of church expan-sion; not least the twentieth-century tools of management and marketing strategy. Wells has been one of the harshest critics of this approach:

The growth and prosperity of Evangelical institutions during the 1970s and 1980s have brought with them much bureau-cracy and bureaucracy invariably smothers vision, creativity and even theology. Leadership is now substantially in the hands of the managers, and as a consequence the evangelical capital is not being renewed. The only semblance of cohesion that remains is simply tactical, never theological.[78]

David Fitch argues that the desire to create large congregations in which numbers signify success reveals evangelicalism's reliance upon two 'sacred cows' of the USA: 'the autonomy of the individual and the necessity to organize for economic efficiency'.[79] He argues that these values reflect more the principles of modernity than they do the values of the body of Christ and are evidence of evangelicalism's complicity with modernity. It is of immense significance that many of the emerging radicals were themselves nurtured in such mega-churches; their protest is very much against the impact of modernity upon those churches.

Impact of charismatic renewal

Another significant trend within evangelicalism in the second half of the twentieth century was the charismatic renewal and its subsequent effect on worship and the development of 'new' churches. Within the American context, the Episcopalian priest Dennis Bennett had a seminal influence in the USA and his subsequent book *Nine O'Clock in the Morning* became the textbook for those wishing to embrace the baptism in the Spirit experience and a freer expression of worship. Within the UK context, a similar experience was had by Revd Michael Harper while curate at All Souls Church in 1963. The impact of Pentecostalism transcended denominational boundaries, influencing Catholics, Anglicans and evangelicals alike; its influence upon evangelicalism wrought significant changes.

Where the charismatic movement held most significance was in the explosion of the house church movement which grew from the 1970s to the 1990s. For ecumenical charismatics, 'renewal' was the key word, indicating their belief in the possibility of change within existing denominations. However, for the house church movement the key word was 'restoration' as they sought the advent of a pure church which would reflect the authentic biblical church more than existing denominations could.

Bryn Jones became the figurehead for restorationists, influencing many who found the task of seeking renewal arduous to create new churches from scratch along Paul's five-fold ministry principle in Ephesians ch. 5. Thus the difference between renewal as advocated by the Anglican Harper and restorationism as championed by Jones was essentially a difference of ecclesiology. This desire for a new church was strongly linked with the eschatological belief in the end times as the locus of the restoration of the one true church, central to which was their belief in the reinstatement of the ministry of apostoles, of which Bryn Jones was considered the first. The Dales Bible Weeks in Harrogate attracted thousands and became the showcase for restoration ministry. The rapid church growth that Jones pioneered in Bradfield was replicated in the South through the ministry of Tony Morton, Terry Virgo and Dave Tomlinson. It is also important to observe that what was happening within restorationism in the UK was part of a much larger movement occurring in the USA pioneered in the 1960s by the Fort Lauderdale Five.[80] While they sought to implement their doctrines both within and without the traditional churches, emphasis on shepherding divided the American Renewal movement in two. Restorationism succeeded in establishing a significant number of new churches in the UK, but Walker suggests it declined from the mid 1980s. Walker attributes this deceleration in growth to the diminishing numbers of Christians defecting from other churches, along with the popularity of Spring Harvest as an ecumenical initiative.[81] Similarly, the popular ministry of John Wimber in the UK 'empowered' charismatics within mainstream denominations to stay put and embrace charismatic spirituality without some of the more dogmatic emphases of restorationism, with the emphasis being placed on a ministry of 'signs and wonders' rather than baptism in the Spirit. This also marked a shift in emphasis between those churches in the North of England that opted for a more authoritarian leadership style, more akin to the heavy shepherding legacy of the USA, and those in the South, among which there was a certain level of disunity and discontent with the direction and leadership of the movement. It is significant to mention here that one of those early restorationist movement leaders was Dave Tomlinson, who left the movement in the 1980s believing it had adopted an unhealthy ghettoized mindset regarding cultural change. David Smith suggests that part of the attraction of restorationism was that it provided an antidote to the moral decline of society and that the community and immediacy of restorationism was 'attractive to people who despaired of finding meaning in the secular city'.[82] Tomlinson's departure is significant because now, as an Anglican minister, his voice is heard as part of the emerging church's endeavour consciously to redress theological thinking in the light of cultural trends, in stark contrast to the House Church leaders whom Tomlinson suggested were reluctant to 'see evangelicalism dragged into the late twentieth century'.[83]

A secondary contribution of the charismatic movement to the development of evangelicalism that must be mentioned is the impact it had upon corporate worship and song-writing. Under the auspices of The Fountain Trust, spearheaded by Michael Harper and an American group called 'the Fisher Folk', large services were held in various cathedrals pioneering worship influenced by popular music as the organ and robed choir made way for the worship band. This renewal within corporate worship was further developed through the Spring Harvest conferences, and in particular through the songwriting of Graham Kendrick, who sought to adopt a more contemporary rock style. Walker writes of Kendrick that he 'has had a greater influence on British Christianity than all the new church leaders put together'.[84] The story of evangelicalism's development can be told through the history of its songwriting as the theological emphasis becomes reflected in a shift from the communitarian worship songs of the 1970s such as *Bind Us Together* to the more individualistic songs of the 1990s such as *I Will Worship*.[85]

One further aspect of the impact of charismatic spirituality upon evangelicalism is the phenomenon that became known as the 'Toronto Blessing'. In the mid 1990s at the Vineyard ministries near Toronto Airport reports were made claiming an outpouring of the Holy Spirit in miraculous and peculiar ways – ways which were described as a 'cross between a jungle and a farmyard'.[86] Many evangelical churches both in Britain and the USA sought to 'catch the fire' of this new movement, but its impact was short-lived. Bruce observes that the mass conversions promised by this outpouring did not materialize and so it became referred to as a time of 'refreshing' rather than 'revival'.[87] The disillusionment with the failed promises of another movement predicting change and growth may partly explain the desire of some within the emerging church to find new ways of seeking change.

While the emerging church holds vastly different theological emphases to the aforementioned restoration movement, the similarities between the two in terms of motivation and form are noteworthy. The restorationists were discontent with the restrictive environment of the mainstream church; the emerging church is similarly discontent with the modern-influenced rigidity of the mainstream church and both are highly critical of the imperfections of previous generations. Both movements are propelled by a shift in eschatological thinking: restorationism by a belief in the restoration of the pure church in the end times and the emerging church by a less futuristic and more progressive collaborative approach. What is significant here is not primarily the difference in the content of these two eschatologies but rather the power of a shift in eschatological thinking to be the agent of ecclesiological change. It is this eschatological shift which catalyses the move away from the mainstream church. Despite the fact that restorationism explicitly stated that its intention was not to form a new denomination, it ended up doing so. The result of such an approach is that ecclesiology is worked out retrospectively and thus certain practices and values (such as the authoritarian leadership of the house churches) become unintentionally assumed, to the detriment of the movement. One can argue that the coming years will be decisive in establishing whether the emerging church assumes its own denominational form and, if it does, whether it also unintentionally assumes certain ecclesial practices.

Evangelicals facing an identity crisis

The fourth trend which must be considered is evangelicalism's identity problem, regarded by many as its Achilles heel. Grenz describes evangelicalism at the start of the millennium as 'confused', 'divided' and 'unsure of its role in society'.[88] Attempts at defining evangelicalism have proved problematic, an issue that is highlighted by the Stott and Lloyd-Jones debate of 1966 which made apparent the lack of consensus as to whether an evangelical denomination did or even should exist, causing significant hurt. While Stott later regretted using his position as the chair of the National Assembly of Evangelicals to counter Lloyd-Jones' position, retorting that both history and the Bible were against separatism, he never regretted his conviction that evangelicals must stay committed to mainstream denominations.[89] This disagreement cast a considerable shadow over evangelicalism in the following years, revealing two characteristics which were to prove significant in the development of evangelicalism: a propensity towards in-fighting and the gradual erosion of denominationalism that eventually led to a proliferation of new churches and denominations.

The legacy of this debate demonstrates that it is with regard to ecclesiology that evangelicalism has suffered most acutely from an identity crisis. Bebbington's four characteristics of biblicism, crucicentrism, activism and conversionism go a long way in expressing the core convictions of evangelicalism and the Evangelical Alliance's doctrinal basis serves as a suitable centre ground for theological conviction, but it is with regard to ecclesiology that evangelicalism bares its weakness. The increasing diversity of the post-war movement meant that evangelicalism tended to adopt a pragmatic approach to ecclesiology, in which convictions about ecclesiology were expressed primarily in practical application rather than theological discourse: pragmatism being one of the defining features of post-war evangelicalism.

Evangelicals have acted out our convictions about the church more than we have set them out, whether in church planting, parachurch proliferation, cooperative missionary ventures, heresy hunting and schism, liturgical innovation, varieties of pastoral education, the use of mass media, or a hundred other ways. What we haven't much done is reflect on these evangelical ecclesial realities and try to make some theological sense of them all.[90]

The issue of what, if anything, defines evangelical ecclesiology has remained unanswered. At the 1977 National Evangelical Anglican Congress in Nottingham, Stott himself addressed the issue of the evangelical identity problem, maintaining that evangelicals should be identified as people of the gospel:

> 'A gospel which makes us want to sing and dance and leap for joy' as William Tyndale said. Who wants an irreducible minimum gospel? . . . Let's celebrate it with uninhibited joy in our worship.[91]

Murray argues that evangelicalism's commitment to ecumenism downplayed the theological distinctiveness of evangelicalism, contributing significantly to the amorphousness of its identity.[92] Wells similarly suggests that while the loose denominational ties and less formal organizational approach of the evangelical movement may look widespread within American society it actually belies a superficiality and lack of theological substance:

> People thought they saw an invincible religious army composed of the one-third of the American population who claimed to have experienced spiritual rebirth poised to sweep before it all its cultural and religious opponents but the perception was a mirage. The sea that looked to be a mile wide turned out to be only an inch deep.[93]

The erosion of denominationalism has, arguably, played a role in the lack of evangelical identity; evangelicals have often found greater affinity with other evangelicals than with others in their own denomination. This identity crisis is further exacerbated by the rise of parachurch organizations that have become typical of evangelical activity, particularly with regard to mission. Lints suggests that the combination of parachurch movement and expectations of revival have led to the downplaying of ecclesiological concerns. Hart identifies Graham's evangelistic ministry, Dobson's 'Focus on the Family' and La Haye's 'Left Behind' publishing phenomenon as the three most influential parachurch organizations operating within the USA. Hart considers such parachurch initiatives to require little from the participant in terms of commitment, which has a diluting effect on evangelical spirituality. Since there is no binding relationship between the individual and the parachurch organization, the relationship is more akin to that of consumer and service provider.

> The parachurch, by virtue of its size, sends a message about evangelicalism that may actually impede its religious objectives: to be an evangelical is to be in a perpetual frenzy of trying to get more – more money, more contributors, more access, more zeal, and of course more believers.[94]

Churches, by contrast, have creeds, authority structures and liturgical resources which provide a more accountable form of discipleship. The minimal demands of evangelicalism stem from its reliance upon such parachurch expressions of faith, with minimal creed and more abstraction than concrete ecclesial corporate life. This is why, in the USA, the numbers of those who consider themselves evangelical is significantly higher than the numbers of church members. Indeed, Bruce considers that part of the numerical success of evangelicalism is that membership of it demands little in terms of lifestyle change and behavioural distinctiveness.

> Diffuse religion cannot sustain a distinctive way of life. Where there is no power beyond the individual to decide what should be the behavioural consequences of any set of spiritual beliefs, then it is very unlikely that a group will come to agree on how the righteous should behave [. . .] The language of discovering yourself and getting in touch with the God within can, and is, used to justify almost any sort of behaviour.[95]

It must also be noted that many of the movements for renewal or revival within evangelicalism over the past 60 years have held either an opposing or a disregarding attitude towards ecclesiology. For example, the Jesus Movement in the 1970s fused fundamentalism and elements of the charismatic movement, but its lack of formed ecclesiology contributed to its short-lived existence. The emerging church emerges out of a similarly amorphous and fragmented evangelicalism; however, its desire to engage with ecclesiology is to be received warmly, yet the substance of that ecclesiology remains of vital significance and will form the basis for a later discussion.

Lack of clarity about mission

Since the days of Wesley and Whitefield, evangelicalism's commitment to mission has been its defining feature, although the fervency of that pledge has waxed and waned during its history. Guder observes that none of the major confessional documents of western Christianity before the twentieth century had any developed doctrine of mission. Thus evangelicalism's later emphasis on missiology is a necessary redress to this balance; however, its lack of clarity on the subject may stem in part from its historical lack of precedent. During the post-war period one is aware of both periods of fervency and periods of apathy with regards to evangelism, leading to the conclusion that there has been a lack of consensus among evangelicals as to both the nature and the methods of missionary engagement. The following three characteristics illustrate the fluctuating approach of evangelicals towards mission.

Missiology divorced from ecclesiology

As previously stated, the 1950s heralded a period of optimism and confidence in which the new brand of evangelicalism could flourish and stabilize, within which the priority of evangelism featured strongly, making evangelicals deserving of Bebbington's 'conversionism' epithet. In the USA the most significant figure was Billy Graham, whose international evangelistic ministry endured for over 60 years. Amid high-profile scandals of other evangelists, Graham managed to avoid any hint of such disgrace, which may partially account for both the longevity and the popularity of his ministry. Hart considers Graham to be 'the institutional centre holding the evangelical movement together' and he questions whether evangelicalism can survive without Billy Graham.[96] Graham led evangelistic rallies in Britain, beginning with nightly preaching at the 12,000-seat greyhound track at Harringay in 1954, which attracted numbers on a scale unprecedented in religious gatherings in Britain, and even preached at Windsor Castle at the invitation of the Queen. The numerical success of these rallies affirmed evangelical predilection for this type of evangelism and was repeated again in Graham's 'Mission England' visit in 1984, in which Graham preached to more than a million people at full football stadiums. I myself remember attending Villa Park as a young child to hear Graham preach, accompanied by a testimony and music from Cliff Richard. There wasn't an empty seat to be found. The mass evangelism model was emulated by others such as Luis Palau and Dick Saunders and replicated the preaching for an appeal which has been a characteristic feature of evangelical mission. However, some remain sceptical as to the number of genuine conversions such rallies produced.[97] Yet not all within the evangelical movement warmed to Graham's style and theological sympathies and those liberal evangelicals who refused to endorse his ministry became increasingly isolated from a mainstream evangelical movement with the conservative group at its core.

These rallies also illustrate that, for evangelicals, mission was not something that the church did per se but rather something evangelicals did in partnership with other like-minded believers or organizations. One of the largest and most effective parachurch organizations of the second half of the twentieth century was the University and Colleges Christian Fellowship (previously known as Inter-Varsity Fellowship), which has had a thriving evangelistic ministry among students. However, despite the enthusiasm and success of such high-profile evangelistic ministries, they expose a weakness in evangelicalism's relationship to mission. Mission, increasingly initiated by parachurch partnerships, became subsequently detached from the life of the congregation, and church life became increasingly submerged in issues of pastoral and practical maintenance.

The dominance of pragmatism within mission

The second feature of evangelical mission is the dominance of pragmatism within mission. For example, in the Billy Graham rallies the altar call became a crucial mark of mission with the sinner's prayer as the litmus test for genuine conversion. In addition, Graham's evangelistic rallies, and other smaller ones like them, demonstrate the connection evangelicals drew between mission and holding events and the emphasis placed on the invitational nature of evangelism. If a Christian had friends or neighbours who weren't Christians then the onus was on them to bring them to an event to hear the gospel preached by an evangelist. Likewise, the flagship churches of the church growth movement such as Willow Creek promoted the notion of seeker services in which the style and tenor of the service is regarded as crucial to its accessibility and therefore its success. In a similar way, the global success of the Alpha course is one of the triumphs of evangelicalism, and its popularity is arguably partly due to its pragmatic approach, which, along with its professional marketing and training profile, makes it an easy tool for churches to utilize. Pete Ward has suggested that the Alpha course operates according to the rules of predictability, calculability, efficiency and control and in doing so, capitulates to consumerist values.[98] Ward's critique demonstrates the important role that pragmatism has played in the development of evangelical mission.

Faddism and mission

While a commitment to mission has been a hallmark of evangelical conviction, the balance between proclamation and social action adhered to by its forefathers, Wilberforce and Shaftesbury, has not been a tension easily maintained. Post-World War I pessimism about the possibility of human progress readily fuelled an eschatological shift that devalued social involvement, and thus the emphasis lay on proclamation as the core missionary conviction. However, the 1960s witnessed a shift towards greater social responsibility, with a lessening of millennial conviction, and a greater concern for poverty being promoted, particularly through parachurch organizations such as 'Tearfund' and cemented in the 1974 Lausanne Statement that 'evangelism and socio-political involvement are both part of our Christian duty'.[99] Yet a certain amount of debate continued to rumble on as to the precise nature and extent of that social action, particularly in the political sphere. Fluctuating positions on the nature of mission has often resulted in a lack of resources devoted to mission, particularly among Anglican evangelicals. There have been several attempts to address this, but these have met with marginal success. For example, under the leadership of Archbishop George Carey, the 1990s were declared the Decade of Evangelism, which sparked a number of optimistic books about the nature of this evangelistic endeavour. However, it is largely acknowledged that the only lasting initiative to come from this undertaking was the Alpha course. Reasons for the lack of success of this initiative are plentiful, not least the absence of effective teaching and catechetical education about the nature of mission, which contributed significantly to the corporate ecclesial paralysis. It is my contention that where evangelicalism has failed to offer a confident theological account of mission it has made itself arguably vulnerable to faddism and the inherent temptation to attach itself to the latest craze, believing that each new technique will unlock the power to evangelistic success and even revival. Examples of such fads would be the seeker services of Willow Creek, Wimber's 'power evangelism', 'random acts of kindness' and 'servant-evangelism'. Alpha arguably benefitted from the evangelical propensity towards faddism in its early days. One of the most powerful examples of evangelicalism's tendency to latch onto particular trends or fads is in the publishing phenomenon that is the *Left Behind* series. Though the theology of dispensationalism was primarily outlined by Darby in the 1890s, its popular application through the *Left Behind* novels has propelled this particular eschatological scheme into the forefront of American evangelicalism. While the impact of the *Left Behind* series will be explored further later on, it must be mentioned in any account which seeks to provide a context to the emerging radicals' protest and theological revision.

This propensity towards faddism means that evangelicalism is often open to new movements or practices which promise missiological innovation or renewal. In many ways, this mindset has made evangelicalism receptive to the emerging conversation. However, I will also explore in a later section whether the missiology it offers is different from the passing fads which preceded it.

Discontent with the perceived status quo

The final feature of post-war evangelicalism that provides a context to the inception of the emerging church is a sense of discontent with the current state of affairs and desire to effect change. Some of the most significant movements in the history of the church have stemmed from such stirrings of dissatisfaction that have led to revival or reformation. Yet not all such movements end up producing the genuine expression they envisaged, since the pendulum of reactionary theology can often swing to the opposite extreme. This kind of discontent has become an increasing part of the evangelical psyche in recent history, leading to some significant and popular movements for change and some less successful ones too. It is arguable that the evangelical identity problem lends itself to such theological restlessness on account of its lack of cohesive direction and distinctiveness. One of the most popular new initiatives of this nature, which thrives on its alternative and quasi-rebellious identity, is the Greenbelt Festival. Started in 1974, it seeks to combine theology with artistic expression, while attracting a broader spectrum of speakers and contributors and subjects than more mainstream evangelical gatherings would consider. The popularity of Greenbelt is evidence of the resonance these issues have with young people in particular. The birth of alternative worship also grew from a discontent with predictable, unimaginative and restrictive forms of traditional worship and sought to explore more creative and culturally aware expressions of worship. Such movements for change serve as a wake-up call to the church's tendency to guard its institutionalism and resist change. If the mainstream church will not sanction such expressions of creativity within its own walls then they will simply occur outside. However, discussion about alternative worship must acknowledge the infamous catastrophe of the Nine O'Clock Service in Sheffield in the 1980s.

Created by dissatisfied Christians, NOS was a wake-up call to the Church. It suggested that the meta-narrative of the traditional church should be replaced by a postmodern process of individuals exploring spirituality together, learning from a variety of sources.[100]

However, with regards to NOS, what began as discontent with a stultifying and predictable church experience, a desire to engage with young people and harness multimedia technology and contemporary music, ended up as 'one of the biggest sex scandals the church in England has ever seen', as many young people experienced sexual and pastoral abuse under the self-appointed leadership of Chris Brain.[101] Nevertheless, before the wheels started to come off the NOS project, it had already served as a catalyst to expressions of alternative worship throughout the UK that have not succumbed to the same errors.

One of the foremost voices expressing significant discontent with the perceived evangelical status quo has been that of Dave Tomlinson, whose book *The Post-evangelical* arises out of immense frustration with the theologically and socially restrictive nature of evangelicalism in Britain and seeks to raise questions about the future of faith in the West. In many ways *The Post-evangelical* serves as a prototype for the kind of discontent with evangelicalism that fuels the emerging church. Many of the features of post-war evangelicalism that we have considered provide the backdrop to its protest and discontent. The following quote from McLaren makes clear the perception of the inherited forms of evangelicalism against which the emerging church makes its protest:

It's a conversation about what it means to be 'a new kind of Christian' – not an angry and reactionary fundamentalist, not a stuffy traditionalist, not a blasé nominal, not a wishy washy liberal, not a New Agey religious hipster, not a crusading religious imperialist, and not an overly enthused

Bible-waving fanatic, but something fresh and challenging and authentic.[102]

The emerging church's desire to create 'a new kind of Christian' is one that must be listened to and taken seriously. However, it also raises serious questions about the emerging church's future relationship to the evangelicalism in which it was birthed but from which it now seeks to emerge. Bebbington argues that while evangelicalism has, throughout its history, adapted and changed to adjust to the changing cultural landscape, it has maintained its fourfold commitment to biblicism, crucicentrism, conversionism and activism, passed down through the generations. Evangelicalism, at the start of the twenty-first century, is more disparate and ambiguous than ever before and we must consider whether this new movement, which has gathered momentum within its walls, still reflects those four identifying values and, if not, whether its departure from them is also a deliberate rejection of them or merely evidence of the increasing diversification of the evangelical identity.

It is clear that the emerging church in no way sees itself as supporting the evangelical status quo, but instead offers a radical agenda for change. Its relationship to culture is its most defining characteristic and this is what ultimately causes a revision of evangelical eschatology, missiology and ecclesiology. While Bebbington's four characteristics are not explicitly addressed, they all fall within these three areas of theological revision. It can be argued that the emerging church continues in the trajectory of a movement that has always sought to respond and adapt to cultural change. However, its distinctive and more radical approach to culture distinguishes it from the movement out of which it is emerging.

Notes

1 McLaren, *Reinventing your Church*, p. 13.
2 There are three main aspects of postmodern ideology which shape the emerging conversation. They are:

1 Deconstruction: a new understanding of the way language operates is essential to the postmodern ideology and has developed out of literary criticism. Language is not capable of representing truth in an objective way and is understood in terms of power and oppression. The process of deconstruction, therefore, seeks to subvert and unmask what lies hidden beneath. Oden summarizes it as *'the dogged application of a hermeneutic of suspicion to any given text, where one finds oneself always over against the text, always asking the skeptical question about the text, asking what self-deception or bad faith might be unconsciously motivating a particular conceptuality'*. (See Oden, *Two Worlds*, p. 79. For a full exploration of the process of deconstruction see Derrida, *Of Grammatology*.)

2 Post-foundationalism: a way of thinking which acknowledges that the grand narratives that have governed modern western history have now broken down. (See Harvey, *The Condition of Postmodernity*, p. 9.)

3 Social constructionism: the belief that societies or groups create meaning through language follows on from deconstruction. (See Anderson, *Reality Isn't What It Used To Be*, p. 6. This will be explored in greater depth in Chapter 5.)

3 Quoted at www.the-next-wave-enzine.info/issue121.

4 Jones, *The New Christians*, p. 46.

5 I use the term 'radical' because Tony Jones himself, in response to Andrew Jones' blog statement that the emerging church has ceased to be radical, argues that the 'Emergents' are the radicals in the emerging church. He uses a definition of Marxism to describe what it means to be 'radical' and understands it to mean catalysing a revolution that will overthrow the status quo. He argues that it is the 'emergents' who have been declaring that the 'emperor has no clothes', the emperor being the mainstream church. (For the full description of the term radical see Jones, *Lonnie Frisbee and the Non Demise of the Emerging Church*.)

6 Dan Kimball considers the term to have become so broad that it has ceased to be meaningful and uses it as a historical term rather than futuristically. (Kimball, *The Emerging Church*.)

By contrast, Jason Clark's decision (as a lead figure of the emerging church in the UK) to move away from 'emerging church' and embrace 'deep church' was driven by his belief that the emerging church had become too narrow. (Clark, *Reflection*.)

7 Rollins, *How (Not) to Speak of God*, p. 6.

8 McLaren, *The Church on the Other Side*, p. 197.

9 Stetzer, *A Missiological Perspective*, p. 56.

10 Gibbs and Bolger, *Emerging Churches*, p. 28.

11 Tuama, *Take a Second to Unravel.*

12 McLaren, *A Search for What Is Real*, p. 164.

13 Jones, *The Church Is Flat*, p. 36.

14 McLaren, *Extended Interview.*

15 For example, Doug Pagitt talks about the heavy-handed and anti-emotional indoctrination that he received when he first came to faith and even includes a copy of the illustration drawn for him 25 years ago. See Pagitt, *A Christianity Worth Believing*, p. 24.

16 For example, McLaren mentions an individual who stood outside his meeting handing out flyers denouncing McLaren as a false teacher. See McLaren, *A New Kind of Christianity*, p. 2.

17 In his critique of the modern church, Rollins relies heavily on Derrida's notion that any appeal to the natural order of reason is logo-centric. For a detailed discussion of the impact of Derrida's deconstructionism upon theology see Hart, *The Trespass of the Sign*, p. 92.

18 Rollins *How (Not) to Speak of God*, p. 8.

19 Rollins, *How (Not) to Speak of God*, p. 12.

20 See Pat Robertson's comments on the Haiti earthquake and Haiti's pact with the devil at http://www.youtube.com/watch?v=f5TE99sAbwM&feature=related

21 Hatch, *The Democratization of American Christianity*, p. 212.

22 Olsen, *Is the Emerging Church Movement a Real Movement.*

23 Buckeridge, 'Profile: Brian McLaren'.

24 Webber, *The Younger Evangelicals.*

25 Webber (ed.), *Listening to the Beliefs of the Emerging Church*, p. 16.

26 Dickens, *A Tale of Two Cities*, p. 1.

27 Balleine, *A History of The Evangelical Party in The Church of England*, p. 21.

28 Bebbington, *Evangelicalism in Modern Britain*, p. 55.

29 Ibid., p. 65.

30 Grayson, *Anglican Evangelicals*, p. 39.

31 Bebbington, *Evangelicalism in Modern Britain*, p. 5.

32 Brown, *The Death of Christian Britain*, p. 37.

33 Hilton, *The Age of Atonement*, p. 26.

34 Balleine, *A History of the Evangelical Party*, p. 13.

35 Noll, *Turning Points*, p. 221.

36 Brantley argues that Wesley should be understood as the pivotal figure in the eighteenth century who bridges the gap between the Age of the Papacy and the Age of Romanticism. He argues that Wesley held together both the empiricism of Locke, yet also believed the Christian experience could be expressed in poetry and prose. Brantley describes Wesley in the following terms: 'He was somehow sensationalist, empiricist and at the same time free-willist, religious, optimistic, idealistic,

intellectualistic, and generally reasonable though never rationalistic'. See Brantley, *Locke, Wesley and The Method of English Romanticism*, p. 15.

37 Gabriel, 'Evangelical Religion and Popular Romanticism', p. 34.

38 In the first year of her project, Hannah More received over £1,000 in support from wealthy benefactors such as Wilberforce which enabled the literature to be widely distributed. See Pederson, *Hannah More meets Simple Simon: Tracts, Chapbooks and Popular Culture in Late Eighteenth-Century England*, p. 84.

39 One of the most influential of the RTS's publications was a biographical tract by Revd Leigh Richmond entitled *The Dairy Man's Daughter*. This fictitious tale about a young woman's conversion, untimely death yet assurance of salvation communicated many key evangelical tenets. In the first 50 years after it was published there were reputedly 4 million copies in circulation in 19 languages. See Roberts, *Locating Popular Religion in the Evangelical Tract: the roots and routes of the Dairyman's daughter*.

40 Balleine, *A History of the Evangelical Party*, p. 159.

41 As well as being known as the Clapham sect they also received the nickname 'the Saints', indicating they were known for their religious zeal as well as their political involvement. See Martin (ed.), *Christian Social Reformers of the Nineteenth Century*, p. 68.

42 It is interesting that not all members of the Clapham sect were committed evangelicals; William Smith for example was a staunch ally in the abolitionist cause but doctrinally was a Unitarian. While Wilberforce lamented his theological stance he was still willing to partner with him in political endeavour. See Hennell, *John Venn and the Clapham Sect*, p. 176.

43 Wilberforce records in his diary on 28 October 1787 the following conviction: 'God Almighty has set before me the two great objects, the suppression of the Slave Trade and the Reformation of Manners.' See Hennell, *William Wilberforce*, p. 1.

44 Wilberforce believed that social transformation was not possible without proclamation of the Evangelical faith. 'But fruitless will be all attempts to sustain, much more to revive, the fainting cause of morals, unless you can in some degree restore the prevalence of Evangelical Christianity.' See Wilberforce, *A Practical View of the Prevailing Religious System of Professed Christians*, p. 264.

45 Russell, *Household of Faith*, p. 232.

46 Overton, *The English Church in the Nineteenth Century*, p. 93.

47 Noll, *A History of Christianity in the United States and Canada*, p. 166.

48 Wolffe, *The Expansion of Evangelicalism*, p. 90.

49 Ibid., p. 174.

50 The concept of evangelicals as transformers of culture during the nineteenth century is a complex one as the issues of sabbatarianism and temperance indicate. See Wolffe, *The Expansion of Evangelicalism*, pp. 170–8.

51 Balmer, *The Making of Evangelicalism*, p. 3.

52 Hatch, *The Democratization of American Christianity*, p. 199.

53 Ibid., p. 197.

54 Ibid., p. 199.

55 Ibid., p. 7.

56 Ibid., p. 212.

57 Balmer, *The Making of Evangelicalism*, p. 4.

58 Ibid., p. 25.

59 Bebbington, *The Dominance of Evangelicalism*, p. 68.

60 Ibid., p. 137.

61 Tate, *Evangelical Certainty*, p. 27

62 Pollock, *The Cambridge Seven: A Fire in China*, p. 41.

63 Barclay, *Evangelicalism in Britain 1935–1995: A Personal Sketch*, p. 20.

64 Finstuen, *Original Sin and Everyday Protestants*, p. 13.

65 Green writes about the significance of the 'Bash Camps' in his own Christian discipleship and also in the development of the future generation of church leaders. See Green, *Adventures of Faith*, p. 22.

66 Warner, *Reinventing English Evangelicalism*, p. 122.

67 McGrath, *Evangelicalism and the Future of Christianity*, p. 26.

68 Hart, *Deconstructing Evangelicalism*, p. 133.

69 Bebbington regards the IVF as the single most influential factor in the development of a confident post-war Evangelicalism. See Bebbington, *Evangelicalism in Modern Britain*, p. 259.

70 Barclay, *Evangelicalism in Britain 1935–1995*, p. 54.

71 In 2005 Time Magazine listed John Stott in the top 100 people of influence in the world. (Graham, *The 2005 TIME 100*.)

72 Stott, *The Contemporary Christian*, p. 29.

73 Stackhouse, *The Gospel-Driven Church*, p. 5.

74 Chandler, *Customer Poll Shapes a Church*.

75 Kwon, *Willow Creek Sets Record Straight on Mission Focus*. Lints states that in the light of these findings, the leaders at Willow Creek concluded that converts needed to be taught to be self-feeding and learn how to mature their own spirituality without the church. Lints, *Renewing the Evangelical Mission*, p. 146.

76 http://www.saddleback.com/aboutsaddleback/history/

77 Warren, *The Purpose Driven Life*, p. 412.

78 Wells, *No Place for Truth*, p. 133.

79 Fitch, *The Great Giveaway*, p. 33.

80 The Fort Lauderdale Five were Ern Baxter, Derek Prince, Bob Mumford, Charles Simpson and Don Basham.
81 Walker, *Restoring the Kingdom*, p. 308.
82 Smith, *Transforming the World?*, p. 99.
83 Tomlinson, *The Post-evangelical*, p. 18.
84 Walker, *Restoring the Kingdom*, p. 309.
85 Ward, *Selling Worship*, p. 189.
86 http://www.catchthefire.com/About/History
87 Bruce, *God is Dead*, p. 172.
88 Grenz, *Renewing the Center*, p. 12.
89 Dudley-Smith, *John Stott*.
90 Stackhouse (ed.), *Evangelical Ecclesiology: Reality or Illusion?*, p. 9.
91 Lloyd, *Evangelicals, Obedience and Change*, p. 9.
92 Murray, *Evangelicalism Divided*, p. 252.
93 Wells, *God in the Wasteland*, p. 18.
94 Lints, *Renewing the Evangelical Mission*, p. 125.
95 Bruce, *God is Dead*, p. 94.
96 Hart, *Deconstructing Evangelicalism*, p. 111.
97 Brown, *The Death of Christian Britain*, p. 173.
98 Guest, *Evangelical Identity and Contemporary Culture*, p. 47.
99 Stott, *Issues Facing Christians Today*, p. 10.
100 Till, 'The Nine O'Clock Service'.
101 Ibid.
102 McLaren, *Everything Must Change*, p. 2.

2

The Emerging Church and Culture

The most defining characteristic of the emerging church is its deliberate and self-conscious attempt to outline a vision for a church that can survive and even thrive in a postmodern world. This statement by Tony Jones aptly expresses one of their core convictions:

> Postmodernism is neither something to fear nor something to embrace. It's simply the water in which we swim now.[1]

The liquid metaphor is a fitting one and the emerging radicals are not the only ones to utilize it.[2] Postmodernity is not something 'out there' to be dissected and rebuffed. It simply is, for the emerging radicals, a way of life and the context in which the church must find its home or else cease to convey meaning in the contemporary world. It is the drum beat to which the church must now dance. In many ways, the emerging radicals are to be welcomed in their recognition that the church does not exist in isolation from cultural context, to suggest so is naïve and tends towards a defensive or reactive approach to culture. Hunter believes that the emerging church adopts a 'relevant to' posture towards culture, along with the seeker-sensitive church, an approach in which initiatives 'take their cue from the culture around them, and offer little clarity for the confusion of the times'.[3] However, my conviction is that the emerging radicals operate in a distinct way from the seeker-sensitive movement and are not interested in culture as a tool to be utilized or commandeered in a bid for relevance. The emerging posture towards culture is a complex and nuanced one and its contribution must be listened to, yet we must also recognize that the scale of theological revision called to in the light of perceived cultural change warrants critical engagement. This is no mere stylistic change, adapting the form and leaving the content undisturbed.

Central to the emerging church's raison d'être is the conviction that times have changed and that radical action is required if the western church is to survive in the twenty-first century. Bruce paints a gloomy picture of the impact of secularization upon the West:

> Christianity is now but a pale shadow of its former self. Rural churches are converted to houses; city churches become nightclubs and carpet warehouses; church commissions examine the entrails for signs of hope; and sympathetic commentators publish studies with titles such as 'The Tide is Running Out' (Brierly 2000).[4]

Brown similarly argues that the defining aspect of the contemporary milieu in Britain is the death of any sense of Christian culture and heritage. The emerging radicals, however, are more positive about the changes taking place and describe this new cultural era as 'postmodern', although the terms post-Christian, post-Constantinian, post-structuralist, and post-foundational also surface frequently.

The emerging radicals respond to this perceived cultural crisis in two ways. First, they believe that they are uniquely placed to rid the church of the modern influences which dominate it.

> Many in church leadership today – not to mention everyday believers – feel that the church made a wrong turn somewhere in the twentieth century. At the dawn of a new century, the emergents are one of the few groups offering a way out of this mess and lots of people are listening.[5]

Second, the emerging radicals believe that the voice of postmodernity is critical to the development of the Christian faith in the twenty-first century. As McLaren states:

We need a deep shift, not merely from our current state to a new state but from a steady state to a dynamic story. We need, not a new set of beliefs, but a new way of believing; not simply new answers to the same old questions, but a new set of questions instead.[6]

In contrast to the rationalism of modernity, the postmodern climate is welcomed as an arena offering new possibilities and freedoms:

Western Christianity went to sleep in a modern world governed by the gods of reason and observation. It is awakening to a postmodern world open to revelation and hungry for experience.[7]

It is the positivity with which postmodernity is viewed that is characteristic of an emerging approach, in contrast to a more traditional evangelical approach that has often seen postmodernity as the enemy of orthodox truth. To regard postmodernity as a place of promise rather than peril is central to the emerging approach. Postmodernity is welcomed as a place in which Christian life and faith can be reimagined and can flourish.

Influential to the emerging radical's understanding of cultural change is Phyllis Tickle's book *The Great Emergence*, which divides history into four eras, each 500 years long. At the end of each era the church holds a 'rummage sale' to decide which doctrine or dogmas are no longer tenable. Tickle argues that three upheavals have already taken place: the collapse of the Roman Empire (around AD 500), the Great Schism (circa AD 1000) and the Reformation in the 1500s. Tickle maintains that at the dawn of the third millennium the church faces another cultural shift which she classes as 'The Great Emergence'. It is ironic that a movement opposed to linear and confining forms of history should give so much credence to a theory that divides history so neatly and conveniently into four equal social and cultural epochs. Nevertheless, Tickle's premise illustrates the magnitude of the 'moment' that the emerging radicals believe they find themselves in.

Central to the emerging radicals' acceptance of the postmodern turn is their conviction that postmodernity is a reaction against modernity, in particular the Enlightenment project, and therefore acts as an ally in ridding the church of its modern viruses. In many ways they regard their protest against the modern church as mirroring the protest of postmodernity against modernity.

At the heart of the emerging church is the self-belief that they can 'read the times' better than any other Christian movement and that they understand how to relate to this burgeoning new era. Rollins considers the emerging church uniquely equipped with 'the conceptual tools' to move beyond modernistic interpretations of Christian faith and to respond to postmodern culture in a way that 'offers the potential of a dramatic revolution in religious thought'.[8] This approach marks a significant departure from the church–world dichotomy that has often hampered an evangelical approach to culture. The discussion around Fresh Expressions within an Anglican context has raised crucial questions for how the church responds to this dilemma. However, both Brewin and Rollins are dismissive of Fresh Expressions' reliance on the security of the institution and its attempt to make church accessible without championing radical change. Rollins is critical of those who seek to be sanctioned and accepted by the wider church, since the cost of doing so may be 'restriction' and even the 'perversion' of the message they seek to communicate.[9] Brewin's incarnational model, which will be explored further in a later chapter, offers a more radical approach to cultural engagement that is not reliant on pre-established connections.

Thus, it is with regard to postmodernity that the emerging radicals make their distinctive contribution; the postmodern context is not regarded as the new setting in which theology must be contextualized but as a whole new world which must redefine theology itself. This is no intention to merely rebrand timeless theological truths in trendy packaging; the perceived scale of cultural change is far too drastic for that and warrants a more radical response:

You see, if we have a new world, we will need a new church. We won't need a new religion per se, but a new framework for our theology. Not a new Spirit, but a new spirituality. Not a new Christ, but a new Christian. Not a new denomination but a new kind of church in every denomination.[10]

However, there are those who would question just how endemic postmodernity is in shaping twenty-first-century life and whether it remains the academic currency of the educated elite. Steve Bruce is of the opinion that in overplaying the impact of postmodernity too much attention is given to philosophy:

> If social science taught us anything, it is that there is often a huge gulf between what the 'chattering classes' think and do and the lives and worldviews of ordinary people.[11]

While it would be foolish to deny the existence of a postmodern shift, perhaps Bruce's observation that conversations taking place in academia are not necessarily normative for wider society carries some weight. Vanhoozer's suggestion that postmodernity is largely 'conversation and rhetoric' could lead us to question whether such intellectual ideology is unduly shaping this current conversation.[12]

Some critics have been vocal in their suggestion that through its reliance upon postmodern ideology, the emerging church over-prioritizes the voices of the white middle classes. John Piper scathingly referred to the emerging church as an 'upper-middle-class white departure from orthodoxy'.[13] A similarly biting charge against the cultural homogeneity of the emerging church is made by Soong-Chan Rah:

> So there I was, sitting in yet another workshop led by yet another blonde-haired, perpetually twenty-nine, white male with a goatee.[14]

In all fairness, Rah's criticism is directed more at evangelicalism in general and how the dominance of the white middle classes has been allowed to triumph unchallenged. The church in the West may lament over statistics of its decline, but such statistics fail to acknowledge the dynamic growth taking place in the global south, something which is also reflected among the immigrant communities of America. Rah suggests that a preoccupation with postmodernity means that the 'white captivity of the American church' continues unchallenged without due consideration being given to the fact that the future of evangelicalism does not lie in the West. In support of his argument, Rah lists what he considers to be the 17 most influential books published under the emergent village imprint, the majority of which are written by white males who constantly make reference to one another.

It appears somewhat ironic that the emerging church's obsession with postmodernity and its inherent freedom and elevation of stories from the margins, has resulted in such reproach from those who critique it. Rah suggests that one of the most significant problems the emerging church faces is its propensity to see itself as an entirely new entity and its failure to recognize that it is a product of North American evangelicalism and is therefore still a carrier of some its vestiges. Rah does concede that, to the emerging church's credit, there is some rhetoric about diversity, but he believes that in practice this extends to little more than tokenism which ultimately only strengthens the dominant culture.

The response of the emerging radicals to such accusations is varied and some are quicker to defend this seemingly glaring inadequacy than others. Tony Jones admits, in his PhD research published under the title *The Church is Flat*, that 93 per cent of the emerging church is predominantly white. His direct response to Rah's accusation is that he does not see this as a problem since the emerging church is 'about a particular people trying to solve a particular problem'.[15] This point is backed up further by his statement that:

> The EC is not an evangelistic movement. I don't mean that in reference to the gospel, but to the movement itself. The EC is not about growing the EC. It's about catalyzing an ecclesial and theological conversation and about building a network

of friendship in which these conversations can safely take place.[16]

This statement identifies Jones' belief that the emerging church exists to cater for those who are disillusioned by the church under modernity. Perhaps this aim means that there is less willingness to incorporate other and external influences. And yet, in fairness to many within the emerging church, a deliberate desire and intention to seek wisdom from outside the recognized voices, is apparent. Individuals such as Brian McLaren work very hard to ensure that voices other than his own are heard as part of the emerging conversation, as his partnership and friendship with the late Richard Twiss, a Lakota Sioux, demonstrated. If the emerging church is to be charged with paying closer attention to the theological voices arising from the remarkable church growth in the global south, this cannot be a charge laid exclusively at their feet and is one to which mainstream evangelicalism must also attend. The presence and influence of such voices ensure we embrace Sanneh's perspective that it is always in engagement with the 'other' that Christianity has grown, facilitating the important recognition that no one particular culture has the monopoly on how the gospel can be expressed and inhabited.

However, perhaps a question needs to be raised about the over-reliance on the insights of postmodernity in directing the emerging conversation. Vanhoozer questions whether postmodernity is a 'culture into which the gospel can be translated, or [. . .] a condition from which the Gospel must be liberated?'[17] In the rush to welcome postmodernity as that which can redeem the church from its syncretism to modernity, has something of this nuance been neglected?

Keller suggests that the propensity to regard postmodernity as capable of freeing the church from modernity, fails to critique sufficiently those aspects of the postmodern culture which the church should reject:

An over-emphasis on the post-ness of our situation can lead us to celebrate the greater tolerance, the end of 'Christendom', the fall of Reason-capital-R, and the openness to the spiritual without seeing that it is based on a kind of hyper-modernity that is perhaps more antithetical to Christianity than ever.[18]

This observation is further expressed in the propensity to pit modernity versus postmodernity, evidenced by the list of contrasts regularly drawn between the two. McLaren dedicates one of his books to 'the many people who love God or want to love God but have been repulsed by ugly, unworthy images of a cruel, capricious, merciless, tyrannical deity'.[19] Aside from the 'strawman accusation', such binary oppositions seem to express the very system of thought that they seek to depose. Derrida himself rejected such binary oppositions as oppressive and believed that the role of deconstruction was to alleviate such confinement. Carson, on the other hand, suggests that the utilization of false antitheses is characteristic of deconstruction itself. Similarly, Eagleton regards binary oppositions as an 'illusion of postmodernism' and that despite postmodernists' claim for plurality, 'postmodern theory often operates with quite rigid binary oppositions'.[20] The construction of false antithesis is one of the ways that the emerging radicals demonstrate the assimilation of postmodern values into their theology.

In addition, the creation of false antithesis is not the only weakness of the emerging radicals' critique of modernity. It is my supposition that the emerging radicals' disaffection with the American mega-church of the 1990s skews their understanding of modernity; the failings and weaknesses of this movement are read back into their account of modernity. The emerging radicals should heed Erdozain's advice that, although historical reflection may lay open the pathway to valuable resources, it must remain open to complexities and paradoxes, and must not be pigeon-holed for convenience.[21] Arguably, there are negative ways in which the church has been influenced by modernity, and it is a critique to which we must listen and take heed, but to suggest that these weaknesses provide an adequate framework for evaluating modernity, or that every expression of Christianity during this period falls foul of these weaknesses, is not easily justified.

While we must not dismiss the validity of the emerging radicals' critique of the church under modernity, we must nevertheless challenge the tendency to draw comparison between modern Christianity, which is culturally conditioned, and Christianity in postmodernity, which is authentic. Just as Rollins accuses the modern church of claiming to reject the secularizing tendencies of the Enlightenment, but 'mirroring its underlying suppositions', the danger of following suit within a postmodern context remains.[22]

Percy suggests that the consumerism prevalent in postmodern society unduly affects church life, in that believers begin to behave like consumers with regard to spiritual practices, engaging with them but doing so inconsistently. While his argument is directed at the house church movement, his suggestion that a lack of theological foundation makes a religious movement susceptible to enculturation in which 'social relevance is a trademark' is nevertheless pertinent.[23] This raises a significant question about whether a lack of doctrinal core makes this new and emerging movement more susceptible to cultural incarceration and whether this lack results in its uncritical acceptance of certain postmodern values. In fact, some have argued that this approach means that, despite their emphasis on community, emerging churches remain fragmented and weak:

> Churches which embrace a self-consciously postmodern identity are more likely to be fissiparous and socially fragile.[24]

Gerhard Lohfink is highly critical of any approach which seeks to embed the church too deeply within human culture, since he does not think it can result in the transformation of society. He argues that the people of God have always understood themselves to be a 'contrast society', a point he argues scripturally and through textual evidence from the first two centuries.

> Christ is someone absolutely different and new, in whom the holiness and truth of God have become definitively present in the world. Wherever his word is believed and life is based

on his truth, something new and different, the sacred realm of truth, emerges in the midst of the world.[25]

Themes of contrast between darkness and light do not sit easy with the emerging radicals' inclusive approach. However, Lohfink argues that many scriptural passages addressing the identity of the church utilize contrasting themes, often contrasting the church's call to holiness with the depravity of the world (1 Peter 2.9; Phil. 2.15). However, the commitment to contrast is not for the sake of contradiction but because of its missiological imperative:

> Precisely because the church does not exist for itself, but completely and exclusively for the world, it is necessary that the church not become the world, that it retain its own countenance.[26]

It is only by maintaining its distinctive Christ-centric identity that the church can be the agent of transformation for the rest of society, pointing away from itself towards Christ. However, Lohfink's approach rests upon the church–world dichotomy that has often been characteristic of an evangelical approach to culture and is perhaps equally problematic, resulting in a tendency either to wholeheartedly resist the influence of culture, or to plunder its resources in a bid for relevance.

The classic text in the modern era for understanding the relationship between gospel and culture was Niebuhr's *Christ and Culture*. Many scholars have since criticized Niebuhr's taxonomy of the relations of understanding Christianity and culture, offering alternative perspectives in its wake.[27] Nevertheless, Niebuhr's seminal work continues to provide a useful framework through which such alternative theories can be viewed. *Christ and Culture* describes the 'double wrestle' of the Christian seeking to balance loyalty to Christ against allegiance to culture, espousing five different approaches. Niebuhr's transformation type has had a strong legacy of evangelical affinity, an approach which Niebuhr believed aspired to a positive attitude towards culture that is motivated by a theological approach which seeks to hold together creation, incarnation and redemption:

> The effect of this understanding of the work of Christ in incarnation as well as creation on conversionist thought about culture is unmistakable. The Word that became flesh and dwelt among us, the Son who does the work of the Father in the world of creation, has entered into a human culture that has never been without his ordering action.[28]

In support of this position, Niebuhr uses Calvin's conviction that every aspect of human life can be permeated by the gospel with its aim of 'the transformation of mankind in all its nature and culture into a kingdom of God'.[29]

Carson seeks to revisit the Christ and culture theme for the postmodern age and, while he recognizes the importance of Niebuhr's work, he takes issue with the biblical basis of the assumption that any model can be chosen if deemed most appropriate. Carson is critical of approaches to church which do not take political and social involvement seriously and he continues to use the language of transformation as descriptive of the missional identity of the church.[30] Carson also expresses the conviction that where the perceived attitude of culture influences the content of the message, the implications for the fidelity of the transmission of a timeless message are serious.

> If we control our evangelism by analysis of market 'needs' the result is virtually always a domesticated gospel.[31]

Carson's critique of Niebuhr is both rigorous and insightful; nevertheless, he fails to propose any genuine alternative to the five positions offered, a failure which is unfortunately often characteristic of the conservative responses to the emerging church. However, Duncan MacLaren's critique of Niebuhr offers a genuine alternative. MacLaren suggests that instead of Niebuhr's five categories it is more helpful to think in terms of three categories that are derived from the analogy of responding to the current of a river: tension, momentum and significance. These three categories are helpful in enabling us to explore some of the complexities of the church and culture debate.

Tension

Tension strategy is characterized by the distinctiveness in which the church has sought to stand firm while the river flows fast in another direction. When the church has operated within a tension strategy it has been marked by uncompromising behaviour and doctrinal preservation. Such churches present a high threshold for new members to cross, since expectations of discipleship are high. MacLaren argues that this position is exemplified in sectarian mega-churches where church membership involves a full schedule of activities leaving little time for relating to the 'world outside'. However, Tilby argues that fourth-century monastic movements demonstrate that retreating from society can benefit the church, by maintaining authentic Christian spirituality and challenging the wider church to consider where it has lost distinctiveness. Tilby argues such ascetic movements were fuelled by the conviction that 'the culture needed converting to Christ as well as the people' and so 'they held out a vision of society derived from and dependent on the gospel' which led to missionary expansion.[32] Thus, it is perhaps unfair to associate distinctiveness with a retreat from society when argument from history prevails.

Momentum

The momentum strategy which MacLaren summarizes as 'culture-Christianity' is on the opposite side of the spectrum. This strategy typifies an approach in which the church mirrors the values and norms of its surrounding context. The symbiotic relationship between church and culture means that little distinction can be drawn. Some within the emerging church argue that this strategy was typified under Constantine where values of the Roman Empire became normalized as Christian virtues and vice versa, negating the need for a counter-cultural approach. However, the similarities between the momentum strategy and the emerging radicals' own approach cannot be ignored, rendering their summation of the Christendom period somewhat ironic:

> Why is Christendom 'bad' but culturally relevant emerging church 'good'? Are we not guilty of what C. S. Lewis calls 'chronological snobbery'?[33]

MacLaren observes that those who so vehemently oppose the modern influence upon Christianity are often the most willing to accommodate Christianity in the present postmodern situation and yet regard their immersion as bold and courageous. Croft believes that some within the emerging church think that the church must change in identical ways to culture in order to chasten its decline. MacLaren sees the momentum strategy as particularly harmful to missiology.

Significance

MacLaren's final strategy is the intention to 'achieve significance through engagement in the public sphere', offering the consumer society as an example of how the church can participate within the public arena, winning public attention and thus legitimizing their claims. The church may be able to harness certain aspects of the consumer culture such as choice, novelty and abundance for the Christian faith. He even suggests that perhaps the consumer culture has something to teach the church:

> Whereas the street preacher is anachronistic and, ultimately, fails to gain our attention, the billboard adverts, corporate logos, television exposure, press releases and national campaigns of consumer religion succeed in gaining some public attention. We instinctively understand their language. In this way, consumer religion is able to enter into public conversation both avoiding the stigma or sectarian religion, and demonstrating it has relevance for contemporary people.[34]

MacLaren's 'significance strategy' paves a way through the two extremes of sectarian seclusion and cultural immersion. However, this approach raises the question as to what the criteria are for deciding which aspects of the consumer culture can be harnessed by the church and which should be rejected. For example, while the consumerist value of choice can be harnessed by the church since it finds its origin in the doctrine of creation, the consumerist value of self-gratification may not be so uncritically incorporated.

MacLaren's study raises important questions about how the emerging church relates to culture and the process of discernment required. McGrath expresses the importance of finding norms and standards apart from our own cultural setting, arguing that scripture plays a crucial role in this process:

> To allow our ideas and values to be controlled by anything or anyone other than the self-revelation of God in scripture is to adopt an ideology, rather than a theology; it is to become controlled by ideas and values whose origins lie outside the Christian tradition – and potentially to become enslaved by them.[35]

This challenges Pagitt's argument that there are no biblical norms and values apart from our cultural location.[36] Webber's solution that the church should reject 'ideologies of culture' yet find points of connection within culture has much to commend itself in this regard.[37] Similarly, Wells stresses the importance of a contextualized approach to cultural engagement, which he understands in terms of the church's mandate to speak truth to the issues that rise to the surface of contemporary culture. He argues that the church should not hide within culture but must 'also speak to that culture from outside itself'.[38]

Yoder also offers a rigorous critique of Niebuhr's *Christ and Culture*, arguing that this typological approach cannot help in the complex question of culture and ecclesiological formation. Yoder challenges Niebuhr's assumption that culture is 'monolithic', regarded as 'every realm of human creative behaviour' and as such 'autonomous', standing independent of Christ and therefore also challenges the viability of a consistent approach. Instead he sees the challenge for the church being that of developing 'categories of discernment' in the light of the confession of Christ's lordship through which different value dimensions can be distinguished:

> There is no reason that what we should do about war, and about farming and about epic poetry, about elementary education and about pornography, about mothering and about heavy metal, would gain by our trying to treat each of those segments of culture in the same way. What we need is rather a capacity for moral discernment.[39]

In a concluding comment, which he unfortunately fails to explore, Yoder also criticizes Niebuhr's preference for the transformational typology of failing to take seriously the power of evil prevalent within the world, a criticism which can perhaps also be levelled at the emerging radicals' tendency to welcome postmodernity with such positivity.

In my opinion, it is the notion of cultural discernment which is most critical to this conversation. Leonard Sweet's use of the EPIC acronym to describe what is distinctive about emerging churches serves as a case in point. For Sweet, the four themes of Experiential, Participatory, Image-driven and Connected are both biblical and culturally resonant. Yet such characteristics demonstrate the necessity of the discernment to which Yoder alludes. It could be argued that these four characteristics are more immediately located as postmodern values than they are biblical ones, from which you would perhaps expect categories around holiness, unity and mission-orientation to be prioritized in ecclesiological definitions. While Sweet considers EPIC characteristics to be morally neutral, they actually mask a particular postmodern agenda. For example, how do we ensure that image-consciousness does not merely mimic culture's obsession with appearance? Where is the gospel invited to prophetically critique and subvert such obsession? The 'capacity for moral discernment' is pertinent. There is a very real danger that in the laudable attempt to free the church from its cultural entanglement with modernity, postmodernity simply becomes the next ensnarement.

Bretherton suggests that some within the emerging church have lost the 'separateness of Church', becoming so submerged within the cultural context that they cease to provide a place where believers can 'interpret our context in the light of the death and resurrection of Jesus Christ'.[40] Bretherton challenges the perception of many emerging practitioners that their gatherings take place in 'neutral' spaces. A café, for example, may be chosen on account of its neutrality in contrast to a 'religious' venue; however, even a coffee house plays a role in a capitalist consumer culture and cannot be neutral:

> Churches, as a community and a place are, of their nature, hybrid spaces. What sets them apart from non-church gatherings and places are how a particular time and place are transfigured or translated through orientation of those gathered to the Christian tradition of belief and practice and to the actions of Christ and Spirit in creation.[41]

Perhaps a more radical approach to cultural engagement, which allows the church to exist as its own culture shaped by the values and expectations of the kingdom of God, holds potential here. This idea is prevalent in the writing of Hauerwas, who believes that the church exists to build its own culture, which reflects the very nature of God himself, and in so doing bears witness to Christ who lies beyond culture:

> The most important social task of Christians is to be nothing less than a community capable of forming people with virtues sufficient to witness to God's truth in the world.[42]

Hauerwas emphasizes the character and virtues of the new community, which stands in contrast to much of the emerging rhetoric that is about cultural immersion and structural adaptability. Tomlin adds the warning that new expressions of church that reflect the surrounding culture will eventually become indistinguishable from it, a religious alternative of that which is already available. However, where the Christian community embodies a radically different and at times antithetical life from its surrounding culture, then 'they can have an exciting future'.[43]

The emerging radicals' approach to postmodern culture also raises a further point about the possibility of the unaccommodating nature of the gospel. While Grenz maintains that the offence of the gospel does not evaporate in the postmodern context, he also suggests that the church must guard against the assumption that we already know where the offence lies and that a 'cautionary stance' is equally risky.[44] However, I am not convinced that Grenz has the full measure of the risk the emerging radicals take with their presentation of the Christian faith and the extent to which they allow the postmodern matrix to define not only the way the Christian faith is articulated but how its core terms are being defined. Carson's central criticism of the emerging church is that its immersion in culture has sacrificed doctrinal fidelity on the altar of accessibility. He contrasts this approach with that of James Smith who, while seeking to rid the church of its modern cultural influence, sees the postmodern moment as a catalyst for change rather than the agenda which governs the form of that change:

> The church will have this prophetic countercultural witness only when it jettisons its own modernity: in that respect postmodernism can be another catalyst for the church to be the church.[45]

The difference between Smith's approach and that of the emerging radicals is subtle yet significant. They both rehearse the need for the church to banish its cultural captivity to modernity, regarding the postmodernity as a *kairos* moment of change, but for Smith postmodernity serves as a catalyst to rediscover the authentic church, whereas for the emerging radicals postmodernity becomes the new matrix through which their theology is sifted, resulting in a version of the gospel that is in danger of being stripped of any offence. For Stackhouse, the church can only be shaped by a gospel which both contradicts and affirms culture and the greatest challenge facing the church is not structural but confessional: 'to have faith that the gospel is able to do its own work, create its own structures and fashion its own distinct community'.[46] There is a danger that the emerging radicals' immersion in the postmodern matrix results means that they suffer from what Angela Tilby describes as the propensity to 'turn the gospel into something agreeable'.[47] Stackhouse argues that a church which reflects the existential longings of the culture cannot also adequately reflect the 'confrontational scandal of the gospel'.[48] The notion of the 'offence' of the gospel is perhaps unpalatable to postmodern sensibilities; however, Paul reminds us that the gospel is often seen as foolishness in the eyes of the world, and yet within it we discover the wisdom of God (1 Cor 1.17).

For Rowan Williams, the relevance of the church depends, to some extent, on its difference from culture. Somewhat controversially he suggests that any church seeking to act as an agent for the transformation of culture must possess at least some of the 'features of a "sect"'. He affirms the church's unique relationship to the risen Jesus as providing 'the context and the critique for other systems, the irritant that can prevent the world from simply settling down with mutually exclusive and competing tribalisms'.[49] The charge with which he commissions the current institution of the church is the same charge which I believe should face the emerging church: to 'reimagine the church in a more prophetic mould'.[50] Brueggemann's concept of the church as an alternative community has at its heart the idea of the church's prophetic ministry, nurturing and evoking 'a consciousness and perception alternative to the consciousness and perception of the dominant culture around us'.[51] Brueggemann indicates that at the heart of the formation of the church as an alternative community is a two-pronged approach which on the one hand critiques the dominant culture and on the other hand energizes it; he believes that it is in the dialectic of these two approaches that fidelity to the gospel in the contemporary age is forged. The role of the church is to engage in this dialectical prophetic ministry in which it both speaks of God's future hope, thereby resourcing its present context, while also offering a critique of the current social narrative in a way that enables the church community to regard itself as a new social reality:

> The prophetic word concerns a radical turn, a break with the old rationality, and a discontinuity between what has been and what will be.[52]

Perhaps the question of what posture the church takes towards culture is not the right one to be asking, since it assumes that culture is something separate from the church and neglects to acknowledge that any expression of church will always be an expression within a particular culture. Instead, the need is for the church not to adopt a particular stance for or against culture, but to develop the categories of prophetic discernment by which it can maintain its faithfulness to orthodoxy, while also seeking to discern elements of affirmation and of opposition in its particular time and place.

Where the emerging radicals do regard themselves as holding a prophetic role is in speaking out against a dominant church culture that they believe is antithetical to the authentic Christian faith; a perspective which must be heard and responded to by those in the mainstream. It is this sense of protest which propels their theological revision in the areas of eschatology, missiology and ecclesiology. However, this critique must not stop at the church but must be extended further, lest we fall into the trap of assuming postmodernity is the saviour which can release the church from its captivity to modernity, rather than a catalyst of change providing a new cultural setting in which the dialectic of the prophetic ministry can be performed. This propensity to mimic rather than critique postmodern culture could seriously jeopardize the direction of the emerging church movement. One of the critical challenges facing the emerging radicals is that of applying their critique not only to the mainstream church from which they have emerged but to the culture into which they are becoming immersed and in which they are finding fertile new ground for an expression of Christian faith. If the same rigorous critique is not applied to the context in which they are immersing themselves as to that from which they are emerging, then their beliefs and practices will be as captive to postmodernity as they believe their evangelical ancestors were to modernity.

If ever there was a time for pioneers, prepared to journey forward in new and courageous ways, it is now. Yet at the heart of that pioneering spirit must be this understanding of the prophetic nature of the church as the community of God that prayerfully discerns and seeks which aspects of its particular time are to be confronted and which are to be affirmed. It is the role of this community to give itself to the prophetic task of sifting God's foolishness from the often dazzling chimeras of worldly wisdom. The primary call of the missionary church in any age must be the call to Spirit-filled biblical and prophetic discernment, not only of its own theological assumptions but also of its present cultural context.

Notes

1 Jones, *Postmodern Youth Ministry*, p. 231.
2 Pete Ward uses the metaphor of liquid church.
3 Hunter, *To Change the World*, p. 217.
4 Bruce, 'The Demise of Christianity in Britain', p. 53.
5 Jones, *The New Christians*, p. xvi.
6 McLaren, *A New Kind of Christianity*, p. 23.
7 Sweet, *Postmodern Pilgrims*, p. 29.
8 Rollins, *How (Not) to Speak of God*, pp. 2, 6.
9 Rollins, 'Biting the Hand that Feeds', p. 84.
10 McLaren, *Reinventing your Church*, p. 13.
11 Bruce, *God is Dead*, p. 230.
12 Vanhoozer, *Pilgrim's Digress: Christian Thinking On and About the Post/Modern Way*, p. 73.
13 https://www.youtube.com/watch?v=MkGq5A4QEjg&feature =player_embedded
14 Rah, *The Next Evangelicalism*, p. 108.
15 http://www.patheos.com/blogs/tonyjones/2012/05/08/how-white -is-the-emerging-church/
16 http://www.patheos.com/blogs/tonyjones/2010/04/06/is -sojourners-for-straights-only/
17 Vanhoozer (ed.), *The Cambridge Companion to Postmodern Theology*, p. 22.
18 Keller, *Late Modern or Post Modern?*.

19 McLaren, *The Last Word and the Word After That*, p. x.

20 Eagleton, *The Illusions of Postmodernism*, p. 27.

21 Erdozain, 'Emerging Church: a Victorian Prequel'.

22 Rollins, *How (Not) to Speak of God*, p. 8.

23 Percy, 'A Place at High Table? Assessing the Future of Charismatic Christianity', p. 102.

24 Guest and Taylor, 'The Post-evangelical Emerging Church'.

25 Lohfink, *Jesus and Community*, p. 129.

26 Ibid., p. 146.

27 For two more contemporary frameworks see Lynch, *Understanding Theology and Popular Culture and Bevans, Models of Contextual Theology*.

28 Niebuhr, *Christ and Culture*, p. 193.

29 Ibid., p. 218.

30 Carson, *Christ and Culture Revisited*, p. 146.

31 Carson, *The Gagging of God*, p. 466.

32 Tilby, 'What Questions Does Catholic Ecclesiology Pose for Contemporary Mission and Fresh Expression?', p. 85.

33 MacLaren, *Mission Implausible*, p. 166.

34 MacLaren, *Mission Implausible*, p. 181.

35 McGrath, *A Passion for Truth*, p. 63.

36 Pagitt, 'Response to John Burke', p. 77.

37 Webber, *Ancient-future Evangelism*, p. 134.

38 Wells, *Above All Earthly Pow'rs*, p. 308.

39 Yoder, 'How H. Richard Niebuhr Reasoned: a Critique of "Christ and Culture"', pp. 33, 83.

40 Bretherton, *Beyond the Emerging Church?*, p. 41.

41 Ibid., p. 43.

42 Hauerwas is cited in: Tomlin, *Can We Develop Churches That Can Transform the Culture?*, p. 71.

43 Tomlin, *Can We Develop Churches That Can Transform the Culture?*, p. 77.

44 Grenz, *Renewing the Center*, p. 22.

45 Smith, *Who's Afraid of Postmodernism?*, p. 30.

46 Stackhouse, *The Gospel-Driven Church*, p. 76.

47 Tilby, *What Questions Does Catholic Ecclesiology Pose for Contemporary Mission and Fresh Expression?*, p. 84.

48 Stackhouse, *The Gospel-Driven Church*, p. 22.

49 Williams, *On Christian Theology*, p. 238.

50 Ibid.

51 Brueggemannn, *The Prophetic Imagination*, p. 13.

52 Ibid., p. 105.

3

The Emerging Church
and Eschatology

Introduction

Eschatology is pivotal to the pursuit of a 'new church for a new world' and is the first of the theological areas we will explore that the emerging church seeks to revise for the post-mortem age. Eschatology is traditionally understood as the doctrine of the 'last things': final judgement, death, resurrection and the parousial return of Christ. However, limiting eschatology to questions of post-modern existence fails to do justice to the breadth of eschatology as the framework through which we understand the unfolding of human history into the future towards what Tom Wright describes as 'God's new world of justice, healing and hope'.[1] The scope of eschatology is far-reaching, making it essential to Christian faith and theology in the twenty-first century because 'its implications reach to the depths of the conditions of the world, of the dynamics of history and of human life'.[2] Defining eschatology is critical to the discovery of what it is to be human, in defining the nature of the pilgrimage of human existence. Theologically, it is foundational to an understanding of what the church is, sharpening and defining its missiological mandate. Yet surprisingly, this subject is often either neglected as a sermon topic or subjected to fantastical imagery far removed from the earthy struggle of human existence. In current discussions about new expressions of church, much is made of the link between missiology and ecclesiology, yet little is made of the primacy of eschatology in this dynamic process. Tom Wright reminds us of the critical interrelation between these three theological themes:

> The way forward is to rediscover a true eschatology, to rediscover a true mission rooted in anticipating that eschatology, and to rediscover forms of church which embody that anticipation.[3]

The emerging radicals, perhaps unbeknownst to themselves, demonstrate the importance of the link between eschatology and missiology and, subsequently, ecclesiology. While few emerging church publications address the subject of eschatology explicitly, the implicit references are strong and it can be suggested that it is eschatology which is the hidden agenda providing commonality to this largely disparate movement. In fact, Tony Jones asserts eschatology as one of the defining features of the emerging church:

> So, I've poked around, trying to figure out exactly what is going on in the emerging church, and in Emergent Village in particular. And if there is one core conviction that I can put my finger on, it's an eschatology of hope.[4]

The emerging radicals exchange traditional evangelical eschatology in favour of what they consider a more collaborative or participative approach. If eschatology is, as I have suggested, pivotal to theological enquiry, then it will also be the case that a shift in eschatological thinking ultimately drives changes in the emerging church's missiology and ecclesiology also. To what extent emerging eschatology is genuinely 'hopeful', and to what extent it offers a good way forward for the mission of the church, is the subject of this chapter.

The emerging church's critique of dispensationalism

We have already established that, at its heart, the emerging church is a protest movement. In terms of eschatology, this protest is most explicitly directed at the theology of dispensationalism exemplified in the *Left Behind* novels. However, we must pause to acknowledge the differences between US and UK contexts when it comes to discerning currents in eschatological thinking. Tom Wright argues that the UK church is enshrouded by confusion about eschatological issues and he cites, as evidence, readings chosen at church funerals as often more reflective of a Buddhist non-material concept of the afterlife than a Christian one. Such readings serve as an attempt to ameliorate the horror and travesty of death rather than proclaiming the resurrection as the ultimate triumph over it.

Confusion about the afterlife was epitomized in the 2009 BBC drama *All the Small Things* which portrayed a rural parish church in the Peak District where a trendy new curate tried to shake up the stridently held status quo. The programme was a tragic caricature of rural Christianity but displayed its greatest confusion when addressing the subject of heaven. A mural was painted in which each church member contributed their idea of what heaven meant to them. The resulting picture was heaven fashioned in the likeness of personal preference; the pastiche of images of singing, painting and surfing were collaged together like eschatological bricolage. Many cite the UK's public reaction to the death of the Princess of Wales in 1997 as demonstrative of this confusion about the afterlife. Similarly, the mass outpouring of grief at the unexpected death of the singer Michael Jackson in 2009 exposed a wishful-thinking mentality that exhibits further this bewilderment about the afterlife, as tributes were offered with the hope that 'His star will shine forever'.[5] This lack of clarity about eschatological issues in the UK has meant that there is a fertile ground for the planting of a new emerging eschatology.

By contrast, in the USA eschatological considerations have most recently become dominated by the popularization of dispensational theology through the marketing of the *Left Behind* series. The scope and impact of this apocalyptic narrative should not be underestimated, nor should the extent to which a rejection of it shapes and drives the emerging church's eschatological revision.

The impact of the *Left Behind* series

The *Left Behind* series has been a Christian publishing phenomenon quite unlike anything else, with an introductory video
on its website claiming that 'lives are still changing, someone
near you could be next'.[6] The ninth novel *Desecration*, claimed
to be the world's top selling hardback fiction book in 2001.
Yet it is not simply the novels that have gained cultural credence but the subsequent films, clothing and other merchan-
dise. When visiting America I was intrigued by the array of
'rapture' products available, from t-shirts and belts to bumper
stickers warning that the driver may be raptured any moment,
so one had better drive carefully. The *Left Behind* series offers
an imaginative narrative exploration of the theology of dispensationalism that has become dominant within American evangelicalism. Dispensationalism proposes that Jesus Christ could
return visibly at any moment and 'rapture' to heaven all who
are true believers; those *left behind* enter a seven-year period
of 'the tribulation' during which the 'Antichrist' will carry
out savage persecution until his defeat at the second return
of Christ when Christ will rule on earth for 1,000 years. The
books narrate the experience of those '*left behind*' and their
journey of discipleship through the 'tribulation', in which they
experience intense persecution and the heightened presence of
evil. The first book *Left Behind* commences with the rapture;
pilot Rayford Steele, while thinking lustfully about an air host-
ess, is *left behind* as his wife, son and one third of the pas-
sengers on his Boeing 747 are raptured to heaven. The books
include several apocalyptic Bible passages which are given definite historical interpretations, making it hard to know where
the exposition ends and the fiction begins, though arguably
that is the point. While the novels have made some inroads
into the UK market, the reception has been nothing like that
in the USA. The *Left Behind* books are pertinent to our exploration of emerging eschatology because they represent the dispensationalist perspective in which the emerging radicals were
predominantly schooled and against which they make their
protest. The title of Pagitt's publication, *A Christianity Worth*

Believing: Hope-filled, Open-armed, Alive-and-well Faith for the Left Out, Left Behind, and Let Down in Us All cannot be coincidental in its references to it.

The popularity of the *Left Behind* series is extraordinary and the extent to which its portrayal of dispensationalism has influenced and shaped the culture of the evangelicalism in which the emerging radicals were schooled should not be underestimated. Bennett's research identifies eight beliefs as essential to *Left Behind* eschatology, which correspond to John Nelson Darby's formulation of dispensational eschatology in the mid nineteenth century.[7]

1 A futuristic interpretation of the book of Revelation;
2 a total distinction between Israel and the church;
3 belief in the imminent return of Jesus;
4 a rapture (possibly secret) in which the chosen are taken to heaven before the tribulation begins;
5 a two-stage return of Christ prior to the millennium;
6 an Antichrist-led tribulation;
7 a millennium in which Christ will reign on earth; and
8 the return of the Jews to Palestine prior to the return of Christ.

The influence of Darby, a prominent leader in the Plymouth Brethren, warrants mentioning, which, along with the publication of the Schofield Reference Bible, saw these ideas largely adopted within American Protestantism. Yet, Bennett is keen to suggest that the testimony of church history stands against this scheme and that while the early church affirmed belief in the imminent return of Christ and an Antichrist-led tribulation, the rapture is strikingly absent. Millard Erickson suggests that such lack of evidence is not necessarily problematic since the church's eschatology has often been implicit rather than explicit. However, he contends that the stronger argument for its rejection is the false dichotomy it places between both Israel and the church and the Kingdom of Heaven and the Kingdom of God.[8]

The emerging radicals are in good company in their rejection of the pre-millennial dispensationalism of the *Left Behind* series since both the Presbyterian Church in the USA and the Lutheran Church–Missouri Synod have publicly denounced this apocalyptic scenario.[9] Not surprisingly N.T. Wright has stepped into the fray to offer his critique of what he calls the 'Left Behind Myth' and in particular the doctrine of the rapture which he comically describes as 'a pseudo-theological version of Home Alone' and reliant upon poor scriptural exegesis:[10]

> Paul's mixed metaphors of trumpets blowing and the living being snatched into heaven to meet the Lord are not to be understood as literal truth, as the Left Behind series suggests, but as a vivid and biblically allusive description of the great transformation of the present world of which he speaks elsewhere.[11]

However, to explore the books purely in terms of their theological themes perhaps misses the point. Amy Johnson Frykholm's sympathetic, yet critical, research highlights the social nature of these texts and the pivotal role apocalypticism plays in American religious history.[12] Gribben similarly suggests that the novels act as 'a barometer of cultural and political attitudes within the evangelical movement'.[13] We must read the emerging radicals' protest with this in mind; their protest is most keenly directed where fiction expresses reality, as typified in this comment by Left Behind author, Tim La Haye:

> We're in a religious war and we need to aggressively oppose secular humanism; these people are as religiously motivated as we are and they are filled with the devil.[14]

Left Behind dispensationalism is not primarily rejected by emerging radicals for its poor exegesis or lack of historical precedent, but rather because of how its embodied ideology within American evangelicalism has detrimentally shaped its missiological and ecclesiological practice. The emerging protest is galvanized by two particular features of Left Behind dispensationalism: pessimism and exclusivism.

Left Behind pessimism

The emerging radicals are vocal in their rejection of the deterministic reading of the future offered in the narrative of *Left Behind* dispensationalism. By contrast, McLaren describes his compatriots as those who 'share my belief that the versions of Christianity we inherited are largely flattened, watered down, tamed . . . offering us a ticket to heaven after death but not challenging us to address the issues that threaten life on earth'.[15] On reading the *Left Behind* series, it is not difficult to imagine what McLaren has in mind as this version of Christianity.

The *Left Behind* world is overwhelmingly evil and irredeemable; the earth is on a steady path to destruction and nothing can be done to prevent it. *Left Behind* dispensationalism regards the new creation as taking place after the destruction of the present world and therefore entirely discontinuous from it.

> Jesus will have as His canvas an entire globe that has been shaken flat – except Israel. Around the world, debris from the planetary earthquake will lie hundreds, sometimes thousands, of feet deep. Rock, foliage, buildings, and water will create a residue that coats the earth, leaving everything at sea level.[16]

In light of this imminent destruction, the plight of the individual becomes the primary concern of Christian ministry. Endeavours in ecology and social reform are ultimately futile and the 'winning of souls' trumps other ministry concerns.[17]

In a stinging critique, McLaren calls *Left Behind* dispensationalism an 'eschatology of abandonment', regarding it as a product of modern Christianity which, in the light of industrial progress and rising secularism, could only imagine the decline of the church and global destruction. The sole solution was the imminent return of Christ to transport believers to a non-material existence in heaven:

> Their only hope? A skyhook Second Coming, wrapping up the whole of creation like an empty candy wrapper and

throwing it in the cosmic dumpster so God can finally bring our souls to heaven, beyond time, beyond messy matter, beyond this creation entirely. There is virtually no continuity between this creation and the new heavenly creation in this model: this creation is erased like a mistake, discarded like a non-recyclable milk carton. Why care for creation? Why get sentimental about a container that's served its purpose and is about to be discarded into the cosmic trash compactor of nothingness?[18]

McLaren argues that this mindset made perfect sense in the progress-driven and consumerist modern world. However, he argues that in order for this theology to survive it had to spiritualize Old Testament prophecies which spoke about the future harmony of creation; in so doing modern Christianity allowed its theology to be influenced by a cultural proposition which would be later shown to be vacuous.

By contrast, emerging eschatology is positively world-affirming. Through his fictional character Joe, a homeless figure representing God in *The Word of the Lord to Evangelicals*, McLaren makes clear his rejection of the notion of heaven as a place of escape from the decaying world:

> The only salvation I have ever been interested in is global salvation, the restoration of all things. All this talk about saving souls and damning everything else – it did not come from me. That is something you made up.[19]

Rollins' writings contain a similar emphasis on the affirmation of the world in contrast to versions of Christianity which regard salvation as world-escapism. In *Insurrection* Rollins writes a lengthy apocalyptic parable which is a parody of rapture-influenced thinking in which God separates the wheat from the chaff, calling up to heaven all those who have 'turned from this suffering world by calling out "Lord, Lord"'. However, the twist in Rollins' parable is that God chooses to return to earth and to spend eternity with those who have forsaken 'heaven in order to embrace the earth'.

And so it was that God and the heavenly host left that place to dwell among those who had rooted themselves upon the earth; the ones who had forsaken God for the world and thus bore the mark of God; the few who had discovered heaven in the very act of forsaking it.[20]

While Rollins' use of parody is intended to shock and entertain, it reveals a shared concern with McLaren in its rejection of a futuristic world-escaping eschatological framework in place of one which embraces and affirms the world in the present.

The emerging radicals replace dispensationalism's belief in the imminent destruction of the world with an emphasis on the continuity of the old and new creations in which ecology is imperative. In addition, emphasis on the individual is replaced by social and global concern. There is much that is to be welcomed in the emerging radicals' rejection of this schemata, and their emphasis on the goodness of creation and its positive future is a helpful redress to a negative and imbalanced theology. Wright believes that many expressions of Christian theology have misinterpreted the idea of believers being 'citizens of heaven' (Phil. 3.20) to imply that it is a destination that we escape to, rather than the hidden realm where God's promises are stored and which one day will be united to the newly restored earth.[21] The biblical emphasis lies not in believers escaping to heaven, but in Jesus coming to earth and bringing together the renewal and restoration of the earth, as heaven and earth are united in God's act of cosmic transformation. However, we will also explore later where the emerging radicals' rejection of pessimism can tip over into an optimism that is equally unsubstantiated.

Left Behind exclusivism

The second aspect of the *Left Behind* series which galvanizes the emerging radicals' protest is its obsession with exclusivism. Binary thinking dominates the novels; there is a strong emphasis on deciding whether one is 'in' or 'out' in the light of the impending judgement which is, coincidentally, characterized by a high level of retributive violence. However, the rapture brings surprises as some find themselves unexpectedly left behind, not least the minister who, it turns out, experienced serious doubts. This dual emphasis upon the imminent destruction of the world and exclusivism means that mission is expressed almost exclusively in terms of individualistic, soul-saving evangelism. Determinism is another feature of *Left Behind* exclusivism and is epitomized in this statement from *Desecration*: 'The script has already been written. I have read it. You lose.'[22] McLaren regards this emphasis on 'insiders' and 'outsiders' as a product of modernistic thinking 'when theological controversy and competition, combined with a penchant towards control reinforced . . . motivation by exclusion'.[23] This rejection of boundaries is replaced by the principle of inclusivism which pervades emerging rhetoric.

The emerging radical's rejection of *Left Behind* exclusivism is, however, more complex and problematic for missiology. Since judgementalism and arrogance cannot exist alongside the Christian gospel, one can appreciate the emerging radicals wishing to distance themselves from evangelical leaders who have found it permissible to talk about encouraging the US President to 'blow away enemies in the name of the Lord'.[24] Nevertheless, the validity in their protest must not prevent us from similarly challenging what is formed in its place. What replaces judgementalism, in the emerging account, is not attitudinal transformation but a theological shift to inclusivism which negates the need for final judgement. Wright comments that while the talk of judgement may offend liberal or postmodern sensibilities, God's judgement is welcomed in scripture as the time when wrong will ultimately be put right:

In a world of systematic injustice, bullying, violence, arrogance and oppression, the thought that there might be a coming day when the wicked are firmly put in their place and the poor and weak are given their due is the best news there can be. Faced with a world in rebellion, a world full of exploitation and wickedness, a good God must be a God of judgment.[25]

We must question whether, in the attempt to move away from a theology of judgementalism, a crucial theological doctrine has been lost and the hope of the Christian gospel is in danger of becoming emasculated, replaced by a naïve evolutionary optimism that supposes everything will work out in the end. This shift has significant consequences for how mission is interpreted and Scot McKnight suggests that ambiguity about boundaries has detrimental consequences for evangelism:

> This emerging ambivalence about who is in and who is out creates a serious problem for evangelism. The emerging movement is not known for it, but I wish it were. Unless you proclaim the good news of Jesus Christ, there is no good news at all – and if there is no good news, then there is no Christianity, emerging or evangelical.[26]

If the emerging church wishes to be taken seriously as a missional movement then it cannot hide in ambiguity about boundaries, particularly one with soteriological implications. Eschatology is the fuel to the fire of missiology and any lessening or weakening of eschatology can result in an impoverished missiology.

The immaterial eschatology of the *Left Behind* series leads to an immaterial evangelism which pursues the salvation of the soul above social concern. Such an approach is a far cry from articulating mission in terms of *Missio Dei* as

> God's Self-revelation as the One who loves the world, God's involvement in and with the world, the nature and activity of God, which embraces both the church and the world, and in which the church is privileged to participate.[27]

Affirming the centrality of the kingdom of God to the ministry and teaching of Jesus means that a broader vision of mission including social justice and transformation must be embraced, and indeed appears to be part of a positive shift within evangelicalism more generally in recent times. However, we must also question whether, in allowing the *Left Behind* caricature of the gospel to catalyse their protest, the emerging radicals have neglected a vital emphasis on evangelism. The ministry of Jesus holds emphasis upon the injustices of society and the needs of the individual in perfect tension. He challenges the exclusivity of the religious establishment but also offers personal forgiveness and calls for repentance. In an attempt to move away from a crude stereotype of the gospel, has the simple yet all-demanding call of Jesus to 'come follow me' been forgotten?

While there is much to be listened to in the emerging radicals' rejection of the pessimism and exclusivism of *Left Behind* dispensationalism, we must now consider the eschatological framework which they offer in its place and question whether it offers anything more substantive than the dogmatism which they reject.

Participatory eschatology: a key theme for the emerging church

In place of *Left Behind* dispensationalism, the emerging radicals offer an alternative eschatological framework which can be defined as 'participatory eschatology', a phrase used by McLaren to affirm the effectiveness of human activity and countermand the determinism of dispensationalism. McLaren emphasizes partnership and collaboration, regarding the overarching biblical narrative as 'the story of the partnership between God and humanity to save and transform all of human society and avert global self-destruction'.[28] McLaren's 'participatory eschatology' resonates strongly with Wright's 'collaborative eschatology', yet there are two significant divergences. The first is that participatory eschatology is influenced by the insights of process theology and the second that participatory eschatology is not anchored in a theology of physical resurrection which is so pivotal to Wright's account of the new creation.[29]

In 'participatory eschatology', a converging theological agenda between the emerging radicals and process theology becomes discernible. Process thinking is a way of looking at the world that incorporates organic development and recognizes that ideas are not static but evolving.[30] Process theology's idea of an undetermined and open future finds a common point of protest in dispensationalism. Bruce Epperly, who claims that his theology is in the spirit of Brian McLaren as he seeks to proclaim 'a new vision of God and the world as inspirational for a 'new kind of Christian', describes a friend who was distressed by the *Left Behind* books' presentation of the impending destruction of the world and for whom process theology was the perfect antidote to such divine arbitrariness.[31] While Epperly writes at a popular level, his ideas reflect a more traditional understanding of process theology as construed by Hartshorne and Whitehead, developed during the end of the nineteenth century, influenced by a growing awareness of the evolutionary nature of the world.[32] Hartshorne used the phrase 'panentheism' to describe how God is not removed from creation but operative within the whole creation.[33] In order to understand more deeply what the emerging radicals mean by 'participatory eschatology', we will consider three defining themes and their points of convergence with process theology.

The openness of the future

McLaren is keen to distance himself from popular eschatologies which regard the primary purpose of the Bible as being 'to provide a detailed timeline for the end of the world'.[34] Participatory eschatology counteracts dispensationalism's tendency to evaluate the events of world history in terms of how they match apocalyptic prophecies, advocating instead an open-ended schemata. The future is imagined not as a pre-planned event but a collaborative journey between God and humanity. McLaren describes this non-deterministic relationship between God and humanity in familial language:

> God intended to create our universe the way a parent gives birth to a child; the child is given limits and guidance, but she also has freedom to live her own life. That means that the future of the universe is not determined as if it were a movie that's already been filmed and is just being shown to us. Nor is it completely left to chance like dice on a table.

Rather, God's creation is maturing with both freedom and limits under the watchful eye of a caring parent.[35]

Epperly suggests that since the future is unknown to God, its outcome will be as surprising to God as to us and there are no guarantees as to what will evolve.[36] In fairness to emerging radicals I do not think that their uncertainty about the future extends this far, since McLaren clearly envisages the ultimate defeat of evil: 'I believe God has made promises that will be fulfilled and in that way God is ultimately going to win.'[37] Yet, while there is some sense in which the final outcome is already decided there is a fair amount of flexibility as to how it will play out, with the future expressed in terms of promises fulfilled rather than God's will being done.

McLaren's predilection to talk about God's promises rather than God's will exposes how semantic preference can mask theological changes. McLaren's reactionary eschatology is directed against the straw man of hyper-Calvinism where individual choice is irrelevant. McLaren uses the image of God as a parent to explain how he regards the future. However, it can be argued that where paternal imagery is found in scripture it is more commonly used to illustrate God's compassion for his children; biblical passages addressing the future of God's kingdom prefer the images of king, judge and lord. McLaren's picture of God as a watchful parent means that we cannot speak with certainty about the future of the universe, other than trusting God will intervene if things go too far out of control. However, this cannot provide an adequate answer to the question of how evil will be dealt with. Furthermore, this emphasis upon flexibility and possibility with regards to the future challenges the assurance of the long-treasured Christian hope that evil will, at the end of time, be conquered. Perhaps we must also question whether there can be genuine hope for the future if it is governed not by God's will but by his dreams and desires. Since the twentieth century witnessed more bloodshed than any in the church's history, how can we honestly say that creation is 'maturing with both freedom and limits'?[38] In the quest to find a suitable replacement for the pessimism of dispensationalism it appears that the equally extreme position of evolutionary optimism has been embraced. This also holds consequences for the doctrine of the resurrection since surely an open view of the future means we cannot say with confidence that Jesus' resurrection provides the grounds of hope for future resurrection. The optimism inherent in the biblical account of hope seems to be anchored not in the correct conditions for the maturing of creation but rather in the promise and expectation of the dynamic and miraculous intervention of God in the Day of resurrection, which will one day come and for which the whole of creation waits and longs to see (Rom. 8.20).

The creation of destiny

Participatory eschatology elevates the role of humanity in the evolution of the future to that of collaborators and creators. For Whitehead it was the belief that God was at work within the constantly evolving universe that enables humanity to collaborate in its future development:

> Creation is a continuing process, and 'the process is itself the actuality', since no sooner do you arrive than you start on a fresh journey. In so far as man partakes of this creative process does he partake of the divine, of God [. . .] His true destiny as co-creator of the universe is his dignity and his grandeur.[39]

Pagitt adopts this notion of humanity as partakers of the divine, concluding that over time God and humanity can collaboratively bring about the eradication of evil on earth:

> God's intention for individuals and for collective humanity is to bring together full integration of God's agenda with our world . . . Sin is dis-integration, while God's intention is integration. When participation is reduced, we are more likely to disintegrate than to become fully integrated in the things of God.[40]

Participatory eschatology is optimistic, suggesting that humanity is gradually evolving towards greater integration with God, which means that any contrariety between the present world and the future is similarly being eradicated. Rollins also affirms participatory eschatology, agreeing that human beings are not pawns in a divine providential drama, but creators of destiny in communion with the divine:

> Destiny no longer refers to some predetermined reality that history conforms to, but rather comes into being through our direct participation in the transformation of the world. In short, we participate in the creation of the eternal itself.[41]

Rollins here exhibits an important conviction of participatory eschatology – it is not that human beings discern the will of God and then work in partnership with him, but rather by their own actions become active initiators of the future of the divine. Thus the future is not fulfilling a pre-determined timetable but being shaped through dynamic interplay between God and humanity in which humanity plays a determining role.

If the *Left Behind* motto is 'everything is doomed' then the motto of the emerging church is 'things can only get better'. Participatory eschatology means that God and humanity are working collaboratively to establish God's Kingdom of love and justice on earth. Initially, this appears to cohere with Jesus' teaching that his followers should pray 'your kingdom come, your will be done on earth as it is in heaven'(Matt. 6.10). However, a deeper exploration of participatory eschatology reveals the exaggerated importance placed upon the role of humanity in this process.

Moltmann's statement that hope sets action in motion raises a critical question about the outworking of participatory eschatology within the Christian community. Eschatology has always influenced the role evangelicals have played in society.[42] Since the emerging radicals regard themselves as standing on the precipice of a major moment in church history, then we must explore how their participatory eschatology operates as a catalyst to action. McLaren, in particular, is to be praised in his endeavour to reawaken the church to its vital role as an agent of change in the world. Getting one's hands dirty is the outworking of McLaren's eschatology and as such serves as a pertinent and prophetic challenge to the church in the world.

Nevertheless, one of the problematic features of participatory eschatology is the lack of attention given to elements of discontinuity between present and future creations. While the emerging radicals are justified in rejecting the dispensationalist agenda that condemns this present world to destruction, their idea that the current world is moving towards increasing integration with the purposes of God fails adequately to account for the present reality of sin and evil. We must question whether optimism has been substituted for hope. Pagitt's basic premise that humanity is gradually evolving towards greater integration with the things of God has surprising modernist overtones. This evolving agenda does not appear to cohere with the biblical concept of hope as being certain of that which cannot be seen (Heb. 11.1) or trusting in that which is experienced only partially in this life (1 Cor. 13.12). In removing the dichotomy between the present age and the age to come, the potency of hope as an agent of transformation is reduced. This dichotomy does not mean that we understand the world as beyond redemption, but as marred by sin yet still capable of reflecting the beauty of God as a foretaste of the world that is to come. Biblical hope does not require passivity but co-operation in the mission of the coming kingdom. As Hart comments:

> To live by faith as a disciple of Christ, as a citizen not just of this world but the kingdom of God, is to live life in accordance with a reality which is not yet fully present, but which we imagine, long for and hope for, and which, in the meanwhile, we strive to make known already in the patterns of our being and acting in the church and in the world.[43]

Emerging optimism is, therefore, a poor substitute for hope, downplaying the decisive role that God plays in the final outcome of creation. The overarching biblical narrative is arguably progressive, but cannot be represented as an incline from segregation from God towards eventual full integration with the agenda of God. The narrative of scripture commences with Creation as a place of integration with God, followed by segregation in the Fall. Both the journey of the people of Israel and the beginnings of the church, notwithstanding the cataclysmic events of the life, death and resurrection of Jesus, are also marked by the ups and downs of integration and segregation. To suggest that the church might eventually evolve towards full integration with God, without the decisive cosmic intervention of God, fails to acknowledge the nuances of the biblical narrative and the inconsistency of humanity's past record.

The lack of attention given to the resurrection further heightens this excessive continuity between the present world and the age to come. The resurrection provides a way of discerning elements of both continuity and discontinuity between the two creations. While glimpses of the age to come are experienced anticipatorily in this age, there will also be a cataclysmic act of God in the resurrection of all people from the dead and the final destruction of evil. It is the Holy Spirit which provides the critical link between these two ages; the first instalment of the life that is to come (Rom. 8.23) and a deposit which guarantees our inheritance (Eph. 1.14) However, a developed pneumatology is noticeably absent in participatory eschatology, which severely hampers its ability to link present reality to the future reality of God's kingdom.

Balance between continuity and discontinuity significantly affects the church's relationship to its surrounding culture. Newbigin's notion of the church as the pilgrim people journeying towards the grand climax of God's consummation is one that resonates strongly with me since it demonstrates that the church is not static but 'in via', pioneering the new future for the whole of humanity. The doctrine of the physical resurrection is a stark reminder of the death and decay still present in our world, which means that the church will be always on the move until Christ returns to restore creation. Eschatology provides the church with the confidence to seek signs of God's kingdom breaking into its present existence while also explaining why elements of difficulty and opposition will characterize its life until the final act of resurrection. The conviction that God would one day intervene cosmically and definitively has been a tenet of faith which has emboldened the church's witness through times of persecution.[44] In addition, it is through its eschatological identity that the church gains the courage and tenacity to be both 'at home' and 'not at home' in the world (John 17.16). This reminds us once again of the importance to the church of developing categories of discernment through which it can determine which aspects of the world it can be 'at home' in. This most critical exercise in discernment must be done through the lens of eschatology, ensuring that the tension between discontinuity and continuity is preserved.

Participatory eschatology is also in danger of laying too much emphasis on the role of humanity in securing the final outcome of creation, an overemphasis which stems from a lack of prominence on the resurrection and its correlative understanding of the lordship of Christ. Without due recognition of Christ as risen lord, humanity appears to hold all the power as creators of their own destiny rather than in obedience to and in partnership with the risen Christ.

Novelty prized over tradition

Participatory eschatology also has significant implications for the way the emerging radicals regard the church. For Pagitt, the conviction that the world is steadily evolving towards greater integration with the will of God means that he can be more optimistic about the church in the future than he is about its past:

> I am a Christian but I don't believe in Christianity. At least I don't believe in the versions of Christianity that have prevailed for the last fifteen hundred years, the ones that were perfectly suitable in their time and place but have little connection with this time and place [. . .] I am not conflicted because I struggle to believe. I am conflicted because I want to believe differently.[45]

Pagitt even suggests that there is nothing as 'beautiful, attractive, or fitting as a progressive agenda of God' and that as the church reinvents itself it mirrors God's evolving agenda.[46] Thus, priority is given to the new and surprising over the traditional and established in emerging rhetoric about the church. This penchant for novelty is evidenced in the titles of McLaren's publications: *A New Kind of Christian*, *Everything Must Change* and *A New Kind of Christianity*. These titles indicate that the pursuit of the novel and the new is a significant outworking of emerging eschatology.

Developing a biblical eschatology means the church understands how it relates to its past as well as its future. Doerksen considers McLaren's preference for novelty as one of the most problematic aspects of his approach since 'he proceeds as if the things bound up with postmodern culture should determine the understanding of a new kind of Christian'.[47]

The preference for novelty has significant implications for ecclesiology also. The premise that the church is increasingly becoming integrated with the purposes of God neglects the continuing faithfulness of God to his gathered people despite their failings and mistakes. A less future-oriented eschatology assumes that here and now is most important and so the church is free to reinvent itself afresh with every generation. However, eschatology which is based on the premise that God's people are on a journey until the Lord's return encourages the church to be bold and creative but without the liberty to reinvent itself according to present cultural sensibilities. This is what lies at the heart of the Anglican declaration of assent and the commitment of its ministers and leaders to 'proclaim afresh in each generation' the Christian faith as declared in the creeds. It appears that the vital tension, evident in both the gospels and the Pauline epistles, between the 'already' and the 'not yet' of the Kingdom of God has been replaced with a 'steadily evolving' version of eschatology. Hoedemaker imagined two extreme positions regarding ecclesiology that are pertinent here. The first is the church that defines its existence in terms of its beginnings, is characterized by nostalgia for its past experience and continually tries to recreate what it once was. The second position is that of the church that is defined by its emergence, anticipating what it can and could be, and it is into this category that the emerging radicals are in danger of falling. A perspective that dismisses whole swathes of church history can become unanchored from the past, prizing novelty above tradition, driven by the dazzling chimeras of social trends rather than the unchanging gospel of Christ. A resurrection-oriented eschatology can guard against this susceptibility by its conviction that elements of God's future have already broken into the past. This provides the church with a context in which it can learn from its past experience, both good and erroneous, and also look to its future as it seeks signs of God's kingdom breaking through.

The emerging church and the 'last things'

As stated earlier, eschatology is traditionally understood as the doctrine of the 'last things'; however, it seems important to establish from the outset the broader framework of the church as the pilgrim people of God journeying towards their final climax. Nevertheless, the matters of final judgement, death, resurrection and the parousial return of Christ remain critical to the pursuit of a serviceable eschatology for the twenty-first century.

It is in their discourse on eschatology that the emerging radicals have caused the greatest stir, generating vast controversy in the blogosphere. The brouhaha caused by the publication of Bell's *Love Wins* in 2011 illustrates the depth of emotion that surrounds such theological issues and debate, a debate that was reported upon in the mainstream press.[48] Arguably, the promotional video of *Love Wins* acted as a publicity stunt to provoke conservative evangelicals, several of whom were easily snared, offering vitriolic denouncements of Bell before even reading the book.[49]

However, the heated and often unpleasant controversy that has been generated should not detract from the importance of the issues lying behind them. The issues of judgement, death, resurrection and parousia remain at the heart of any eschatological framework and significantly shape and direct our understanding of the role the church should play in the world today. In order to consider what the emerging church has to offer to the formation of eschatology for the twenty-first century, some evaluation of its presentation of the last things, and in particular its interpretation of the return of Christ, must be given.

The last things

When it comes to the controversial subjects of judgement, heaven and hell, the emerging radicals frequently prefer to express what they do not believe, primarily the modern church's obsession with post-mortem soteriology. Emotions run high when the emerging radicals express their opinion of the way they perceive the concepts of heaven and hell have been abused within evangelicalism. McLaren denounces the way an exclusivist position has been employed as a licence for complacency and judgementalism, making the following remark after listening to a sermon on hell: 'I got this strange feeling that they actually were glad that all these people were going to be destroyed.'[50]

Rob Bell also portrays the exclusivist position in this way through his depiction of Christian pastors who have tirelessly engaged in 'God's work' while other people are having fun; hell then becomes a form of relief knowing that unbelievers are getting what they deserve.[51] Similarly, Bell commences his book *Love Wins* with the story of an art display in church in which someone had used a quote by Mahatma Gandhi, to which a note had later been added, saying 'reality check – he's in hell'.[52] Such examples provide the basis for McLaren and Bell's uneasiness with ungenerous expressions of faith that lead to a feeling of superiority or self-righteousness.[53]

McLaren's tendency to define himself by extreme versions of what he does not believe makes it difficult to extrapolate his position on the subject of judgement. Indeed Scot Mcknight criticizes him for using his interpretation of western evangelicalism as his foil.[54] McLaren's caricature of the exclusivist delighting in the eternal punishment of others is both ugly and unfair. While there may be extreme examples of those who misunderstand the nature of the gospel in this way, one would struggle to find such sentiments in either the early evangelicals like Wesley or in more recent evangelical leaders such as John Stott, who regard judgement as something that Christians should be prepared for as much as unbelievers.[55]

There are also stylistic challenges to expounding Bell's beliefs, not least his perpetual use of questions. In many ways, Bell appeals precisely because he dares to ask questions that have long been considered unsuitable subjects for evangelicals to voice in public. He provides a platform for doubts that have often been brushed under the carpet for fear of not appearing spiritual enough and his approach is perhaps a timely pastoral rebuke to a sometimes stultifying evangelical culture. However, despite its initial appeal, the questioning approach is also problematic when it relies on extreme rhetoric to assume the rejection of a theological position which is not truly representative of evangelicalism in the first place. For example, in the anecdote about Gandhi, Bell responds with the questions: 'Reality check: He's in Hell. What? Really? Gandhi's in Hell?' Yet, in doing so he fails to deal fairly with the issue and leaves the assumption that this statement is representative of evangelicalism unchallenged.

Both Bell and McLaren's rhetorical style means it is easier to define what the emerging radicals do not believe about judgement and hell than what they do. While some conservative critics have been quick to brand Bell a universalist, others have been more cautious, and Bell's argument is clearly more nuanced than many give him credit for. Newbigin highlights the tension within universalism which denies life both its seriousness, with regard to the eternal consequences of sin, and its hopefulness, by presenting an overly optimistic account of human progress. The issue of human freedom takes centre stage and raises the question whether God's ability to melt even the hardest of human hearts is a denial of human freedom. Interestingly, it was C. S. Lewis's commitment to the principle of human freedom that persuaded him of the necessity of hell:

I would pay any price to be able to say truthfully 'All will be saved'. But my reason retorts, 'Without their will, or with it?' If I say 'Without their will', I at once perceive a contradiction; how can the supreme voluntary act of self-surrender be involuntary? If I say 'With their Will', my reason replies 'How if they will not give in'.[56]

The critical issue in Bell's reluctance to talk about judgement stems from the way sin is articulated as the effect of brokenness in the world rather than human culpability. Because Bell misrepresents human sinful culpability in this way, hell is then interpreted as the vindictive action of a God who does not get his own way. Portraying God in terms of love only fails to do justice to the richness of scriptural imagery which also addresses God as spirit (John 4.24), light (1 John 1.5) or even a consuming fire (Heb. 12.29). Failure to present this holistic understanding of God means that God can be unfairly caricatured as loving and gracious one minute and then vicious and cruel in the next, rather than understanding the justice of God as the means by which these seeming dichotomies must be reconciled. Similarly, the emerging tendency to portray God's justice as only employed against social evils and never against individual human culpability, is hard to reconcile with Jesus' challenging call to personal repentance.

Both McLaren's and Bell's reluctance to directly address soteriological questions, believing that such discussions detract from responding to human suffering in our present world, nevertheless reveals the theological agenda from which they are taking inspiration.[57] The influential framework which underlies emerging eschatology is the preference to focus on present realities rather than future ones. For example, Bell argues that Jesus understood heaven and hell as present experiences and the 'continuation of the kinds of choices we make here and now'.[58] Hell is not to be understood as a post-mortem destination but as the 'big, wide, terrible evil that comes from the secrets hidden deep within our hearts all the way to the massive, society-wide collapse and chaos that comes from when we fail to live in God's world God's way'.[59] Bell presents this present-oriented eschatology in his exegesis of the parable of the prodigal son in which the two different brothers exemplify the two different realities of heaven and hell in this life. Hell is depicted in the older brother's resentment and reluctance to see all that the Father has already given him, refusing to 'trust the Father's version of his story'.[60] Hell and heaven are interconnected and co-existing, 'bumping up against each other' and Bell states that 'we create hell whenever we fail to trust God's retelling of our story'.[61]

In some ways, the emerging eschatological preference for the present over the future acts as a corrective to spurious forms of the gospel that have prioritized a spiritual future at the expense of compassionate engagement with the present. As is often rightly pointed out, Jesus teaches more about the priority of the poor than he does the specifics of hell. However, one could argue that interpreting heaven and hell primarily as present realities ultimately diminishes the future horizon towards which the narrative of scripture points.

Bell vividly illustrates the idea of hell as the horrendous consequences of erroneous decisions in this life by the devastating and horrific scenarios witnessed in the rape and genocide in Rwanda. However, it is hard to see how this argument adds up when in reality it is more often the victims who suffer the consequences of hell while the perpetrators are exonerated and in reality face 'no hell in this life'.[62] Judgement cannot adequately be expressed in terms of natural consequences of humanity's actions since all wrongs are not ultimately put right in this life; divine action is also required.

While the emerging radicals offer a helpful critique of a perverse use of judgement to frighten people into submission, we must ensure that, through fear of offending our postmodern sensibilities, we do not lose the demanding and arresting challenge of the Gospel of Jesus. Newbigin again reminds us that judgement serves not only as an impetus to mission but as a challenge to the integrity of believers' own lives:

> It follows that the grave and terrible warnings that the New Testament contains about the possibility of eternal loss are

directed to those who are confident that they are among the saved. It is the branches of the Vine, not the surrounding brambles, that are threatened with burning. It is those who had their invitation cards to the wedding banquet who will find themselves outside, while the riffraff of the streets and lanes will be sitting at table.[63]

Resurrection

We have already observed that the resurrection does not feature prominently in the emerging radicals' writings. Bell explains the resurrection as part of the cyclical 'death-and-life mystery' that is 'built into the very fabric of creation'.[64] McLaren echoes Bell's cyclical understanding of life and death as essential to the mechanism of the universe and its 'dynamic dance of give and take, procreation and death, production and recycling, thriving and struggle, and extinction and evolution'.[65] He describes death as a seamless transition between living in God's presence in the present, to another way of living in the future:

I expect to experience death as a passage, like birth, like passing through a door. I don't know how that passing will come [. . .] like a slow slipping away in disease, like a sudden jolt or shock in an accident, like losing my grip and feeling that I'm falling, only to discover that I'm not falling out of life, but deeper into it.[66]

It is the lack of attention given to the doctrine of the resurrection that is, in my opinion, the most serious shortcoming in emerging eschatology. The preference to talk about a cyclical account of life and death does not sit easily within a biblical framework and stems from a more general emerging emphasis upon original goodness, neglecting the Fall as the place where sin and death entered the world. This leads to a failure to make a crucial distinction between natural death, which is part of the created world, and 'spiritual death' which is expressed in terms of exile and separation from God. Expressing life and death as part of the fabric of creation belittles Wright's understanding of death as a 'real and savage break' and 'the horrible denial of the goodness of human life'.[67] It is when death is understood as a 'real and savage break' that the doctrine of the resurrection carries its greatest potency. While the emerging radicals are evidently influenced by Wright's eschatology, there are certain aspects of his theology which they neglect, an emphasis on the resurrection being most crucial. The doctrine of resurrection entails two core convictions: that resurrection has uniquely happened to one person and that the first resurrection was an anticipation of the final resurrection at the end of history.

> There will come a time, which might indeed come at any time, when, in the great renewal of the world which Easter itself foreshadowed, Jesus himself will be personally present, and will be the agent and the model for the transformation that will happen both to the whole world and also to believers.[68]

Physical resurrection, therefore, is essential to Christian hope. Without the resurrection, Christianity is rendered impotent and futile. The doctrine of resurrection has two significant implications which are pertinent to our exploration of emerging eschatology, one of which we have already noted in the discussion on participatory eschatology. First, the doctrine of resurrection makes sense of the discontinuity and continuity between this world and the world that is to come. The doctrine of the resurrection enables an affirmation of the physical nature of the world and its potential for redemption and restoration (which *Left Behind* eschatology neglects), while also identifying its propensity to sin and decay (which emerging eschatology neglects). The doctrine of physical resurrection means that we do not have to choose between these two opposing scenarios. It is the doctrine of physical resurrection which enables us to hold to the original goodness of creation while also acknowledging the existence and the extent of evil in the world without needing to capitulate to a dispensationalist view of the spiralling decay of creation.

Second, the resurrection has implications for an understanding of mission. Wright observes that historically within evangelicalism belief in physical resurrection has 'always gone with a strong view of God's justice, and of God as the good creator', leading to a determination to oppose injustice in the world.[69] Conversely the times when evangelicals were cautious in their belief in physical resurrection, instead spiritualising the world to come, their social engagement also dwindled. This argument must appeal to the emerging radicals' desire to distance themselves from notions of heaven as an escape route. However, it is actually a theology of resurrection that provides the firm foundation from which such otherworldly scenarios can be challenged. In Christological terms, without the resurrection, Christ can be understood as a teacher or prophet whose death was at best exemplary and at worst tragic. However, with the resurrection, Christ can be understood as the risen and exalted Lord, an appellation which does not feature strongly in emerging Christology. This neglected emphasis is important because it provides both missionary motivation and the conviction that the new era inaugurated through the death and resurrection of Christ will be a place where injustice and sin will one day be entirely vanquished. The resurrection does not advocate followers of Christ to rest on the laurels of their secure salvation but invites them to be active in hastening God's new creation.

In contrast to the other emerging radicals, Rollins places the resurrection as a dominant feature of his world-affirming eschatology. For Rollins, the cross is the place of atheism: the place where the existential experience of the loss of God is expressed and a way is provided for followers of Jesus to move out of religious certainties into a place of forsakenness and loss. The resurrection is not, Rollins argues, the solution to the problem of the cross. Instead, it opens the way up to religionless faith in which securities are removed and we can embrace ourselves and the world:

We must read the Resurrection in its full radicality; as the state of being in which one is able to embrace the cold embrace of the cross. If the crucifixion marks the moment of darkness, then the Resurrection is the very act of living fully in this darkness and saying 'yes' to it.[70]

This experience of saying 'yes' to the darkness is understood as a life-affirming choice. Rollins talks about the resurrection as being stripped of securities and certainties and entailing the affirmation that we are creators of destiny and not pawns in the purposes of God. Rollins also elaborates upon his understanding of doubt within the context of the cross and resurrection. He refers to doubt as 'a holy Saturday experience' and suggests that it is in that place of uncertainty and darkness before the resurrection that the decision to follow Jesus is made authentic:

> A faith that can only exist in the light of victory and certainty is one which really affirms the self while pretending to affirm Christ, for it only follows Jesus in the belief that Jesus conquered death . . . A real follower of Jesus would commit to him before the crucifixion, between the crucifixion and the resurrection and after the resurrection.[71]

It is in this way that the resurrection is not offered as the basis of faith but one aspect of an ongoing journey of authenticity that incorporates both faith and doubt.

While Rollins and Wright share the same revulsion of salvation as world-escapism, their versions of resurrection as the antidote could not be more different. For Wright, the physical resurrection of Christ provides the assurance of future resurrection along with immense missional impetus. Conversely, Rollins talks about the resurrection as being stripped of certainties and affirming humanity's role as creators of destiny. However, Rollins' emphasis on humanity's experience of resurrection elevates human beings to centre stage rather than Jesus as resurrected lord; sacrifice and obedience are replaced by freedom and creativity. This account of the Christian faith is far removed from the stories of martyrs who lost their lives because of their conviction and belief in the resurrected Christ. Rollins' theology is noticeably born in an environment removed from the costly experience of such sacrifice and persecution. Furthermore, Rollins' emphasis on the authenticity of the holy Saturday experience seems to contradict the Apostle Paul's idea that faith follows the act of resurrection: 'If Christ has not been raised, our preaching is useless and so is your faith' (1 Cor. 15.14). Christian faith is specifically resurrection faith. It begs the question whether Rollins is demanding more from his readers than Jesus himself expected of the first disciples. Holy Saturday was marked by fear and doubt and it was only after either seeing the resurrected Christ or hearing testimony of his resurrection that faith was born. Wright himself comments that if Jesus had not been raised from the dead then his life and words possess no relevance beyond his death.[72] Christian faith is ultimately a response to the unique and definitive act of Christ's resurrection from the dead. Doubt is never demonized in scripture, but unbelief is the very antithesis of resurrection faith. Jesus did not affirm Thomas in his unbelief but invited him to 'stop doubting and believe' (John 20.27). It was the experience of the physically resurrected Christ that enabled the disciples to emerge from despair, embrace hope and embark upon their task of mission. Perhaps the time is right for the church to gather courage once again in the missionary mandate that the resurrection of Christ provides.

The return of Christ

It is the doctrine of the return of Christ that has perhaps been most radically rethought by emerging eschatology. The portrayal of the second coming of Christ in popular dispensationalism is considered especially damaging by the emerging radicals because of its inherent link to a scenario that foretells the destruction of the current world:

> This eschatological understanding of a violent second coming leads us to believe that in the end, even God finds it impossible to fix the world apart from violence and coercion; no one should be surprised that those shaped by this theology behave accordingly.[73]

The return of Christ cannot be considered a question of *adiaphora* and therefore rethinking it has serious implications for whether the emerging church considers itself orthodox. The doctrine of Christ's return is attested to in the Apostolic, Nicene and Athanasian creeds, which declare that 'He will come again in glory to judge the living and the dead and his kingdom shall have no end'. While mainstream denominations may hold differing opinions on the rapture, the millennium and so forth, the return of Christ in glory is held by all as a major doctrinal tenet. However, it is the depiction of the return of Christ in vengeful and violent imagery that has caused the emerging radicals to reimagine this aspect of eschatological belief.

Yet in McLaren's desire to rightly reject a violent and coercive portrayal of Jesus, he fails to make a distinction between the manner of Christ's return and the character of the Christ who returns. Although the character of Christ is not different in his return, his mode is decidedly changed and what was once hidden and 'laid-aside' is now manifested. As Travis comments:

> One of the purposes of Christ's coming will be to reveal what is now hidden, to make clear-cut what is open to doubt, to demonstrate the glory of Christ in contrast with the 'incognito' element in his first coming.[74]

I am not certain that in rejecting a false stereotype of a returning Christ, emerging eschatology offers anything substantive in replacement of it. Participatory eschatology seems to emphasize the gradual evolution of the completion of the kingdom, negating the need for any future decisive or cataclysmic action on God's behalf.

As well as refuting popular dispensationalism's version of the returning Christ, McLaren criticizes those who regard the future as a movie that has already been recorded, which we are simply watching play.[75] In place of a deterministic reading of scripture, McLaren suggests that prophetic teaching operates as a system of warning about the consequences of actions rather than as predictions about events. Thus the prophets warn what will happen if their word is not heeded in the hope that their 'prediction' will not come true. Their words 'wake us up – to realize that serious consequences could flow from our current carelessness'.[76]

Yet this definition of prophecy as warning rather than future prediction seems tendentious since there are scant occasions within scripture of prophetic warnings and promises that did not come to pass. Arguably, Nineveh heeded Jonah's reluctant warnings and repented and thus disaster did not fall upon them but this was exception rather than norm.

Critical to an understanding of the emerging account of the 'last things' is the eschatological agenda which Perriman outlines in *The Coming of the Son of Man* since this appears to express the broad schemata which shapes the emerging radicals' ideas about the return of Christ. McLaren's writing pays heed to it in footnotes and his thoughts reflect in summary what Perriman writes in detail. Perriman defines his position as post-eschatological, meaning that the majority of the eschatological drama of the New Testament has already taken place.[77]

Perriman maintains that the New Testament has three future horizons in view. The first is the destruction of Jerusalem in AD 70 which is what the majority of Jesus' apocalyptic teaching addresses. The second horizon is the less sharply defined situation of the collapse of Roman Imperialism and the elevation of Christ to a place above Ceasar, which he regards as the parousia. He contends that the New Testament focuses on these two horizons and that the third horizon of judgement and new creation is 'barely discerned beyond the dark billowing visions of impending crisis'.[78] The parousia is then understood as referring to the authority that is given to Jesus at the inauguration of the new age ushered in by the events of AD 70.

While the emerging radicals do not offer a rethinking of parousia in the depth of detail that Perriman does, many convergences remain and they present some theological ramifications of this position. If the parousia has already taken place through the non-physical reign of Christ on earth, then the cosmic return of Christ as judge and king can no longer be a feature of theological expectation. This explains the absence of emphasis upon future judgement and McLaren's preference to interpret salvation as escaping 'the chain of bad actions and bad consequences through forgiveness'.[79]

However, a post-eschatological perspective which suggests that the parousia has already taken place is a theory challenged by many. Both Michael Green and Leon Morris maintain that Jesus, in the Gospels, references two horizons indicating that while some predicted events were to occur in the disciples' lifetime, others were not, most significantly the return of Jesus. In fact, Morris even goes so far as to suggest that Jesus actively dissuades the disciples from expecting his return imminently.[80] Green implies that while AD 70 is a critical part of the apocalyptic narrative in Matthew, Jesus' teaching is 'primarily about the end of the world's history'.[81] The biblical arguments are complex and extensive and cannot be explored fully here; however, the impact of a spiritualized concept of the parousia upon emerging theology cannot be underestimated and the parallels between emerging eschatology and the realized eschatology of the Social Gospel movement become apparent.[82]

It is worth comparing the reinterpretation that this doctrine underwent at the hands of modernity when scholars, such as Bultmann, sought to demythologize the parousia. The parousia was then understood to mean that 'Christ comes to me' as an existential encounter in response to the Christian message. Despite the emerging church's endeavour to rid itself of the vestiges of modernity, one wonders whether what is offered in this reimagining of the parousia is anything more than a social version of the individualistic parousia offered by modernity.

This rethinking of the concept of the coming of the Son of Man is hugely significant for emerging eschatology and we must question what is lost in the spiritualization of a key theological conviction.

By contrast, the return of Christ is integral to the gospel events, the final piece of the jigsaw that completes all that has gone before. The Christian hope in the return of Christ is the logical outcome of faith in God's activity through the life, death and resurrection of Christ and it is hard to see how there can be meaningful progression without that end.

In order to maintain that the biblical narrative from Creation, through Israel and latterly the church, is part of a linear account of history, it must also have a completion. The cataclysmic intervention of God in judgement, resurrection and re-creation is integral to this biblical view of history. The return of Christ ensures that we are not left with a cyclical view of history in which it is impossible to see how the promise of the new heavens and earth will ever become reality. The gospel is dependent on Christ's return to complete its story. The future physical resurrection of the dead, of which Christ is the first-fruit, is reliant upon Christ's return in glory, as is the final conquest of evil and the devil. We must also perhaps question what is lost in a post-eschatological account of the parousia.

It was Newbigin who said that 'the implication of a true eschatological perspective will be missionary obedience'.[83] The return of Jesus has always featured prominently as a motivation to mission, not least among the missionary expansion of the eighteenth century which propelled people to take the gospel overseas to nations who had not yet heard of Christ. Taking Jesus as the returning judge out of the gospel schemata means missiology can readily be reframed purely in terms of social concern and environmentalism. Evangelism becomes an optional extra.

Moreover, the parousia holds relevance to the development of ecclesiology. Integral to the identity of the church is the sense that the Christian community is a partially fulfilled reality; Paul describes the church as the bride of Christ, being prepared for the final consummation that is to come (Eph. 5.27). The church that no longer anticipates that final day of consummation can easily become shaped and fashioned by the present culture in which it exists. As we have already explored, it is the faith in the final and definitive work of God in Christ that enables the church to stand firm and serve with compassion and conviction as she makes her journey towards that final day.

In conclusion, the return of Jesus is paramount in the development of both missiology and ecclesiology and thus any attempt to reinterpret the return of Jesus will impact the future life and witness of the church. Genuine missional ecclesiology must be rooted in an eschatology which holds out the hope of a Christ who will return in glory. The emerging church may believe it offers an 'eschatology of hope', but without the visible and glorious return of Christ that hope can never be realized. If eschatology really is the fuel to the missionary fire, then the implications of this new account of the parousia for missiology and ecclesiology could be troubling indeed.

Notes

1 Wright, *Surprised by Hope*, p. 134.
2 Fergusson and Sarot, *The Future as God's Gift*, p. 151.
3 Wright, *Surprised by Hope*, p. 267.
4 Jones, 'A Hopeful Faith', p. 130.
5 Wardrop, *Michael Jackson*.
6 http://leftbehind.com/
7 Bennett, *The Origins of Left Behind Eschatology*.
8 Erickson, *Contemporary Options in Eschatology*, p. 111.
9 Frykholm, *Rapture Culture*, p. 176.
10 Bashir, *Bishop's Heaven*.
11 Wright, 'Farewell to the Rapture'.
12 Frykholm, *Rapture Culture*, p. 14.
13 Gribben, *Writing the Rapture*, p. 21.
14 Quoted in Frykholm, *Rapture Culture*, p. 175.
15 McLaren, *Everything Must Change*, p. 3.
16 LaHaye and Jenkins, *Kingdom Come*, p. xiii.
17 Gribben, *Rapture Fiction*, p. 87.
18 McLaren, *A Generous Orthodoxy*, p. 237.
19 McLaren, *The Word of the Lord to Evangelicals* (Kindle edition) ch. 5, paragraph 35.
20 Rollins, *Insurrection*, p. 138.
21 Wright, *Surprised by Hope*, p. 26.
22 LaHaye and Jenkins, *Desecration*, p. 179.
23 McLaren, *More Ready Than You Realize*, p. 89.
24 Quoted in McLaren, *Everything Must Change*, p. 152.
25 Wright, *Surprised by Hope*, p. 150.
26 McKnight, *Five Streams of the Emerging Church*.
27 Bosch, *Transforming Mission*, p. 10.
28 McLaren, *Everything Must Change*, p. 94.
29 This phrase originated with Dominic Crossan. For their debate on the nature of the resurrection see Stewart (ed.), *The Resurrection of Jesus*.
30 Pittenger, *The Lure of Divine Love*, p. 3.

31 Epperly, *Emerging Process*, Introduction; Epperly, *Process Theology*, p. 7.

32 For a review of the core philosophical concepts of Whitehead's process thought and an exploration of its implications; for theology, see Moluf, *The Whiteheadean Foundation of Process Theology*; Pittenger, *The Lure of Divine Love*, p. 7.

33 Hartshorne, *Divine Relativity*, p. 96.

34 McLaren, *Everything Must Change*, p. 94.

35 Ibid., p. 173.

36 Epperly, *Process Theology*, p. 21.

37 Interview with Krish Kandiah at the 'Reaching the unchurched network', 18 June 2008.

38 McLaren, *Everything Must Change*, p. 173.

39 Price (ed.), *The Dialogues of Alfred North Whitehead*, p. 297.

40 Pagitt, 'The Emerging Church and Embodied Theology', p. 132.

41 Rollins, *Insurrection*, p. 133.

42 Bebbington, 'Eschatology in Evangelical History', p. 86.

43 Hart, 'Eschatology and Imagination', p. 137.

44 Daley, *The Hope of the Early Church*, p. 1.

45 Pagitt, *A Christianity Worth Believing*, p. 2.

46 Pagitt, *The Emerging Church and Embodied Theology*, p. 136.

47 Doerksen, *The Air Is Not Quite Fresh: Emerging Church Ecclesiology*.

48 Marrapodi, *Christian Author's Book Sparks Charges of Heresy*.

49 Perhaps the most significant example of this was John Piper's 'Farewell Rob Bell' tweet which sent ripples through cyberspace. Piper, *Farewell Rob Bell*.

50 McLaren, *The Last Word and the Word After That*, p. xxiii.

51 Bell, *Love Wins*, p. 180.

52 Ibid., p. 1.

53 McLaren, *A Generous Orthodoxy*, p. 109.

54 McKnight, *The Ironic Faith of Emergents*.

55 Stott, *The Contemporary Christian*, p. 373.

56 Lewis, *The Problem of Pain*, p. 95.

57 McLaren, *A Generous Orthodoxy*, p. 112.

58 Bell, *Velvet Elvis*, p. 147.

59 Ibid., p. 93.

60 Ibid., p. 169.

61 Ibid., p. 173.

62 Galli, *God Wins*, p. 103.

63 Newbigin, 'Cross Currents'.

64 Bell, *Love Wins*, p. 131.

65 McLaren, *Everything Must Change*, p. 131.

66 McLaren, *Making Eschatology Personal*.

67 Wright, *Surprised by Hope*, p. 21.

68 Ibid., p. 148.

69 Ibid., p. 38.

70 Rollins, *Insurrection*, p. 112.

71 Rollins, *How (Not) to Speak of God*, p. 34.

72 Wright, *Jesus and the Victory of God*, p. 659.

73 McLaren, *Everything Must Change*, p. 144.

74 Travis, *I Believe in the Second Coming of Jesus*, p. 86.

75 McLaren, *The Secret Message of Jesus*, p. 172.

76 Ibid., p. 175.

77 Perriman, 'NT Imminence of Parousia'.

78 Perriman, *Re:Mission*, p. 5.

79 McLaren, *A Generous Orthodoxy*, p. 96.

80 Morris, *The Gospel According to Matthew*, p. 434.

81 Green, *The Message of Matthew*, p. 250.

82 Rauschenbusch, *Christianity and The Social Crisis in the Twenty first Century*.

83 Newbigin, *The Household of God*, p. 181.

4

The Emerging Church
and Missiology

Introduction

Mission has long been considered one of the hallmarks of evangelical spirituality and while the fervency with which it has pursued its missionary calling has ebbed and flowed, mission has always been a feature of evangelical activism. Prior to the eighteenth century, Protestantism was not known for its missionary prominence, with the Puritan emphasis more on preaching the word and prayer, but through the events and individuals of the evangelical revival, mission soon became one of the principal attributes of not only evangelicalism but Protestantism itself. However, while mission flourished and prospered in the eighteenth century it was not regarded as integral to the domestic life of the church and had little influence upon the formation of ecclesiology. In addition, the call to mission was not initially understood to extend beyond the boundaries of Christendom. However, with the establishment of European colonies in Latin America, Asia and Africa, the chance arose to reach territories which were previously untouched by the gospel message. When coupled with the rise of the voluntary society, this new opportunity contributed to the explosion of Protestant missionary activity that took place in the nineteenth and twentieth centuries.[1] The 'activism' that Bebbington assigns to evangelicalism was typically manifested in this desire to take the gospel to the unconverted, a conviction exemplified by the Cambridge Seven: a group of intelligent and able individuals who left behind the prospect of promising careers to establish evangelical witness in China in 1885. It is in this way that mission has become one of the defining features of evangelicalism, being understood not merely as the calling of a select few, but as the duty of all who would call themselves Christian.

The origins of mission in North America are particularly relevant to the development of the form of evangelicalism from which the emerging radicals emerge. Contrary to popular misconception, American mission did not originate in the ministry of Carey and Adoniram Judson in the nineteenth century. Missionary endeavour was birthed in New England Protestantism and the belief that it was the church's destiny to expand via small pockets of believers who would convert and civilize indigenous communities. These early Protestants believed that the return of Christ was imminent but that before this happened there would be a third and final epoch in which the church would be expanded and the Antichrist defeated.[2] Properly locating this missionary origin is informative in two ways. First, it demonstrates that American missionary activity began with a concern for expansion and extension and, second, it acknowledges that eschatology played an important role in catalysing missionary activity.

This chapter explores how the emerging church regards its missionary heritage and considers the distinctive contribution that the emerging church is making to contemporary discussions about mission. One preliminary observation must, however, be made about the emerging church's contribution to missiology. Some question whether or not the emerging church should be considered a missiological movement at all or whether it simply caters for those disenfranchized by mainstream expressions of Christianity rather than those for whom church is not an existing feature of life.[3] While that may sound harsh, the sentiment is actually echoed by one of the emerging church's own leading voices: 'Emergents start new churches to save their own faith, not necessarily as an outreach strategy.'[4] It is possible to argue that it is not missiology that drives the emerging church but rather a desire to cater for disillusioned Christians who have seen the failures of the mega-church movement and no longer feel that this approach adequately meets their spiritual needs.

Thus, the emerging church responds to those who no longer identify with mainstream evangelicalism and yet still wish to identify with Christian discipleship. Publications such as Tomlinson's *The Post-evangelical*, Alan Jamieson's *A Churchless Faith* and Pagitt's *A Christianity Worth Believing* reflect this spirit of disillusionment and disappointment with mainstream evangelicalism and highlight the need for alternative expressions of faith. As the emerging church addresses the needs of disaffected Christians it also becomes an attractive alternative for interested seekers who are put off institutional Christianity, and missiology becomes a by-product. However, a case can be made that when church is tailored for those who have been long disenfranchised by institutional Christianity, it can overlook some of the central tenets of the Christian faith in the process. These considerations must be borne in mind when looking at the contribution of the emerging church to missiology.

Notwithstanding such caveats, an exploration of emerging missiology is warranted not least because it is in the formation of missiology that it becomes apparent what is understood by the gospel of Jesus Christ itself. In order to critique the emerging church's approach, I will explore two themes that lie at the heart of emerging missiology.

Why the emerging church prefers 'missional' to 'mission'

The term 'missional' has been adopted by the emerging radicals to signify a new understanding of mission, its deployment – most commonly in conjunction with the word 'church' – also signifying a new understanding within ecclesiology. However, the emerging radicals are not the only ones who have adopted this term and it is being used more widely. 'Missio' originates from the Latin for 'sending' and has been employed within Christian theology to denote the sending of the Son within a trinitarian framework. In the sixteenth century, 'mission' was only used to refer to the activity of the church to promulgate the gospel for the purposes of expansion, whereby it became associated with colonization and 'magisterial commissioning'.[5] One common thread among all those who embrace the term 'missional' in an emerging context is its use to denote a departure from previous definitions of missions and missionary. Rejection of the associations with western imperialism and colonialism arises out of what McLaren describes as 'post-colonial embarrassment with the term missionary'.[6]

While definitions of 'missional' vary greatly, there are four strands that appear consistent across a relatively broad evangelical theological spectrum which provide an appropriate understanding of the term while also illustrating its positive contribution.

First, the term missional demonstrates the impact of *Missio Dei* on contemporary understandings of mission practice. Missiologists have increasingly been drawn to this phrase because its expresses the conviction that mission is not the responsibility or activity of humanity, but stems from the character and nature of God. Barth first articulated the notion of mission as an activity of God himself at the Brandenberg Missionary Conferences in 1932, but the concept did not really gain widespread acceptance until the International Missionary Conference in Willengen in 1952. *Missio Dei* reflects the conviction that mission stems not only from the activity of God but the nature of the Trinitarian God himself. God is the great missionary who sends his church into the world just as he sent his Son into the world. Thus mission is not the property of the church but rooted in the ontological nature of the sending God. Participating in mission was understood to be participating in the sending love of God himself. In many ways, mission remained church-centric at Willengen; however there were strong voices in opposition.[7] Hoekendijk's paper entitled 'The Church in Missionary Thinking' was hugely influential in this regard, voicing his emphatic criticism that church-centric mission is both illegitimate and easily misdirected.[8] Since Willengen, the term *Missio Dei* has undergone further modification to express something of the breadth of mission to include all aspects of God's work within human creation.[9] Flett, however, argues that the term *Missio Dei* lacks purposeful definition, becoming a catchall for various missiological developments, and cannot escape an anthropological grounding for mission.[10] However, notwithstanding the debate surrounding the definition of *Missio Dei*, the emerging preference for 'missional' arguably continues along this trajectory of thought which seeks to re-orientate the church as an integral part of God's own mission:

> Mission is not just a program of the church. It defines the church as God's sent people. Either we are defined by mission, or we reduce the scope of the gospel and the mandate of the church. Thus our challenge today is to move from church with mission to missional church.[11]

Second, the term missional denotes a contrast with institutional forms and models of church. For the church to be missional it must relinquish its cherished assumptions about ecclesial practice and embrace new and creative expressions of worship. Ray Anderson regards this as one of the distinctive attractions of the emerging church:

> What marks emerging churches as different is that they let go of what the church has been in order to become the church that will be.[12]

Third, the word missional provides a way to breach the divide between evangelism and social action by offering a more holistic approach. Abraham argues that Wesley's missionary legacy was ambiguous and its hazy intellectual foundations meant that in the wake of evangelical revival, ideas of evangelism bifurcated into the dichotomy between evangelism and social action that has subsequently hampered evangelical missiology.[13] The term missional ameliorates this division. In addition, both Brian McLaren and Tim Keller, while representing different streams of evangelicalism, regard 'missional' as offering a third way, capable of transcending the dichotomies of conservatism and liberalism and thus making such labels nonsensical in the postmodern world. Keller believes that it is only the missional church that will be able to survive in the non-Christian West:

In general, a church must be more deeply and practically committed to deeds of compassion and social justice than traditional liberal churches and more deeply and practically committed to evangelism and conversion than traditional fundamentalist churches. This kind of church is profoundly counter-intuitive to American observers. It breaks their ability to categorise (and dismiss) it as liberal or conservative.[14]

McLaren, however, takes his use of the term missional a stage further, suggesting that it can provide a middle way between the extremes of universalism and exclusivism: 'The missional way is better: the gospel brings blessings to all, adherents and non-adherents alike.'[15]

Fourth, the missional church seeks to take seriously its post-Christendom context, believing that it must engage authentically with culture. Murray argues that the Christendom mindset perverted thinking about mission:

Mission now involved ensuring doctrinal conformity, enforcing church attendance, enshrining moral standards in the criminal law and eradicating choice in the area of religion. Methods used included education, persuasion, inducement and coercion.[16]

Murray believes that the church must now reject the unhelpful and unbiblical patterns of mission adopted during the Christendom period. The emerging radicals believe that the church in the West has become syncretized with modernity.

Christian Churches are owned lock, stock and barrel by modernity. They have clung to modern modes of thought and action, their ways of embodying and enacting the Christian tradition frozen in patterns of high modernity.[17]

Jones imagines the youth workers of today as pioneering prophets called to wake the mainstream church from its 'modernistic slumber'.[18] Jones likens conventional forms of the church to the payphone: a 'dead' and obsolete form of communication.[19] Murray vociferously denounces the modern church for exchanging its 'prophetic role' for a 'chaplaincy role' in which it sanctified social occasions and state policies, assuming a primarily pastoral role.[20] The Christendom church saw itself as a moral majority rather than a prophetic minority and used scripture to support rather than challenge the prevailing culture.

In many ways, there is much to be commended in the emerging radicals' preference for missional over mission. Where the term 'missional' is used as a clarion call to a renewed expression of mission in which the church plays a more central role it is to be welcomed. This acts as a helpful redress to a modus operandi which has too often been as an army sending solitary soldiers out on an occasional offensive skirmish while the rest of the army stayed safe in the barracks. In addition, where the word 'missional' is used to encourage creativity and interdenominational collaboration in mission practice then it also has much to offer evangelicalism in the twenty-first century.

Nevertheless, some have questioned the emerging radicals' use of 'missional' and Kimball wonders whether their use of it is anything more than an issue of semantics:

> I have been observing, listening, and asking questions about the missional movement. I have a suspicion that the missional model has not yet proven itself beyond the level of theory.[21]

Richardson goes so far as to suggest that in the desire to stand apart from modern expressions of mission, the term 'missional' has become a 'code word for a claim to the moral high ground'.[22] In their protest against modern mission, the emerging radicals once again demonstrate one of the problematic aspects of their approach: that it is easier to define emerging thinking in terms of what it is against rather than what it is for.

For the emerging radicals, the preference for missional over mission also incorporates reticence about evangelism, a term McLaren says has become so 'bastardized' that he can scarcely bear to use it. The following passage by McLaren illustrates the extent to which he perceives modern evangelism to have injured the portrayal of God himself.

An uptight God who is about black-and-white easy answers and brittle, rigid logic and law, rather than about profound and many-faceted truth, self-sacrificing love, compassionate justice, and profound relationships.

A conceptual God who is encountered through systems of abstractions, propositions and terminology rather than through an amazing story, intense poetry, beauty, experience, experiment and community.

A controlling God who is cold, analytical and mechanistic rather than a master artist and lover who is passionate about good and evil, justice and injustice, beauty and desecration, hope and cynicism.

An exclusive God who favors insiders and is biased against outsiders rather than a God of scandalous inclusion, amazing mercy, and shocking acceptance, who blesses 'insiders' so they can extend the blessing to 'outsiders', thus making everyone an insider.

A tense God who prefers people to become judgmental, arrogant and closed-minded rather than compassionate, humble, and teachable.[23]

This statement not only exhibits the intensity with which McLaren feels the church has 'missed the point' but highlights the issues that catalyse the emerging radicals' protest against modern mission.[24] McLaren's antithetical rhetoric is employed emotively, but theological conservatives such as Carson have criticized him for presenting his argument in terms of antithetical extremes that do not accurately represent either theological position. As McLaren and others present a wooden and one-dimensional portrayal of modernism, so too is their description of the church under modernism caricatured. Thus modern Christianity is explained as propositional truth at the expense of experience, doctrinal correctness at the expense of authentic living and coercive evangelism at the expense of compassion. Carson regards the drawing of false antithesis as one of the most dangerous pitfalls of the emerging approach:

So which shall we choose? Experience or truth? The left wing of an airplane or the right? Love or integrity? Study or service? Evangelism or discipleship? The front wheels of a car, or the rear? Subjective knowledge or objective knowledge? Faith or obedience?

Damn all false antitheses to hell, for they generate false gods, they perpetuate idols, they twist and distort our souls, they launch the church into violent pendulum swings whose oscillations succeed only in dividing brothers and sisters in Christ.[25]

McLaren's tendency to present the contrast between modern and postmodern mission as a list of binary opposites is strikingly ironic since we have already seen how the emerging radicals regard binary thinking as a modern virus. Yet McLaren, in his caricature of the God of modernity, posits binary opposites in his endeavour to reimagine postmodern mission. Thus the choice McLaren presents is between rigid uncaring truth or love and compassion; it is either restrictive conceptualization or it is beautiful narrative. What McLaren does not seem to allow for is the conviction that propositional truth could be also loving and compassionate, or that a concept of God that could be explained in a philosophically rigorous manner is not at odds with a beautiful and creative retelling of the gospel story. These polar opposites present the reader with a false choice between truth and beauty. In a similar way, McKnight suggests that Bell's rhetorical approach – such as his question 'Does Love win or is history tragic?' – as overly reliant on binary oppositions and proposes that he should adopt a more complex approach to such questions, allowing both sentiments to be true: 'It can be true that a good deal of history is tragic and also true that God's love wins in millions and millions of cases.'[26] Furthermore, such reliance upon binary opposites renders the emerging radicals vulnerable to the weaknesses of reactionary theology. Arguably, theology is often developed in reaction to an opposite extreme position and so the history of the church is observed as a series of theological pendulum swings.

This pendulum swing has seldom been more apparent than in the emerging radicals' rejection of the methods of modern mission and their desire to recreate missional identity for the postmodern age. To McLaren, modern mission is characterized by conquest and coercion and legitimized forceful persuasion as a form of church recruitment. In addition, its emphasis on apologetics has narrowed the gospel to a list of philosophical propositions used as 'logical ammunition'.[27] McLaren contrasts modern evangelism's emphasis on argument and logical reasoning with the parabolic approach of Jesus, which, he suggests, was more interested in generating conversation than presenting an argument.[28] The term missional, then, endeavours to leave behind the outdated and coercive model of modern mission and seek to reimagine it for a postmodern age. Where the word evangelism is used it is in connection with 'conversation' and stripped of the fixation with answers, argument and recruitment. The emerging radicals' use of the word missional signifies a rejection of modern mission and the embracing of a new way for evangelism to be incarnated, an approach which McLaren likens to a dance and Webber to a display. Where modern mission focused on offering opportunities for the nonbeliever to explore the Christian message, the missional church in the postmodern milieu operates by 'immersing the unchurched in the experience of community'.[29] Rollins imagines that the emerging church has the 'upper hand' as the uniquely placed expression of church in the twenty-first century that can really relate to and resonate with its context. The emerging radicals often contrast the clarity of modernity with the profundity or 'fuzziness' of postmodernity.[30] Rollins believes that expressing this fuzziness or profundity is an integral part of the emerging church's mission.

> The emerging church is able to leave aside the need for clarity and open up the way for us to accept the fact that we are embraced by the beloved rather than finding agreement concerning how we ought to understand this beloved.[31]

For Rollins, an understanding of the hypernimity of God means that the emerging church is uniquely placed to work in partnership with other churches, since it 'decentres' the idea of one true interpretation held against others, and he ambitiously suggests that this approach can breach the divide between liberal and conservative theologians. Within a missional context, Rollins' belief in the 'hypernimity' of God dissuades the postmodern evangelist from definitive statements about the Christian gospel; he rejects apologetics as a coercive method of evidence-based evangelism, even questioning the validity of answering people's questions:

> The emerging community is in a unique place to embrace a type of communication that opens up thought by asking questions and celebrating complexity . . . the emerging church must endeavour to be a question rather than an answer, and an aroma rather than a food.[32]

In his reimagining of evangelism for the postmodern age in Velvet Elvis, Rob Bell likens the evangelist to a tour guide, opening people's eyes to the reality of what already exists rather than taking Jesus to a place where he is not present.

A more dialogical, creative and relational approach to evangelism is to be welcomed, but once again the dangers of reactionary theology become apparent. Duncan MacLaren identifies one of the flaws in the post-Christendom mindset towards mission as being the speed with which it has sought to throw off the vestiges of Christendom while overlooking the vast cultural inheritance of Christianity in the West and its continuing missional potential.[33] In a similar way, Bruce argues that the current hostility to western imperialism has led to inaccurate stereotyping and the mistaken assumption that Christian mission was manipulated to be the vehicle for commercial and military exploitation.[34] Recent scholarship has demonstrated that many missionaries actually sought to subvert the 'colonial mentality' and that Protestant mission was not always the 'imperialist adventure' that has become stereotypical of the era.[35] This may mean that McLaren's caricature of modern mission is based upon a particular assumption about the nature of that missionary activity and thus, in his desire to rid the church of the methods of modern mission, he may disregard vital insights from western missionaries who sometimes engaged in prophetic counter-cultural mission.

Nevertheless, the emerging radicals' critique of modern evangelism should not be unduly dismissed: they echo the voices of those within mainstream evangelicalism who seek to reject versions of modern mission that dishonour the gospel, not least in modern evangelism's association with phoney TV evangelists, slick strategies and patronizing formulas.[36] While many welcome the emerging radicals' questioning of evangelistic approaches – for example the caricature of the lonely evangelical standing on the street corner announcing that Christians are the sole possessors of truth – others suggest it ultimately leads to the devaluation of the spoken word in evangelism. Nevertheless, it is unfair to characterize McLaren's 'gospel' as reduced to mere 'morality with perhaps a pinch of tolerance for idiosyncratic personal spirituality'.[37] Perhaps those who are quickest to accuse the emerging church of losing its nerve with regards to evangelism need to demonstrate that they have heard the reasons for the emerging church's unease about modern mission and that they are willing to discover new and innovative approaches to evangelism that both sit more easily within a postmodern climate and do not neglect the personal call to repentance and faith in Jesus. Those who wish to critique the emerging radicals' approach of prizing innovation above inheritance need to offer something more proactive in their response than retreat and entrenchment.

Perhaps a better response to McLaren would be to challenge him to take his own resistance to binary opposites more seriously; instead of reimagining evangelism in terms of dance and conversation rather than proclamation and reasoned debate, to embrace a more holistic approach to mission in which all of these different methods have a part to play. What must be gleaned and applied from McLaren's approach is the rebuke of the modern attitude to mission where it has become associated with arrogance and doctrinal correctness at the expense of compassion. However, neglecting the validity of proclamation fails to recognize the multiplicity of methods that scripture commends as the means by which followers of Christ are to embark upon their missionary adventure.

Rollins' emphasis on the 'hypernimity of God' is also hugely significant for the development of emerging missiology. While he offers a 'mystical-emergent-deconstructive' version of the Christian faith, he ironically considers his approach as 'the way' to do theology in a postmodern context. Bauman suggests that postmodern religion is identified by its tendency to rely on definitions that 'conceal as much as they reveal and maim and obfuscate while pretending to clarify and straighten up'.[38] This charge can be levied at Rollins and indicates the extent to which he has capitulated to the postmodern paradigm. Rollins' determination to 'leave aside the need for clarity' also has detrimental consequences for emerging missiology.[39] If the evangelist cannot be certain or assured in any of his or her statements about God, but must instead embrace ambiguity and postmodern 'fuzziness', it is hard to imagine what 'good news' such an evangelist could bring. In addition, Rollins' suggestion that the emerging church is a question rather than an answer is so vague that it lacks substance.

We must also challenge the emerging radicals' reticence about the role apologetics can play in contemporary mission. McLaren does not reject apologetics outright, but nevertheless he argues that postmodernity requires a new apologetic, one which does not offer answers but 'mysteries'. Attempts to explain the faith that are only ever defensive rather than offensive, that are coercive and combative and use circular lines of reasoning, need evaluating and challenging. However, perhaps McLaren's analysis should be taken as a reminder to the apologist herself regarding self-critical evaluation, to ensure that any defence or portrayal of the Christian gospel exhibits the core values of love, humility and compassion and that both the message and the messenger demonstrate the reality of the gospel. It was Newbigin who reawakened the church to its mandate to be a gathering of Christian people that exists not for its own sake but to be a 'sign, instrument and foretaste of God's redeeming grace for the whole life of society'.[40] Perhaps the most powerful apologetic in the postmodern age is not the rational defence of the faith, but a community of grace that lives in unity and hospitality towards the world. However, that is not to say that there is no place for reason or argument and, indeed, Keller is keen to suggest that an apologetic approach in the postmodern world must take the form of a critical appraisal of postmodern culture itself to enable people to hear and respond to the call of Christ while immersed within a postmodern mindset.

> There will be no joy in the grace of Jesus unless people see they're lost. Thus a gospel-shaped apologetic must not simply present Christianity; it must also challenge the non-believer's worldview and show where it, and they, have a real problem.[41]

It is the failure to offer an appropriately rigorous critique of postmodern ideology that renders the emerging church vulnerable in its missional approach and indicates the blindness with which it adopts some aspects of postmodernity into its theology.

However, perhaps we should not be so quick to dismiss McLaren's rejection of modern-influenced evangelism and should instead welcome the suggestion that evangelism needs to be reimagined for a postmodern age. What is needed is not to abandon evangelism per se but rather to discover a better way of expressing what lies at the heart of evangelism, understanding it as something more humble, authentic, conversational and life-giving rather than forced or stilted and reliant upon an 'us–them' dichotomy. There is work to be done by those of us who have evangelistic conviction in a postmodern age for how we develop a better language and expression of what talking about Jesus might look like.

The emerging church and incarnational mission

'Incarnational' is a twentieth-century neologism that has become associated with emerging discussions on mission. It is a term that has been widely used within evangelicalism to relate to the praxis of mission typified by John Stott's statement that 'all authentic mission is incarnational mission'.[42] However, Leonard Sweet uses it alongside 'relational' and 'missional', identifying these as the three words that define the emerging church. Gibbs and Bolger's survey of over 50 key leaders in the emerging church identified emphasis on incarnation as being a defining characteristic of the emerging church and the primary model of mission by which it immerses itself in 'the local cultures of our time'.[43] The doctrine of the incarnation is understood primarily as a Christ-like pattern of mission, and a contrast is frequently made between attractional and incarnational mission; two modes of mission that are outlined most comprehensively by Australian missiologists Hirsch and Frost. In attractional mission the church is dependent upon invitation, employing the latest tailor-made programme as a means of attracting people into the community of faith, an approach the emerging radicals appraise as limiting the agency of God to specific times and places. By contrast, the incarnational model emphasizes the act of going out into the local community rather than drawing people in to the church. As Hirsch and Frost summarize:

> An incarnational mode creates a church that is a dynamic set of relationships, friendships and acquaintances. It enhances and 'flavours' the host community's living social fabric rather than disaffirming it.[44]

The incarnation model often advocates meeting in what Hirsch and Frost call 'proximity spaces' that are deemed neutral and more accessible. These two modes, attractional versus incarnational, are similarly understood as the difference between a bounded set approach to evangelism and a centred approach. In the bounded set approach, it is the Christian who possesses knowledge that must be communicated to the lost unbeliever. However, the centred approach recognizes that every individual is created in the image of God and as such has 'the God-given ability to seek for the truth'.[45] For Perriman, the term incarnational mission is used by the emerging church to move beyond an 'us–them' approach to mission:

> The Emerging Church Movement is concerned to blur – even dismantle – the distinctions between 'us' and 'them' in an

honest endeavour to present a Christ for today. This is no mere intellectual exercise. It is not enough to think as 'they' do: the Church must actively choose to operate beyond its own boundaries – beyond the safety of its own walls – in order to be fully incarnational.[46]

Incarnational mission affirms that Christ is already present within any culture and encourages small indigenous groups to emerge that reflect that cultural setting.

The language of incarnational ministry is common currency within contemporary evangelical discussion about mission, but nevertheless there remain some who question the validity of incarnational mission in the first place. Such critics argue that the incarnation is not primarily about Jesus' ministry but rather his hypostatic relationship with the Father, a unique act that cannot be replicated. Tim Chester asks whether the belief that the incarnation is a model to follow is inherently arrogant in its assumption that we can do as Jesus did.[47] The fallible nature of the church makes it a poor reflection of the perfection of the incarnate Christ.

Todd Billings similarly rejects the incarnation as an appropriate model for mission as he believes it obscures the theological concept of servant-witness and cross-cultural ministry in the New Testament. Billings maintains that John's gospel uses different words for 'sent' to delineate between the sending of the Son into the world and the manner in which the church is sent into the world. What is to be replicated is not the mode of incarnation but its attitude of humility. While we need to listen and learn from other cultures, Billings says that 'we need not pretend to "incarnate" into that culture or to "be Jesus" to that culture'; to do so undermines belief in the work of the Spirit to mediate the presence of Christ in the world.[48]

Though Billings' thesis against incarnational ministry is directed specifically at liberation theology, his observation that incarnational theology is deficient in terms of pneumatology could be levelled at emerging missiology. Brewin, for example, focuses extensively on the Father and the Son, with greater emphasis laid on the birth or emergence of the church than on the active work of the Holy Spirit. Similarly, Bell's *Love Wins* contains few references to pneumatology and talks instead about 'an energy in the world, a spark, an electricity, that everything is plugged into' rather than a personal Spirit.[49] Since the concept of the Spirit as the agent of mission is not strongly featured within emerging missiology, this places greater stress on the need to create the right model of church as the means by which the missionary mandate is fulfilled. It can also be argued that a lack of pneumatological emphasis explains why the emerging radicals are reluctant to emphasize the spoken word, as it is only through the ministry of the Spirit that words can effect genuine change.

Allan Effa argues that any biblical missiology must have a conjunctive pneumatology because the Holy Spirit plays a critical role in empowering the church for mission. Effa further critiques the dichotomization of the attractional versus incarnational models of mission as creating an unhelpful caricature of evangelism as purely about getting people into the church; genuine evangelism is both centripetal and centrifugal:

> Certainly an outwardly-directed incarnational witness that shares life, demonstrates love and compassion and establishes friendship with people who are not following Jesus is supremely evangelistic.[50]

Effa argues that New Testament mission used both attractional and incarnational models and that missiology is impoverished by the acceptance of one to the exclusion of the other. A more holistic approach to mission would ensure against this.

The incarnation of Christ

Notwithstanding the above exceptions from some, an incarnational model of mission is relatively uncontroversial within evangelical thinking about mission. However, it is my supposition that the emerging radicals use the term 'incarnational mission' in a unique way and that this reflects their particular understanding of the doctrine of the incarnation. It is in this way that we can understand emerging missiology as being ultimately directed and governed by Christology. The governing principle of Christology for emerging church writers is the doctrine of the incarnation, and it is this understanding of the incarnation that drives the emerging church's ideas about mission, particularly in regard to culture. Incarnational theology is reaffirmed in response to their belief that evangelicalism has tended to portray a docetic Christology: a Christ who is Lord and Judge but not one of us.

McLaren believes that Christ's incarnation is the model that prescribes how the church should relate to other religions. Once again, the missional way is the third way, this time between the two extremes of disingenuous relationship-building for mission, akin to 'spy work', and religious pluralism that glosses over differences. For McLaren, the doctrine of the incarnation is the ultimate act of inclusion, paving a middle way.[51] He cites Vincent Donovan as his inspiration for understanding incarnational mission as a collaborative approach of mutual learning:

'Do not try to call them back to where they were, and do not try to call them to where you are, as beautiful as that place might seem to you. You must have the courage to go with them to a place that neither you nor they have ever been before.' Good missionary advice, and a beautiful description of the unpredictable process of evangelization, a process leading to that new place where none of us has ever been before.[52]

The emerging author who deals most extensively with the subject of the incarnation is Brewin, in *The Complex Christ*; he is the only writer to tender an account of the doctrine of the incarnation upon which his missiology is based. Brewin uses Fowler's six stages of the psychological development of faith as a means of understanding his own faith journey. This journey moves from the preliminary stages of childlike belief and arrogant certainty, through doubt to the fifth stage, in which one is able to live with the tensions and paradoxes that doubting unearths, a stage generally reached at middle age. The sixth stage is achieved only rarely by enlightened individuals. Brewin applies this model in two different ways. First, he regards the evangelical church as being stuck in stage three, defined by arrogant certainty and, as such, a stifling place for those asking uncomfortable questions. Second, Brewin uses this model to explain how the differing accounts of God in the Old and New Testaments can be understood in synthesis. In so doing, Brewin references Jack Miles' fictional book *God: A Biography*, which portrays God in the Old Testament as a tempestuous adolescent who develops, as Fowler's stages predict, into the mature and more balanced God of the New Testament. It is not clear how far Brewin embraces Miles' suggestion, as he does allow the possibility that what has changed is not the nature of God but merely our understanding of him. However, in a subsequent publication Brewin intimates that this transition is not purely our perception of God but concerns 'maturity and growth within God too'.[53] The incarnation, for Brewin, is of paramount importance as the means by which this transition occurs. It is through the process of taking on human flesh that God 'grows up' and is reborn.

> It is as if we are seeing Jack Miles' teenage God so rampant and delinquent in his rough diamond youth, born again in an immediately more mature and mellowed figure: a stage 3 God who has gone through the intertestamental darkness of stage 4 and been re-born at stage 5.[54]

Brewin regards the temptations of Jesus in the desert as revealing God's inner turmoil, tempted to revert back to his teenage past and to respond through violence and revolution. Brewin sees God's humanity as having had a tempering effect on him, enabling him to choose a new path 'to conjunctivity and beyond'.[55] Brewin advocates that what the incarnation does is demonstrate a new mode of God's self-communication in the light of the failure of the top-down method of the Old Testament; he refers to this as an 'experiment involving trickle down truth', a failure that left God caricatured as a cruel and harsh god who required sacrifices to placate his wrath. Thus,

God knew that the only way to overcome this misinterpreta-
tion was the costly and sacrificial option of the incarnation and
to 'change things by evolution from the bottom up'.[56] So the
church also must embrace an act of rebirth.

> In order to reach humanity God had to re-emerge and be reborn
> into human form. In the same way, we need to re-emerge and
> be reborn into specific places and cultures in order to be truly
> incarnate to them and reach them.[57]

However, before we can even explore the emerging radicals'
conviction that the incarnation of Christ provides the church
with a pattern of mission to follow, we must question whether
their doctrine of the incarnation, upon which this missiological directive is based, actually represents traditional Christian
orthodoxy. While it is beyond the scope of this book to explore
the nature of the incarnation in full, some consideration must
be given to Brewin's portrayal of the incarnation as the process
by which God becomes fully mature. Scot McKnight regards a
deconstructive critique of the God of the Bible to be one of the
chief characteristics of the emerging church:

> Sometimes I hear it in ways that are no more interesting than
> Marcion's old (and heretical) critique of the violent God of
> the Old Testament. Yet upon close inspection, the rumblings
> are subtler and more sophisticated, and the struggle is pal-
> pable and genuine. For some emergents, the Bible includes
> portrayals of God that cannot be squared with their under-
> standing of a God of love.[58]

Though McKnight draws an analogy with Marcionism, he is
quick to deflect the heresy claim by setting it within the broader
context of the emerging church's commitment to love as an
overriding principle that renders aspects of the Old Testament
problematic. Nevertheless, a significant question remains about
the polarity that appears to exist between Brewin's approach to
the Old and New Testaments. In many ways Brewin's perception of the incarnation is Irenaean in emphasis, particularly in

his account of the temptations, which Irenaeus regards as the victory of Jesus the man over the devil. Furthermore, Irenaeus' focus in the incarnation is on the mediation achieved through the life of obedience rather than through atonement. However, this emphasis on incarnation at the expense of atonement, characteristic of emerging missiology, is one of the aspects that I consider most problematic. The incarnation must be understood holistically as an integral and essential part of the whole Christ-event, which begins with incarnation, through atonement, to parousia and eventually to the final defeat of evil. Explaining the incarnation as a necessity in order for God to grow up contradicts this holistic sense of the Christ-event. For Torrance, the disciplines of Christology and soteriology cannot be understood apart from one another.[59] This coherence between the atonement and the incarnation, for Torrance, requires that the work of Jesus, and in particular the concept of redemption, cannot be rightly understood apart from its Old Testament context. The incarnation, therefore, should not be portrayed as either a last-ditch attempt when all others have failed, or, far worse, as a necessity for God's own character development.

Brewin's dichotomy between the God of the Old and New Testaments may stem from a lack of eschatological framework. Chris Wright argues that eschatology enables us to view the God of the Old Testament as working unchangingly and consistently through the act of the incarnation of the Son with the aim of fulfilling the eschatological hope of the Old Testament. Wright believes that the genealogy at the beginning of Matthew's gospel demonstrates that if we accept the fact of the incarnation we also have to accept the history that preceded it as part of the same story:

> The very form of the genealogy shows the direct continuity between the Old Testament and Jesus himself. This continuity is based on the action of God. The God who is manifestly involved in the events described in the second half of Matthew 1 was also active in the events implied in the first half. In Jesus he brought to completion what he himself had

prepared for. This means that it is Jesus who gives meaning and validity to the events of Israel's Old Testament history.[60]

Contrary to Brewin's supposition that the incarnation represents the failure of the 'experiment involving trickle down truth', Wright argues that God's action in the Old Testament is part of a coherent whole in which the incarnation is the final planned instalment rather than an eleventh-hour attempt to put things right. For Wright, the missiological significance of this conjunctive approach demonstrates the unity of the mission of God, of which Jesus Christ is the centre, and provides the key for understanding the purpose and nature of mission in the world today:

> Jesus was launched by a revival movement for the restoration of Israel. He launched a movement for the blessing of the nations. He himself, therefore, was the hinge, the vital link between the two great movements. He was the climax and fulfilment of the hope of Israel and the beginning of the hope of the nations.[61]

Brewin's idea of the evolution of God further demonstrates the influence of process theology upon the emerging radicals. Process theology proposes that God is a relative being in that he responds to and is shaped by human experience. Epperly describes God as 'infinitely flexible and versatile', creatively responding to every moment of experience and 'becoming a "new" God to respond to the novelty of the universe'.[62] This strongly echoes Hartshorne's view that absoluteness and relativity, permanence and change, activity and passivity can all be attributed to God.[63] The belief that God is constantly shaped in response to human interaction means that faith is understood not in terms of obedience to God's revelation but as willingness to welcome new perspectives in the evolving process of life in relationship with him. The implications of this openness for the uniqueness of the incarnation are significant, as while process theologians affirm the revelation of truth through the incarnation, they do not consider it to exclude other experiences of divine revelation.

With Brian McLaren, we must be generous in our orthodoxy . . . God's voice can be heard through an imam's call to
prayer or a Zen Buddhist koan. Bountiful in revelation, the
God described by emerging process also speaks in the careful
voice of the skeptic and the challenge of the atheist and her
vision of a god she cannot believe in.[64]

It is in this way that the incarnation is understood as the ultimate
manifestation of the divine presence in all things and as 'best
revealed in Jesus' identification with human kind and his refusal
to rule the world by coercion and domination'.[65] Following on
from this view, process theology similarly explains the atonement as the ultimate act of identification as Jesus experiences
and shares in the suffering of humanity.

While it would be inaccurate to suggest that all emerging
radicals are process theologians, as I have already sought to
demonstrate, the resonances between the two movements are
nevertheless considerable, not least in Brewin's belief that God
is in a state of change and responds to the evolution of humanity by this ultimate act of identification. Therefore, identifying
the weaknesses of process theology can also indicate some of
the defects in the emerging radicals' approach. We must challenge the presumption that the doctrine of immutability means
that God does not or cannot respond differently in different sit-
uations, as if his infiniteness prevents him from relating personally to creation. Grudem maintains that the God of scripture
is both infinite and personal and that process theology erro-
neously assumes that in order to maintain the personal nature
of God they have to substitute infiniteness for changeability.[66]
In addition, Geisler and Watkins argue that the concept of a
changeable God relies upon poor exegesis of scripture. Passages
such as Exodus 32.14 and Jonah 3.10 are cited by process theologians as examples of instances where God changes his mind,
demonstrating that he experiences change within his nature.
Geisler and Watkins argue that such passages are to be interpreted figuratively and do not require us to conclude that God
is incapable of responding personally to humanity without also
experiencing ontological change.[67] Furthermore, the idea that

God is prone to change raises the possibility that if God could change for the better then we must assume he could change negatively as well.

One final question to be raised about the emerging radicals' formulation of the doctrine of incarnation is the extent to which it is accentuated over and above the doctrine of atonement, emphasizing that the purpose of Jesus' incarnation is identification rather than redemption. Stott states that all incarnational ministry is cross-centred and that the incarnation must be understood as leading to the cross.[68] Torrance takes this argument one step further with his conviction that the doctrine of hypostatic union can only make sense when expressed soteriologically; the union of God and man in Jesus Christ cannot be expressed without relation to the atoning and reconciling work of God the Son in incarnation, death and resurrection. Furthermore, Torrance argues that where incarnation and atonement are not understood in proper relation to one another there has historically been a tendency towards dyophysitism. Torrance argues that the incarnation can only be effective in so far as it is connected to the atonement:

In atonement God has brought about an act at once from the side of God as God, and from the side of man as man; an act of real and final union between God and man.[69]

Rowan Williams similarly confirms an inextricable link between incarnation and atonement, particularly in terms of the shape of the Jesus story, which inevitably introduces an element of conflict:

Belonging with Jesus upsets other kinds of belonging – of family, of status, even of membership of the children of Abraham. Jesus on the cross is consciously portrayed as isolated, condemned by the political and religious communities to which, in one sense, he belonged. An incarnational theology has to deal with the question posed by the cross; it is not enough to say Christus Consummator, in the face of a story of discontinuity and costly separation.[70]

Yet despite the emerging radicals' emphasis on incarnation, the conflict that allegiance to Christ brings to other allegiances goes unmentioned, suggesting that the emerging definition of incarnation focuses on the birth and life of Christ rather than seeing the incarnation as a trajectory leading ultimately to death and resurrection. Thus, we must question whether any version of the incarnation that neglects the atonement can be an adequate basis for missiology. Wright considers that the crucified messiah provides us with an open window to the heart and character of God and is therefore paradigmatic for missionary vocation:

> The task of shaping our world is best understood as the redemptive task of bringing the achievement of the cross to bear on the world; and in that task the methods, as well as the message, must be cross-shaped through and through.[71]

Stott proposes that it is the cross which calls the church to radical, costly evangelism and that the key to church growth lies in suffering: 'it is the seed that dies that multiplies'.[72] Guder similarly states that where the incarnation is detached from the atonement, the gospel message becomes moralistic and the problem of human sinfulness is not addressed and thus 'the dimensions of God's grace and love are never fully expounded'.[73] These comments add support to the perspective that Christ entered the human race not only to identify with humanity but to bring restoration and redemption (Phil. 2.6-11). Thus, any formulation of the incarnation must always be tempered by the cross. In my opinion, the emphasis on incarnation at the expense of atonement is one of the greatest weaknesses of the emerging radicals' missiology and, as we will now see, can lead to syncretism in cultural engagement.

Incarnational mission: immersion and identification

For the emerging radicals, the incarnational model of mission provides a mandate for how new fledgling churches are to relate to culture. At the most basic level, incarnational mission advocates a positive and reciprocal relationship with culture:

> It must become embryonic and re-evolve within a host culture, learning from it, feeding from it and growing to understand it from the inside out.[74]

Brewin proposes the incarnation as a model for how the church should relate to the culture of postmodernity, encouraging the church to 'understand it, learn from it, be in it, love it, listen to it, wait 30 years before speaking to it'. He argues that just as Christ required the earthly world to sustain his physical life, so the church is reliant upon the 'host' culture for its existence and future survival:

> Becoming incarnate will mean the same for us as it did for Christ. We will have to experience being small and defenceless, requiring nurture from our host world just as Christ needed Mary's milk . . . To admit our need as a church, our dependence on our host culture, is a risk. Yet like Christ we must take this risk of interdependence, this risk of being born, this risk of life.[75]

Brewin maintains that if the church is to survive in future generations it must follow this model of incarnational living and become 'wombs of the divine', rebirthing the church within a new cultural context. Brewin understands this relationship to be a matter of dependence – and the only way the emerging church will be capable of serving and ministering. Attempts to merely adopt aspects of culture in order to make the church accessible are not capable of delivering genuine change and transformation: only the act of reincarnation and total immersion within and dependence upon a given culture will be efficacious.

The language of immersion and identification is typical of the emerging radicals' understanding of this symbiotic relationship between church and culture. Ben Edson, an emerging church leader from Manchester, believes that it is this positive attitude to culture that sets apart the emerging church from other examples of contemporary mission that seek relevance rather than authenticity and choose not to adopt the symbiotic relationship between text and context that he proposes:

> We believe that God is already in the world and working in the world. We recognise God's presence in music, film, arts and other key areas of contemporary culture. We wish to affirm and enjoy the parts of our culture that give voice to one of the many voices of God and challenge any areas that deafen the call of God and hence constrain human freedom.[76]

This symbiotic relationship between church and culture, which the emerging radicals favour, is further demonstrated in their rejection of contextualization as a missiological principle. For this, they rely heavily on John Franke's notion of 'pilgrim theology'. In this approach, Franke places as much credence on the discernment of the Spirit's voice through culture as through scripture and believes that in so doing 'new confessions' may develop 'in accordance with shifting circumstances'.[77] Franke proposes that culture should not be understood as the body of beliefs, behaviours and values that mark a way of life for a group of people, but as dynamic process in which people shape and 'construct the worlds we inhabit'.[78] Franke contends that culture-free theology is logistically impossible, since all theology is a 'human enterprise'. Thus he rejects contextualization as a missiological method, since it assumes that there is a Christian universal that functions as the foundation for theological thinking. Franke proposes a more interactive model in which neither gospel nor culture is a presupposed entity but both are seen in dynamic dialogue, shaping and informing one another for 'mutual enrichment'.[79]

In conclusion, the emerging radicals' understanding of the incarnation as both God's transitional act of growing up and his subsequent rebirth within culture shapes their understanding of incarnational mission and the role they believe the church is called to play in identifying with the world.

However, if, as we have already established, the incarnation cannot be expressed solely in terms of identification, incarnational mission cannot either be expressed solely in those terms – yet this is often the way it is presented. Therefore, we need to raise questions about the validity of the emerging radicals' preference to elevate identification as the central idea in their missiology.

Within a missionary context, Harriet Hill's experience working with Wycliffe Bible Translators in the Ivory Coast caused her to question the value of this model of incarnational mission. Hill found the identification approach to result in an impossible conundrum that led to either a false feeling of having achieved identification, when differences between the missionary and the host culture remained glaringly obvious, or guilt that a greater level of identification had not been achieved. While her article addresses a cross-cultural context, she includes anecdotal evidence that what the local people required from the missionaries was not primarily identification but transformation. She describes the shock that she and her husband experienced when the villagers told them they were selfish for their incarnational mentality and that instead of living like one of the villagers they could have done something to improve the village:

> They wanted us only to help them make progress in the world. They could only interpret as selfishness our refusal to do what we could to improve things in the village. We knew a better way to live, but didn't share it with them.[80]

In a corresponding article, McElhannon argues that the Apostle Paul adopted an incarnational mode of mission by becoming all things to all people, but that the difficulties and opposition that Paul faced in his ministry should serve as a caution that the success of incarnational ministry cannot be based upon acceptance.[81] The relevance of this insight can be brought to bear on Brewin's incarnational model, which emphasizes identification and immersion as the core convictions about how the church is to engage with its cultural context.

Describing the incarnation purely in terms of an act of identification fails to acknowledge the more subversive role of the incarnation, whereby Christ became human in order to challenge, transform and redeem culture. A distinction needs to be made between Christ taking on human flesh and Christ adopting Jewish culture and customs. In emerging incarnational mission, the analogy is drawn between Christ's assuming human flesh and the way the church is to immerse itself within the host culture. However, the more accurate parallel is between the way Jesus interacted with Jewish culture and the way the church is to interact with culture. While Jesus did immerse himself in the Jewish culture and religion of his day, he did not give himself entirely to it, flouting many of its customs and regulations, not least in his choice of dinner guests and Sabbath activities.[82] Jesus did not unquestioningly take on board the values and customs of his host culture but instead identified points of disjunction, and it was those points of conflict that set in motion his journey to the cross. When the incarnation is expressed predominantly in terms of identification, mission is not understood in a subversive and challenging way but simply in terms of drawing alongside. Such an approach lacks the tools for prophetic critique of society in our missiological approach. Wright's perspective on the prophetic nature of Jesus' ministry is germane here. By his words and actions, Jesus positively declared his kingdom agenda while simultaneously subverting the agenda of other kingdoms – for example, in choosing to eat meals with those considered beyond the bounds of social acceptance:

> Jesus' welcome symbolized God's radical acceptance and forgiveness; whereas his contemporaries would have seen forgiveness and a God-given start in terms of the Temple and its cult, Jesus was offering it on his own authority, and without requiring any official interaction with Judaism.[83]

Paul's missionary strategy can also be seen as employing both identification and subversion: Paul's contextualized approach is positive about Roman culture, yet whenever he declared Jesus as Messiah he did so as a direct challenge to the authority of Caesar. This highlights the importance of not limiting Christology to the incarnation, as missiology that has no understanding of Christ as Pantocrator or judge cannot be subversive in this way.

A further area of Christology neglected by the emerging church is the doctrine of the ascension, although arguably it is not alone in its failure to give attention to this aspect of the creed and it is perhaps symptomatic of the preference evangelicals have shown towards emphasizing God's immanence. However, its neglect is particularly pertinent when considering how Christology governs and directs missiology. Farrow maintains that where the ascension is overlooked, our understanding of Christ deals only with his influence upon culture and not 'what he himself has accomplished'. By contrast, the doctrine of the ascension prevents us from making Christ into the campaigner of personal causes:

> The 'risen' Christ is today the immanent Christ, the Christ who is ascended into the dynamic of history, into the future of the race, into the evolving cosmos. He is the Aryan Christ, the black Christ, the feminist, queer, communist, capitalist or eco-Christ – whoever we need or desire him to be.[84]

The doctrine of the ascension blows apart the divide between the private and public realm and invalidates the all-too present temptation for the church to allow religion to be relegated to the sphere of personal preference. In his 2010 visit to the UK, Pope Benedict XVI highlighted this tendency for religion to be driven from the public domain, even – and perhaps most especially – among societies that cherish tolerance:

> Religion, in other words, is not a problem for legislators to solve, but a vital contributor to the national conversation. In this light, I cannot but voice my concern at the increasing marginalisation of religion, particularly of Christianity, that is taking place in some quarters, even in nations which place a great emphasis on tolerance.[85]

The ascension provides the theological framework through which the disjunction between private and public can be combated and endows the church with confidence to engage within the public domain. Wright argues that where the church fails to lay due emphasis on the ascension, the result is that the church 'expands to fill the vacuum', which results in either triumphalism or despair.[86] The emerging church must guard against these two temptations: a triumphalist interpretation of church that regards its salvation as being in the power of structural change, or despondency about the failings of the church in the past and its current statistics of decline. David Wells regards some contemporary attempts to precipitate radical change within the structures of church in order to stem the tide as evidence of an overly deferential relationship to culture that emanates from lack of confidence in Christ's lordship:

> The desperate measures being proposed for desperate times are often little more than a case of weak knees and unbelief. We believe altogether too little in God's sovereign control otherwise we would not be in full retreat before the pressures and demands of the postmodern world.[87]

Wells' observations are pertinent and make us aware of the propensity of some leaders to believe that responsibility for the future of the church ultimately lies on their shoulders, therefore succumbing to the temptation to capitulate to the whims of culture in order to ensure the church's survival. This is a temptation that, for all their good intentions, the emerging radicals face; yet without the affirmation of the doctrine of the ascension there is no reason to deter them from this course. Emphasizing incarnation at the expense of ascension leads to the belief that it is the method and form of the church's cultural engagement that will bring about the change required. However, the ascension reminds the church that Christ is Lord even in the midst of decline and disappointment and that while the church has the duty to think creatively, strategically and boldly about what form it should take, the responsibility to grow and continue the church ultimately lies with Christ. Our attempts may aid and accompany but they cannot pre-empt or outsmart him.

This exploration of an incarnational model of mission raises the all-important question about the relationship between church and culture that lies at the heart of the desire to create a 'new church' for a 'new world'. Brewin's language of dependence and immersion implies an uncritical adoption of the host culture, which contrasts with Stott's response to this very debate at Lausanne in which he states that culture must be discerned in two ways:

> Culture is ambiguous because man is ambiguous. Man is both noble (because he is made in God's image) and ignoble (because fallen and sinful). And his culture faithfully reflects these two aspects.[88]

For Stott, one of the most urgent missiological tasks is that of discerning these two different aspects of culture, since 'our cultural heritage cannot be excluded from his lordship'. The need for the church to embark upon both a critique and an embrace of its cultural location is once again pertinent here. Without adequate critique, culture is readily prioritized when a conflict of interest occurs. Those seeking to communicate the gospel within a postmodern culture must be aware of the ambiguous nature of culture and its potential both to open our eyes to aspects of the gospel to which we have previously been unaware, and also to divert our gaze from some of its more radical aspects.

Andrew Walls identifies two principles that are rooted in the nature of the gospel, which, when held in tension with one another, challenge the incarnational identification model. The first is the indigenizing principle, which stems from the gospel conviction that Christ accepts us as social and cultural beings and therefore we should cherish the long-held missiological practice of building indigenous churches that reflect their cultural setting:

> The fact then is that 'if any man is in Christ he is a new creation', does not mean that he starts or continues his life in a vacuum, or that his mind is a blank tablet. It has been formed by his own culture and history and since God has accepted him as he is, his Christian mind will continue to be influenced by what was in it before. And this is true for groups as for

persons. All churches are culture churches – including our own.[89]

The second is the pilgrim principle, which teaches that since the believer has no abiding home, her commitment to Christ will always cause her to be at times out of step with her inherited society, since no culture absorbs the message of Christ without some points of conflict. While the indigenous principle associates the Christian with the particulars of their culture and group, the pilgrim principle associates him or her with things and people outside their culture group, linking them to the wider community of Christ both globally and historically. When either of these principles is stressed at the expense of the other it leads to either syncretism on the one hand or colonialism on the other. Allowing the church in the West to learn from the church in the Global South may provide a way around this conundrum. It is my contention that the emerging radicals focus strongly on the indigenous principle by their commitment to cultural identification, but that their missiology lacks the insights provided by the pilgrim principle; they remain fearful of a prophetic approach, which leads to confrontation and conflict. However, the gospel itself contains both affirmation and confrontation and thus any missiological model which fails to incorporate both elements will inevitably result in either syncretism or judgementalism. There is much to credit the incarnational mission approach, not least where it is employed to encourage sacrificial and costly living for the gospel. Nevertheless, questions must be raised about an incarnational model understood exclusively in terms of identification which can all too easily be adopted as a licence for cultural engagement, which is not costly at all.

Furthermore, the time-honoured missiological question 'What is the gospel?' is not one readily asked by the incarnational model. Yet, if the Christian kerygma has no greater claim to truth than any other worldview, then the task of missiology is redundant at the point of conception. Bosch highlights the missionary task of the church as the outward expression given to 'the dynamic relationship between God and the world, particularly as this was portrayed, first, in the birth, life, death and resurrection, and exaltation of Jesus of Nazareth'.[90] While it is naïve to suggest that the gospel can ever be delivered in a culturally neutral form, the content of the kerygma is of paramount importance. Bosch defines evangelism as 'the proclamation of salvation in Christ to those who do not believe in him, calling them to repentance and conversion, announcing forgiveness of sin, and inviting them to become living members of Christ's earthly community and to begin a life of service to others in the power of the Holy Spirit'.[91] The emerging radicals' reluctance to assert the primacy of the gospel above the cultural situation is problematic for their missiology.

In addition, Franke's 'pilgrim theology', which rejects contextualization as a valid missiological principle in favour of a more dynamic dialogue between gospel and culture, is equally devastating to missiological development. His approach similarly denies the gospel its primacy and subsequently the church its prophetic voice. Graham Cray sees the heart of the Christian message in the crucifixion of Jesus and argues that we must not deny its costly and counter-cultural dynamic:

> We have to hold together an unchanging gospel which is counter-cultural with a deeply culturally costly engagement with culture – following the example of the incarnation so that people can hear the gospel.[92]

Franke's account contains little of this counter-cultural nature of the gospel. Furthermore, understanding missional ecclesiology as the 'pilgrim people of God' requires that one remember the church's ex-centric position in that it is both called out of the world and sent back into the world. While written as a defence of evangelism in the face of modernity, Abraham's argument in *The Logic of Evangelism* can be applied to the emerging radicals.

> Evangelism has never depended on a sunny analysis of the culture it is seeking to Christianise; if that were the case, the West would never have been evangelised in the first place . . . there is no good reason why the evangelist should be intimidated by

prophets of doom who argue that the prospects for evangelism are bleak in the extreme.[93]

For Abraham, missiology's determining factors rest upon the 'internal logic of the Christian gospel' rather than the seeming unfeasibility of the task and is a timely antidote to the cultural bias of the emerging radicals' approach. Newbigin also adds weight to this perspective in his discussion on pluralism, suggesting that attempts to justify Christian mission on the basis of its wider appeal to human unity or liberation have proved futile. For Newbigin, the grounds of authority for mission are rooted in Christology:

> The authority of Jesus cannot be validated by reference to some other authority which is already accepted. The naming of his name calls for nothing less than a fresh and radical decision about one's ultimate commitment.[94]

Newbigin continues that the authority of Jesus means the proclamation of his name stands over 'the whole life of the world – its philosophy, its culture and its politics no less than the personal lives of its people'.[95] This Christological confidence is in stark contrast to the identification model which the emerging radicals draw from their incarnational theology.

Hunsberger considers Paul's self-declaration to be 'all things to all people' to exhibit an incarnational approach in which identification is tempered with spirit-inspired critique and in which a generous attitude replaces triumphalist models of evangelism (I Cor. 9.22):

> Paul's own policy of identification with those among whom he offered the gospel free of charge opposes the tendency to restrict the gospel to a single cultural form. Of course, there is always the matter of the truth and integrity of the gospel, but this Paul preserved, while exhibiting his freedom to be enslaved to other cultural forms and styles . . . Paul's cultural identification was not uncritical but he refined the path of cultural domination and imposition. He was willing to give

the gospel away to new possessors of it and to lose it to their new styles, responses and definitions. There he expected to see it sparkle, startle, surprise and shine.[96]

Here Hunsberger reminds us that a properly formulated incarnational approach can contribute richly to missiological formulation, not least in its advocating freedom and creativity with regards to missiological practice. When properly understood, an incarnational model of mission can ensure that there is congruence between both the message and the method of what is proclaimed. Above all, an incarnational model of mission must be understood as a calling to a pattern of life lived in the footsteps of Christ, a humble attempt to seek an attitude which reflects Christ himself. Langmead suggests that incarnational mission can be a healthy antidote to non-incarnational methods such as proclamation, mass-media evangelism and programme-oriented mission. He argues that there should be three central strands to incarnational mission: being patterned on the incarnation, being enabled by the ongoing power of the incarnation, and joining in the mission of God. However, he also states that incarnational mission should never be used as a licence to elevate presence over the spoken word. A more holistic approach to incarnational mission can guard against this temptation:

> One way to avoid the pride which can be a danger in incarnational mission is to insist on the integration of words and deeds. Wherever possible and appropriate, mission should involve a combination of Christ-like action and verbal witness to the experience of grace which undergirds and enables Christian mission.[97]

In conclusion, the emerging radicals must be encouraged in their emphasis on incarnational mission, which has much to contribute to the formation of missiology. Where their doctrine of the incarnation leads to missionary engagement that requires a symbiotic relationship between words and actions and forces the church out of its comfort zone, it has much to add to the formation of contemporary missiology. However, questions must be raised about their tendency to stress the importance of identification to such an extent that the counter-cultural nature of the gospel is diminished. An incarnational model which emphasizes both identification and subversion would enable an approach to mission which contains both compassionate love and prophetic critique and, in so doing, better reflects the pattern of Christ's incarnation.

In exploring emerging missiology, we have considered both the reactionary nature of the term 'missional' and have also evaluated the implications of incarnational mission for how the church regards itself in the contemporary climate. It is in the desire to be both a missional and incarnational church that the inextricable connection between missiology and ecclesiology becomes apparent. In the pursuit of creating a new church for a new world, the emerging radicals' understanding of culture lends itself most clearly to the task of revising ecclesiology. Thus, it is to this final area of emerging ecclesiology that our focus must now shift in order to complete the picture of the emerging church's theological approach.

Notes

1 McGrath, *Christianity's Dangerous Idea*, p. 179. It is important to acknowledge that Roman Catholics were already having a significant impact on the mission field.

2 Yates, *Christian Mission in the Twentieth Century*, p. 9.

3 DeYoung, 'God Is Still Holy'.

4 Jones, *The New Christians*, p. 197.

5 Bosch, *Transforming Mission*, p. 228.

6 McLaren, *A Generous Orthodoxy*, p. 106.

7 For further see Laing, 'Missio Dei: Some Implications for the Church'.

8 Hoekendijk, *The Church in Missionary Thinking*.

9 Bosch, *Transforming Mission*, p. 391.

10 Flett, *The Witness of God*, p. 77.

11 Guder and Barrett, *Missional Church*, p. 6.

12 Anderson, *An Emergent Theology for Emerging Churches*, p. 199.

13 Abraham, *A Theology of Evangelism; The Heart of the Matter*, p. 22.

14 Keller, *The Missional Church*.

15 McLaren, *A Generous Orthodoxy*, p. 111.

16 Murray, *Post-Christendom*, p. 129.

17 Sweet, *Post-Modern Pilgrims*, p. 28.

18 Jones, *Postmodern Youth Ministry*, p. 5.

19 Jones, *The New Christians*, p. 4.

20 Murray, *Post-Christendom*, p. 81.

21 Kimball, *Out of Ur: Dan Kimball's Missional Misgivings*.

22 Richardson, *Emerging Missional Movements: An Overview and Assessment of Some Implications for Mission(s)*.

23 McLaren, *More Ready Than You Realize*, p. 68.

24 Campolo and McLaren, *Adventures in Missing the Point*.

25 Carson, *Becoming Conversant with the Emerging Church*, p. 234.

26 http://www.patheos.com/blogs/bibleandculture/2011/03/29/for-whom-the-bell-tolls-chapter-four-does-god-always-get-what-he-wants/

27 McLaren, *More Ready Than You Realize*, p. 153. For an example of the approach which McLaren rejects see Sproul, Lindsley and Gerstner, *Classical Apologetics*.

28 McLaren, *The Last Word and the Word After That*, p. xxiii. For a contemporary discussion on the future of Christian apologetics in post-modern culture see Philipps and Okholm (eds), *Christian Apologetics in the Postmodern World*.

29 Webber, *Ancient-future Evangelism*, p. 62.

30 Sweet, *A is for Abductive*, p. 132.

31 Rollins, *How (Not) to Speak of God*, p. 18.

32 Ibid., p. 41.

33 MacLaren, *Mission Implausible*, p. 8.

34 Bruce, *God is Dead*, p. 129.

35 McGrath, *Christianity's Dangerous Idea*, p. 193.

36 Guinness, *Mission Modernity; Seven Checkpoints on Mission in the Modern World*, p. 292.

37 Devine, *The Emerging Church: One Movement – Two Streams*, p. 21.

38 Bauman, *Postmodern Religion?*, p. 55.

39 Rollins, *How (Not) to Speak of God*, p. 18.

40 Newbigin, *The Gospel in a Pluralist Society*, p. 233.

41 Keller, *In Defense of Apologetics*.

42 Stott, *The Contemporary Christian*, p. 358.

43 Gibbs and Bolger, *Emerging Churches*, p. 16.

44 Frost and Hirsch , *The Shaping of Things to Come*, p. 42.

45 Ibid., p. 50.

46 Perriman, 'An Incarnational Missiology for the Emerging Church'.

47 Chester, *Why I Don't Believe in Incarnational Mission*.

48 Billings, 'The Problem with "Incarnational Ministry"'.

49 Bell, *Love Wins*, p. 144.

50 Effa, 'Missional Voices Down Under'.

51 McLaren, *A Generous Orthodoxy*, p. 251.

52 Donovan, *Christianity Rediscovered*, p. vii.

53 Brewin, *Other*, p. 106.

54 Brewin, *The Complex Christ*, p. 43.

55 Ibid., p. 109.

56 Ibid., p. 45.

57 Ibid., p. 49.

58 McKnight, *The Ironic Faith of Emergents*.

59 Walker (ed.), in Torrance, *Atonement: The Person and Work of Christ*, p. xxxvii.

60 Wright, *Knowing Jesus through the Old Testament*, p. 27.

61 Ibid., p. 166.

62 Epperly, *Emerging Process* (Kindle edition), Ch. 2, paragraph 8.

63 Hartshorne, *The Divine Relativity*, p. 120.

64 Epperly, *Emerging Process*, (Kindle Edition), Ch. 3, paragraph 24.

65 Epperly, *Process Theology*, p. 63.

66 Grudem, *Systematic Theology*, p. 167.

67 Geisler and Watkins, 'Process Theology: A Survey and an Appraisal', p. 21.

68 Stott, *The Cross of Christ*, p. 291.

69 Torrance and Walker, *Incarnation*, p. 195.

70 Williams, *On Christian Theology*, p. 229.

71 Wright, *The Challenge of Jesus*, p. 69.

72 Stott, *The Cross of Christ*, p. 290.

73 Guder, 'Incarnation and the Church's Evangelistic Mission', p. 183.

74 Brewin, *The Complex Christ*, p. 48.

75 Ibid., p. 52.

76 Edson, 'An Exploration into the Missiology of the Emerging Church in the UK through the Narrative of Sanctus1'.

77 Franke, J. 'Christian Faith and postmodern theory', p. 115.

78 Grenz and Franke, *Beyond Foundationalism*, p. 147.

79 Franke, *The Character of Theology*, p. 208.

80 Hill, 'Incarnational Ministry; A Critical Examination'.

81 McElhannon, 'Don't Give up on the Incarnational Model'.

82 Mark 2.1–3.6. This section contains five examples of how Jesus challenges and subverts the established cultural and religious assumptions with regard to blasphemy, eating with the 'unclean' and Sabbath activities. It is worth noting that the following section (3.7f) concludes with a large crowd following him – arguably, counter-cultural behaviour was not always unappealing to people.

83 Wright, *The Challenge of Jesus*, p. 27.

84 Farrow, *Ascension Theology*, p. 53.

85 Pope Benedict XVI, *Westminster Hall Address*.

86 Wright, *Surprised by Hope*, p. 123.

87 Wells, *The Courage to Be Protestant*, p. 144.

88 Stott, *The Lausanne Covenant*, p. 26.
89 Walls, 'The Gospel as Prisoner and Liberator of Culture', p. 138.
90 Bosch, *Transforming Mission*, p. 9.
91 Ibid., p. 11.
92 Saunders, *Profile: Graham Cray.*
93 Abraham, *The Logic of Evangelism*, p. 202.
94 Newbigin, *The Open Secret*, p. 16.
95 Ibid., p. 18.
96 Hunsberger, 'Is There Biblical Warrant for Evangelism?, p. 69.
97 Langmead, *The Word Made Flesh*, p. 232.

5

The Emerging Church and Ecclesiology

Introduction

If Hauerwas is correct and 'all theology must begin and end with ecclesiology' then the subject of ecclesiology is of critical importance.[1] Ecclesiology has long been acknowledged as the Achilles' heel of evangelicalism, an assertion attested to by Archbishop Runcie's address to the National Evangelical Anglican Congress in 1988. John Stackhouse observes that evangelicals have more often implied rather than articulated their ecclesiology. Therefore, the fact that the emerging church addresses the subject of ecclesiology is of vital significance and to be welcomed. While we have acknowledged the difficulties in defining the emerging church, to suggest that it is a movement about ecclesiology is arguably valid, since it explicitly advocates ecclesiological change – eschatological and missiological ones are more subtly inferred.

The minimizing of ecclesial thinking within the history of evangelicalism can be attributed to several factors. Evangelicalism's tendency to prioritize soteriological concerns is, arguably, a Reformation legacy. This, combined with a preference for voluntarism along with the theological distinction between invisible and visible church, has meant that evangelicalism has existed as a transconfessional movement with a parachurch modus operandi and little in terms of developed ecclesial doctrine.[2] It could also be suggested that evangelical individualism that exhibits itself in conversionism has also stilted ecclesiological development. Nonetheless, it can be argued that the tide is changing and this neglect is being redressed by a recent surge of books claiming to offer a new ecclesiology for a new age, in which the contributions by the emerging radicals play a significant role. However, it must be considered whether these publications articulate a sufficiently deep ecclesiology or whether, in a bid for postmodern relevance, they merely skim the surface and ride on the coat-tails of theories of social change. While traditional discussions about ecclesiology have focused on the marks of the church, sacraments or ministerial structuring of the church, the emerging radicals have no desire to embroil themselves in controversies that have plagued the church's history and so these issues are conspicuous by their absence. Therefore, rather than addressing traditional ecclesiological themes, our discussion will consider three central ideas that I believe illustrate the emerging radicals' distinctive contribution to ecclesiology.

The need for change: emerging approaches to ecclesiology

Emerging ecclesiology takes its starting point in an intense sense of discontent with the perceived ecclesial status quo. It is not the belief that evangelicalism has neglected ecclesiology that catalyses emerging thinking but the belief that the church became syncretized under modernity and now reflects its weaknesses.

> Our captivity is often a comfortable one . . . the chains, bars and barbed wire that hold us are often invisible. The guards are often disguised in clerical robes or casual suits, and they hold advanced degrees and have mastered techniques of friendly manipulation, always with a penetrating smile and a firm, heavy hand on the shoulder.[3]

The church is perceived to be in a crisis that requires an ecclesiological revolution to rid it of its modernist corruptions. McLaren is optimistic about the potential for change, but he is hugely critical of the church's past mistakes:

I wouldn't be giving my life to it if I didn't think that our Christian faith can still become a saving faith, a life-giving faith, instead of what it has been.[4]

The emerging radicals believe individualism to be one of the vices most endemic within modern Christianity, as McLaren expresses:

In modernity it was me and Jesus, me and my Bible, me and my spiritual approach, me and my salvation. Even where the church came in, it was still about me – getting my needs met, getting my soul fed, acquiring the religious goods and services needed for me and my happiness and my success.[5]

However, we must pause once again and consider the reactionary nature of this ecclesiological 'revolution' and the temptation to read church history through the lens of one's own experience. The complaint McLaren has with the modern church is directed specifically at the mega-church model, and he has a propensity to tar the entire church under Christendom with the same brush. This is demonstrated most clearly in the vehement rejection of individualism as a modern vice. The individualism so vilified in the modern church is the individualism of consumerism, whereby the customer can select and in effect purchase his or her own spiritual experience. However, Bauman regards this kind of rampant consumerism as the property of late modernity or postmodernity rather than modernity.[6] Furthermore, rejecting individualism fails to acknowledge how the pioneers of the evangelical movement used the individualism of modernity to 'emerge' from the hierarchical stiltedness of the church in the eighteenth century. Wesley and Whitefield's conviction that faith must be combined with genuine personal appropriation in conversion arguably led to renewed conviction which, when coupled with the empowerment of lay ministry, enabled them to break free in missionary activity from the confines of the early modern church. Wesley's testimony demonstrates this conviction:

About a quarter before nine, while (the speaker) was describing the change which God works in the heart through faith in Christ, I felt my heart strangely warmed. I felt I did trust in Christ, Christ alone for salvation, and an assurance was given me that he had taken away *my* sins, even *mine*, and saved *me* from the law of sin and death.[7]

It could well be the case that evangelicalism is indebted to individualism rather than enslaved by it and it should be acknowledged that these early evangelicals were also deeply committed to the life of the Christian community, as Wesley's class meetings make clear. An emphasis on the equal dignity of humans and the empowerment of lay ministry was often responsible for the flourishing of the ministry of women, a fact often overlooked by those who would accuse the modern church of being complicit in the subjugation of women. Such individualism is far removed from the consumerist individualism of late modernity. By contrast, as we have already noted in the opening chapter, individualism was a positive feature of early evangelicalism, providing momentum to a time of, among other things, remarkable social reform. That this burgeoning emphasis on the individual later led to an overly elevated account of humanity that, when coupled with consumerism, became a failing in the contemporary church should not negate the beneficial contribution it once made. Instead it should offer a warning that while philosophical ideals can be harnessed for the promulgation of the gospel, this must not be done so uncritically.

Furthermore, the suggestion that the church must return to the model of the pre-Constantinian era, before everything turned sour, is to exhibit what Daniel Williams calls an 'acute problem of continuity'.[8] The emerging radicals exhibit both *progressivist* and *primitivistic* views of history, preferring both the future idea of how church might be and also the original notion of what church once was. However, neither of these approaches acknowledges the presence and work of God through the church during the Christendom period.

Volf's 'kaleidoscopic' view of history, through which he understands that social arrangements shift in various ways without following an evolutionist pattern, is helpful here. This would allow us a more generous approach to church history without glossing over its less than glorious aspects. In a similar way, Clapp understands the church to be part of a narrative trajectory which provides the church with a helpful alternative to an approach which is entirely dismissive of its Christendom past:

> The church is at once a community and a history – a history still unfolding and developing, passing along a story that provides the symbols through which its people gain their identity and their way of seeing the world.[9]

For all its talk of humility, one could argue that an overly critical approach towards the church in history, which implies that only now the church is rediscovering the true gospel, carries a note of self-importance. If it is only in the current era that the church is capable of reflecting God, then one wonders what the church has been doing for the last 1600 years. Healy suggests that attempts to apologize for the mistakes of Christianity's past, while seeming spiritual, do in fact sound empty and false:

> Apologies or confessions . . . ring hollow and devalue true penitential practices, turning them into therapeutic exercises or moral self-congratulation rather than genuine prayers for mercy and forgiveness from our just and loving God.[10]

McLaren considers himself to be ushering in an ecclesiological reformation that will be even more radical than Luther's: 'We need another tipping point . . . we need something more radical and transformative than a new state: we need a new quest.'[11]

The idea of a second reformation is common currency among emerging writings; statements about the scope of the reinvention of the church are often hugely optimistic and ambitious, and central to this is the quest for a suitable ecclesiology. However, the heralding of a second reformation must be premature, since only the passing of time can determine what has been of lasting worth and what is a fleeting fad.

Nevertheless, this 'second reformation' is driven by a conviction that the church must adapt and change to ensure its survival in the changing cultural milieu. Statistics of church decline loom large and the desire to stem the flow of dissent is a real and credible motivator, often creating a 'panic mentality'. The emerging radicals believe that the current form of the church no longer fits the cultural context and that recent attempts by mainstream evangelicalism to address this disjunction are simply insufficient. What is required is not merely the re-marketing of the Christian faith or new missionary methods, but the reinvention of the church itself in which nothing is taken for granted and 'everything must change':

> In the new world, a new ecclesiology will develop that can fit churches of various sizes, and that can actually encourage rather than obstruct church growth.[12]

Emerging ecclesiologies prize newness and innovation, not operating from a blueprint, but developing as missionary engagement unfolds.

However, we must question the assumption that the need for ecclesiological revision is driven by the fact of postmodern culture as a place of flux and change in which the church must 'catch up' in order to survive. Such convictions evidence a subtle form of pragmatism. Webber argues that one of the characteristics of the younger evangelicals is that they represent a move away from the pragmatic evangelicalism that dominated the twentieth century and was 'fuelled by church growth principles, the rise of the mega-church, and the popularity of contemporary worship'. By contrast, Webber believes the younger evangelicals are characterized by 'a ministry not based in programs but on transformed lives'.[13] While I agree with Webber's assessment that the emerging radicals are keen to distance themselves from the values and methodology of the church growth movement and have rightly emphasized the importance of a transformed life, a subtle reliance on pragmatism can still be discerned. It is as if ecclesiology is to be defined once a community has been established in the new cultural context, rather than having preconceived ideas about what the 'givens' of the church must be. Murray describes the secondary nature of ecclesiology which follows in the aftermath of missionary engagement:

> Many emerging churches . . . were not intended to become churches but developed into churches as those involved found their ecclesiology transformed by engagement with the community they were serving . . . They grew into churches as those involved found the culture gap between new Christians and church too wide.[14]

Therefore, the emerging radicals' approach to ecclesiology raises a crucial question about whether the church should necessarily fit comfortably within every cultural context. Is the church subject to the whims of cultural change, forced to compromise and change or risk inevitable extinction? Or is the church to function as a prophetic voice to be followed? The emerging radicals' conviction that the decline of the church will not be offset by persisting with the same methods that brought the decline belies a lack of trust in the power of the gospel to subvert and transform even when it is marginalized. Eschatology plays a pivotal role here since it is the conviction that Christ, as the resurrected Head of the church, is leading his people on a pilgrimage of eternal significance that cannot be thwarted by fear and panic about statistical decline. To neglect the eschatological identity of the church is to become susceptible to a 'panic mentality' elicited by the crisis of decline and easily seduced by the trends of postmodern thought which appear to provide a solution.

Since it is the advent of postmodernity that provides a new era for ecclesiology, postmodern theory is prominent in establishing the shape and direction of emerging ecclesiology. In order to demonstrate this trend I will consider an ecclesiological model which exemplifies this approach and will explore whether it is capable of providing the basis for a sustainable ecclesiology for the future or whether it is merely a postmodern panacea.

Temporary Autonomous Zones (TAZ)

In *Other*, Brewin invites us to consider the notion of TAZ as a suitable model for ecclesiology for a postmodern age. TAZ takes its motivation from the failings of the modern church, in particular its flawed attempts to create a perfect, eternal ecclesial utopia without the taint of modern sinful America. Brewin argues that such endeavours fundamentally misunderstand humanity's propensity to tarnish whatever community we are a part of. Instead, Brewin suggests that we create 'minor' or 'dirty utopias' which do not seek perfection but which, in their brief existence, offer an experience of a different world.[15] Temporality is the distinguishing feature of TAZ's ecclesiology.

Brewin makes known his reliance upon Hakim Bey's theory of Temporary Autonomous Zones in shaping this understanding of ecclesiology. Hakim Bey is a pseudonym for the controversial political anarchist Peter Lambourne Wilson, whose best-selling work *TAZ: Temporary Autonomous Zones* expresses in detail what Brewin alludes to in brevity. Although Bey is not primarily concerned with religion, his ideas resonate strongly with the emerging church:

> The 'Free Religions' as I like to call them – small, self-created, half-serious/half-fun cults influenced by such currents as Discordianism and anarcho-Taoism – are to be found all over marginal America, and provide a growing 'fourth way' outside the mainstream churches, the televangelical bigots, and New Age vapidity and consumerism.[16]

Central to TAZ is a revision of the way pirates have been portrayed through the annals of history. Both Brewin and Bey argue that pirates are misunderstood and should be regarded as a kind of 'heretic', showcasing a new rule of life which the establishment did not have the guts to accept initially, but later accepted as normative.[17] The notion of TAZ is based upon the idea of pirate utopias, which were remote hideouts where ships could take a hiatus in their journey, restocking and trading their booty, living consciously outside the law 'and determined to keep it up, if only for a short but merry life'.[18] Bey challenges traditional notions of pirates as thieves, instead regarding piracy as an act of social resistance against the capitalist establishment that imprisoned them. Brewin sees the attraction of pirate theology in offering 'something that speaks deeply to our human ache for justice'.[19] In essence, TAZ is the ultimate anarchic dream of a free culture and as such an unlikely bedfellow for evangelicalism; however, it is with regard to its temporality that Brewin sees the ecclesiological significance. TAZ enables individuals to be freed both from nostalgia for the past and also wistfulness about the future, in their ability to exist truly in the present moment. Yet Bey regards these intense moments as capable of giving 'shape and meaning to the entirety of a life'. In a similar way Brewin suggests that the church can operate as moments of TAZ: a festival, carnival or gathering that has the power to shape the future:

> It is often too easy to miss the power of a TAZ moment. With loud festivities and people letting their hair down the eye can too easily be drawn to the surface-level mayhem – just as it might have been at the wedding at Cana, or in the feeding of the five thousand. But these carnivals have strong political undercurrents. That slaves could, for a moment, act out their freedom, gave them the imagination and energy to work for true freedom. Carnival, done properly, is a celebration of a better future.[20]

For Bey, TAZ is not rooted in some future ideal but in the present, a concern that resonates with emerging eschatology.

> TAZ wants to live in this world, not in the idea of another world, some visionary world born of false unification (all green OR all metal) which can only be more pie in the sky by-&-by.[21]

It is the temporality of these 'dirty utopias' that is most significant for Brewin's ecclesiology and perhaps his most radical suggestion. He offers instances of miracles in the ministry of

Jesus as being examples of such finite events and suggests that the incarnation is the ultimate example of such a limited period of intensity. He cites festivals such as Greenbelt as providing a taste of how 'the world might be different'.[22] Brewin believes that human life is ultimately a nomadic existence and that we travel a road of constant discovery of both ourselves and others. Thus, in nomadic ecclesiology, the process of journeying is of greater significance than the destination. For Brewin, the explicitly Christian challenge is not to observe the world as a tourist who exploits the world, but as a nomad who reaches out to the 'other' and is himself changed in the process:

> Sent from Eden as nomads until we have learned our lessons, God's constant re-incarnation into those we meet on the road demands that we are active participants in the pursuit of our Lover [. . .] that we quiet our sycophantic choruses of saccharine love, sung eyes shut and hands up high, and instead turn our voices to the poor, the oppressed, the homeless, the lonely and imprisoned and sing tough songs of love and action with our eyes meeting theirs and our hands held out in solidarity.[23]

From the outset, Hakim Bey with his 'potent brew of mysticism, historical narratives, autonomous Marxist politics and French critical theory' is an unlikely voice of inspiration for evangelical theology.[24] A theory that has been used to justify rave culture is not a common choice as a basis for ecclesiology. Yet in many ways, he fits the bill perfectly. Bey calls himself a 'heretic', a label the emerging radicals award themselves for their own rebellious and unorthodox stance. The notion of 'pirate theology' sounds enticing for a generation of individuals tired of bureaucracy and safe sanitized versions of Christianity; it generated immense enthusiasm when Rollins and Brewin spoke on *Pirates and Prodigals* at Fuller Theological College in 2012, evidenced by the number of students turning up dressed as pirates.[25] However, Brewin's deployment of TAZ raises a critical question about the temporary nature of ecclesiology and whether any expression of church should necessarily seek longevity as its goal. Greenbelt is cited as a popular example of this temporary ecclesiology, and while affirming the creative insights and impact of that particular festival it is perhaps a skewed example since the majority of those who attend are likely to be already part of some existing Christian community.

In the light of what he classes 'liquid modernity', Bauman also considers one of the options for the religious community to be the aesthetic or 'instant' community, or TAZ in other words. Yet, Bauman considers such 'carnivals', which offer momentary community without any long-term commitment, as themselves symptomatic of the disorder of liquid modernity.[26] Furthermore, it is striking that for all its appeal to postmoderns, the concept of TAZ seems to have autonomy at its core: 'The TAZ must be the scene of our present autonomy, but it can only exist on the condition that we already know ourselves as free beings.'[27]

David Wells identifies the centrality of the autonomous self to be one of the neglected aspects of continuity between modernity and postmodernity:

> There are important threads of continuity between modernity and postmodernity and not least among these is the fact that at the centre of both is an autonomous self, despite all the postmodern chatter about the importance of community . . . In postmodernity the autonomous being refuses to be fettered by any objective reality outside of itself.[28]

Yet this irony is not detected among the emerging radicals who seek to fashion their thinking about ecclesiology in a manner palatable to the postmodern worldview, and the concept of pirates most illustratively reveals the darker side of this bid for freedom. While Brewin does not advocate the crime and violence of pirates, his concept of dirty utopias is more about a protest against a system than it is an appeal for love or holiness, which would form a more suitable plea as the basis of the Christian community.

It is the nomadic nature of life that is most formative in Brewin's understanding of how the church can operate as TAZ and there are important implications for how this ecclesiology is formed in practice.

Liturgy

Brewin argues that the modern church's obsession with preservation is evidenced in its fixation with liturgies and rituals expressing a desire for permanence. He likens such liturgies to the parable of the persistent widow, 'grinding down God into submission through constant nagging'. While acknowledging the eternal dimension of the church, he believes temporality must triumph, ensuring that no ecclesial expression should be allowed to outstay its welcome and ultimately 'petrify and harden'. This theory is embellished through his idea of cartography. The nomadic nature of the church means that all its incarnations are imperfect and incomplete. Worship and liturgy are acts of 'spiritual cartography', a process of mapmaking which should be dispensed with when the map no longer marks the cultural landscape.[29]

The concept of spiritual cartography illustrates well the value that the emerging radicals place on experimentation and flexibility with regards to liturgy and worship. Brewin offers IKON as an example of church that takes TAZ seriously, guarding the temporality of its existence. In *How (Not) to Speak of God*, Rollins includes an account of a service that exemplifies this experimentation and flexibility. 'Prodigal' incorporated the following elements: a scattering of Mills and Boons novels, a projection of Rembrandt's 'Head of Christ', a creative retelling of the parable of the prodigal son followed by poetry and music on the theme of loss and yearning. The gathering ends with a brief homily on how the revelation of God both exposes and conceals and then a final reading from a verse of Revelation. The blending of scripture or traditional liturgies with contemporary music, art and philosophy is common currency among such gatherings and is fuelled by the conviction that the church is honour bound in every new era to create forms and rhythms of worship that fit the generation. Leonard Sweet has used the EPIC acronym to describe what is distinctive about emerging churches, and the four themes of Experiential, Participatory, Image-driven and Connected serve as an excellent summary of emerging worship.

With regards to liturgy, the creativity exhibited by the emerging radicals is to be welcomed as part of what it means to proclaim the faith 'afresh in each generation'.[30] There is always the need in each new generation for song-writers and liturgists to produce material creatively and imaginatively that can enable and equip the church in its worship and mission. However, the continual pressure to rewrite the maps is costly and laborious and can tend towards an *ahistorical* approach to tradition. While creativity is to be encouraged, the pressure for worship leaders to be constantly rewriting liturgies and music is not sustainable in the long run. Also, Best questions whether even the most creative of worship leaders eventually succumb to habits that become 'liturgically repetitive' over a period of time.[31] Cocksworth maintains that liturgy also has a preservative function and as such is essential to the fidelity and continuation of the church. Without a historically grounded liturgy, new expressions of church are in danger of becoming severed from their historical roots, eventually leading to, at best, irrelevance and, at worst, heresy:

> Without careful scriptural teaching through the systematic reading of scripture, expository preaching of scripture, and scripturally based liturgy and hymnody, our memories will become disconnected from the corporate memory of the church and either hit a blockage and then boredom, or wander into fantasy and then apostasy.[32]

In a similar manner, the use of liturgies that connect the church to the living tradition has the capability of releasing us from what Loren Mead regards as the 'tyranny of the new'.[33] In so doing they can provide stability in the face of the perpetual pressure to reinvent and recreate.

> Praying the prayers of the church is to pray not with second-class material despoiled by time, but handed-on treasures that resist and overcome the corrosions of time.[34]

Furthermore, the desire constantly to rewrite the liturgical maps raises a significant question: if an expression of church exists only for a limited period of time then how does that affect spiritual formation? Once again, the eschatological dimension becomes imperative. Newbigin's concept of 'the pilgrim people of God' means that the church is understood as *in via*, not as either a static or a transitory movement but as participating in a collective journey with a real destination in view. This end view directs and shapes the activities and practices that develop character formation. The eschatological dimension dictates that ecclesiology will always be progressive and never an end in itself. Yet, the concept of the church as the pilgrim people, while sounding similar actually differs importantly from Brewin's concept of nomadic theology, which is less destination-oriented and more focused on the sense of journeying in the present. Brewin passionately conveys the sense of journeying and displacement, but the point of destination remains undefined. It is more akin to the experience of a wanderer than a pilgrim. Donnelly regards fragmentation as one of the key aspects of postmodern life which he refers to as 'the Confetti Generation'.[35] This fragmentation means that there is no overarching narrative to the human story and we struggle to make sense of the differing fragments of our lives and society itself. In many ways, nomadic ecclesiology seems tailor-made for a fragmented society with no overarching narrative. However, while Newbigin and Brewin share an emphasis on discipleship as a journey, for Newbigin it is the end in sight which ultimately governs our missional and ecclesiological identity:

> The Church is the pilgrim people of God. It is on the move – hastening to the ends of the earth to beseech all men to be reconciled to God, and hastening to the end of time to meet its Lord who will gather all into one. Therefore the nature of the Church is never to be finally defined in static terms, but only in terms of that to which it is going. It cannot be understood rightly except in a perspective which is at once missionary and eschatological.[36]

While Newbigin's perspective advocates an adaptable ecclesi-ological approach, he, however, considers the eschatological destination of the church to be more important in defining ecclesiology than the culture surrounding it. The church in the present is to be defined by the vision of what the church one day will be. For Volf, the conviction that the present participation in trinitarian community is an anticipation of the 'eschatological communion of the church with the triune God' is the bedrock of all Christian ecclesiology. Volf's eschatological emphasis enables him to see a strong link between the local and the uni-versal, understanding that both are, by relation to the Spirit, 'a proleptic realization of the eschatological gathering of the entire people of God', a broader perspective that is often absent from emerging preoccupation with the post-Christendom West.[37] This trinitarian understanding of ecclesiology means that the church is not to be imagined as a group of people gathered together by some common will or desire but by an act of incor-poration through faith in the trinitarian communion. Such an understanding adds not only an element of partialness, in that any ecclesial community is only part of a larger universal whole, but also an element of permanence since that whole of which it is a part extends into the future of God's final consummation. Notions of temporality do not sit easily with a trinitarian under-standing of ecclesiology.

How then can this eschatological perspective be reconciled with TAZ? Is it ever right for the church to exist as a temporary gathering without a longer goal? Such discussion begs the ques-tion as to what is the intention of a TAZ expression of church. Where the goal is missiological, however laudable that may be, the temptation is to remove those aspects of ecclesiology deemed inaccessible. However, these are often the very things that can ensure the long-term sustainability of such a grouping. The act of constantly rewriting the liturgical maps may well prevent the church from being the fullest and most authentic version of the peoples of Christ that it could be. It may well be that some of those things considered least relevant or acces-sible in our postmodern age may be the very things required to ensure growth and depth of discipleship in the long term. Stackhouse's critique of this weakness in the church growth movement can also carry resonance here:

> When growth replaces qualitative Christian nurture as the rationale of the church, traditional notions of initiation into the gospel are sacrificed on the altar of expediency, and pastoral care of the saints, in the somewhat ambiguous and messy business of real life; is set in opposition, unnecessarily and unbiblically, to the call to evangelise.[38]

It is interesting to observe that despite its self-confessed rejection of the church growth vision as modernist and formulaic there are aspects of the new emerging theology that have similar values latent within it. When church is centred on the perceptions of those outside the church, there is a high possibility that certain critical vehicles of Christian discipleship or fidelity are disregarded in the name of accessibility. It is not easily apparent how discipleship is to be sustained as a continuous process within a TAZ model of church. Webber uses examples from the first four centuries of the church to support his argument that discipleship should be understood holistically and continuously and not as a post-evangelism activity for those inside the church. He draws particular attention to the terms coined by Hippolytus in the third century to describe this process of discipleship. The four progressional stages of Seeker, Hearer, Kneeler and Faithful with each being marked by a rite of passage, assumed the sequence of discipleship was a journey from believing, to behaving, to belonging. Much has been published on the current reordering of this process from belonging to believing and then behaving within the cultural context, and McLaren explicitly acknowledges this.[39] Without wanting to negate the contribution of this reversal in a cultural climate that aspires to encounter authentic community living, it is, nonetheless, important to consider what is lost in this reversal. Is it the case that some of the harder challenges of genuine discipleship become tamed in the name of accessibility?

It must also be acknowledged that within some strands of emerging theology there is a reintroduction of ancient practices and spiritual disciplines, such as fixed-hour prayer, Sabbath observance and pilgrimage; what some are terming 'the new monasticism'. This is arguably one of the strengths of the emerging church and one of its richest contributions to the contemporary discussion about ecclesiology. McLaren's idea of the rediscovery of faith as a 'way of life' sits comfortably within Webber's holistic approach to discipleship.[40] However, to what extent does it also reflect a postmodern pick-and-mix mentality that selects an eclectic smorgasbord of one's favourite spiritual practices?[41] If these spiritual practices are seen as separate entities and not rooted within some kind of an ecclesial tradition, then what will happen when such practices are no longer in vogue or considered trendy? Such an approach to ancient spiritual practices may prove to be retrievalism or postmodern nostalgia. Carson argues that the emerging church shows its postmodern influence keenly with regard to its pick-and-mix approach to tradition and its reluctance to commit itself to any one longstanding ecclesial tradition:

> As long as you can pick and choose from something as vast as the great Tradition, you are really not bound by the discipline of any tradition. While thinking yourself most virtuous, your choices become most idiosyncratic.[42]

While the current re-emphasis within emerging spirituality on ancient practices should be encouraged as one pathway to genuine discipleship, without anchoring this in any particular ecclesiological tradition, there is no reason to suggest this emphasis will be anything more than a further demonstration of the propensity towards faddism.

Perhaps the most direct demonstration of nomadic ecclesiology is in Brewin's own involvement as one of the pioneering leaders of the Vaux community in London (one of the foremost British examples of an emerging church). Brewin co-led a weekly alternative worship service which sought to relate the

Christian faith to the gritty reality of life in London through multimedia and the arts. Despite its success, Vaux abruptly came to a self-induced end in 2005, and invited its participants to 'a final wake – a meal of bitter herbs and fine wine to send this strange beast to the horizon'. Brewin offered the following reason as explanation for Vaux's cessation:

> No incarnation is ever perfect. For the health of the species, individual manifestations need to die, allowing proper evolution, preventing tired institutionalisation. As soon as something is birthed, it sets off on a journey toward some fixed embodiment, some evolutionary blind alley . . . Vaux didn't want to go that way. So while it still felt good, while it still hadn't hurt anyone, before it became a drag, we shot it dead. Things were beginning to move on: families grew, geographies changed, stages of faith matured. And sometimes you need a new vehicle.[43]

The deliberate cessation of Vaux strongly illustrates the temporality of emerging ecclesiology. Within a nomadic landscape, there is no cause for sentimentality when the model no longer fits. A further example of this nomadic principle is the relatively new idea of 'pop-up' churches. For example, Karen Ward has experimented with an Advent pop-up church in Portland, Oregon which seeks to engage with 'the church-skeptical and church-curious'. Interestingly, this postmodern ecclesial experiment included an advent wreath, incense and reading from the Book of Common Prayer in an attempt to preserve tradition in a 'more chilled-out, smaller way and driven by the desire to be creative and to connect culture and God and the gospel in new ways'.[44] If the church understands itself as a nomad then it is liberated to act in temporary ways that prevent the inevitable stultification of the institutional model.

The concept of 'pop-up' shops and restaurants is increasingly in vogue as a marketing strategy on the high streets of Britain. As a missiological idea it may well have some potential, however, we must also reflect upon its ecclesiological implications. In the example of Brewin's own involvement with Vaux, while one may admire the bravery of an approach that isn't content to provide a service merely for the sake of it, important questions must be asked about the discipleship and support of those within the group. Where the group is made up of a similar demographic of young people and families all in touch via social media, then perhaps the commitment of a weekly meeting seems less important; however, for those on the margins, such gatherings may be essential.

In many ways, Brewin's idea of TAZ is appealing, it allows experimentation and creativity without the need to commit permanently to a particular form or pattern. Within a missiological context it provides the possibility of trying an expression of church without becoming tied up with bureaucracy and process which has hindered many a good ecclesial idea. However, exploring it more deeply, a question is also raised about what ultimately shapes that impermanent form and whether the most powerful and prophetic response might be to offer an alternative to the impermanence of a vastly changing culture. With its rich tradition rooted in the past, the church is to remain a relational institution offering hope and permanence amid the fluctuating changes of the postmodern horizon. It is interesting that in the pop-up generation which supposedly prizes the instant and the temporary, there is an increased interest in monasticism and traditional spiritual practices. Perhaps we should instead suggest that the challenge facing the future of the church is not that of 'keeping up with the times', reflecting them in patterns of worship, but to offer a genuine alternative capable of transcending and transforming those norms? While this must never be used as theological justification for an institutional model of church that is inflexible, hierarchical and unbending, nevertheless, an institutional model that is relational, deeply participative and creative and imaginative may have something permanent and solid to offer in a transient and fluctuating culture.

A commitment to the church in all its forms

Tony Jones lists 'a commitment to the church in all its forms' as one of the four corporate values of the emerging church and in so far as generalizing statements have their merit, this one is considerably useful in discerning the core of emerging ecclesiology. For Jones, the commitment to the church in all its forms stems from what he calls the practice of 'deep ecclesiology', which exhibits a generous approach to other churches and seeks to acknowledge the strengths of other traditions.

> Emergents find little importance in the discrete differences between the various flavours of Christianity. Instead they practice a generous orthodoxy that appreciates the contributions of all Christian movements.[45]

The commitment to 'deep ecclesiology' is based on the conviction that we are in a post-denominational era and is best articulated in the lengthy subtitle to McLaren's *Generous Orthodoxy*: *Why I am Missional, Evangelical, Post/Protestant, Liberal/Conservative, Mystic/Poetic, Biblical, Charismatic/ Contemplative, Fundamentalist/Calvinist, Anabaptist/Anglican, Methodist, Catholic, Green, Incarnational, Depressed-yet-hopeful, Emergent and Unfinished Christian.* This deep ecclesiology manifests itself in an attitude of humility and generosity towards other Christian traditions:

> We seek to be irenic and inclusive of our Christian sisters and brothers, rather than elitist and critical. We own the many failures of the church as our failures, which humbles us and calls us to repentance.[46]

For Pagitt, the use of the term 'post' rather than 'anti' is critical in defining emerging Christianity since it implies something following sequentially rather than reactively. And it is in this sense of the word that he describes himself as 'post-evangelical, post-liberal, post-industrialized and post-Protestant'.[47] On a more pragmatic level, the deep ecclesiology of the emerging church is evidenced in its use of a 'pastiche of worship practices from across confessional boundaries'.[48] One would not be surprised to find an emerging church gathering that incorporates traditional liturgies and liturgical colours, techno-trance music and standing for the reading of the gospel.

However, there is also a missiological agenda at play in the emerging church's 'commitment to the church in all its forms', as this principle is appropriated pragmatically to encourage ecclesial experimentation in order to make church more accessible to those deterred by its institutional form. However, it is the commitment to many different forms of church that makes an exploration of this nature problematic. To suggest that there is *an* emerging ecclesiology somewhat misses the point, because it is the very commitment to a multiplicity of ecclesiologies that demarcates the movement. This approach means that there is no blueprint that the church must follow but an invitation to experiment with different and new forms of church. The result is that emerging churches look quite different from one another. Sweet expresses how this commitment to a multiple approach impacts the way the emerging church understands leadership:

> We anticipate all possible combinations of seminary-trained/ not seminary-trained, formally and informally mentored, paid and unpaid, structural chaos and anarchy, and 'chaordy'![49]

Creativity is also prized in the formation of these new ecclesiologies, which stems in part from the artistic demographic make-up of the emerging church and also from an eschatological conviction that, in being creative, Christians 'participate with God in the re-creation of the world'.[50]

The question of what drives the emerging commitment to the church in all its forms is an important one. In many ways, the missiological impetus that seeks to galvanize creative expression with regards to the form of church is to be welcomed as part of a wider conversation taking place within mainstream denominations also, not least in the Anglican discussion around Fresh Expressions. However, there is also the potential danger that where ecclesiology is driven solely by the practice of mission with no pre-established theology of Christian community, worship or discipleship, the result will be neither a reflection of biblical ideas of ecclesiology nor capable of sustaining long-term disciples. Thus, the question of what is neglected in emerging ecclesiology becomes a question of paramount importance.

On the other hand, the 'commitment to the church in all its forms' is driven by a desire to engage with a 'deep ecclesiology', a phrase that has become popular in theological discussions of this nature but may be seen to hold more than one meaning. For the emerging radicals, their commitment to a 'deep ecclesiology' entails two central threads: first the conviction that we are living in post-denominational times and therefore can accept multiple ideas about church regardless of denominational differences and, second, the desire to retrieve ancient liturgies and practices as formative for the life of the contemporary church. However, breadth in practice does not necessarily entail theological depth and can, as we suggested in the discussion on liturgical innovation, stem from a preference for individual choice, ironically a feature of modernity.

The phrase 'deep church' finds its origin in a letter written by C. S. Lewis to the *Church Times* in February 1952, although his term 'mere Christianity' became more popularly adopted. In this letter, Lewis urged the catholic and evangelical wings of the church to unite against the forces of modernism, arguing that they 'drank from the same well of a common Christian tradition'.[51] For C. S. Lewis this tradition continued through the apostles, to the councils and creeds of the early church, through the Middle Ages and the Reformation, albeit in a truncated and disjointed form. Andrew Walker has brought the theme of deep church to the surface in recent discussions on ecclesiology. Walker argues that while the renewal movement of the 1970s did much to break down many denominational boundaries in the pursuit of common tradition, its inability to deliver all that was hoped by the ecumenical dream extends promise into the current ecclesial scene that such a dream could be realized. The following quote identifies the important way that deep church incorporates both *relevance* to culture and *reference* to history:

The vision for deep church is neither an attempt to simply restate or repristinate the Christian tradition, this is tantamount to ancestor worship; nor does it take its bearings from the emerging culture, to do this is simply to assimilate to the prevailing hegemony; rather, to be a deep church means to stand on the cusp or the breaking-point of both the Christian tradition and the emerging culture, deeply rooted in the former while fully engaged in the latter.[52]

This raises an important question about how the emerging church envisages itself in those dual aspects of relevance to culture and reference to history, and whether the way it does so can be incorporated under the understanding of deep church that Lewis and, more latterly, Walker have in mind.

In the emerging church, the drive to reinvent itself in a plethora of forms is powered by the fluidity and transiency of culture. However, Walker's understanding of deep church locates the fluidity of the church in pneumatological terms, allowing change and adaptation but within a reciprocal relationship with the Christian tradition. This is one further example of where a more formulated pneumatology could help the emerging radicals, providing a way for the emerging church to gain licence for creativity without jettisoning commitment to the deeper tradition. In my opinion, the influential role that culture plays in directing the emerging radicals' adaptable ecclesiology is an indication of its divergence from deep church as Lewis would understand it.

For what Christians need, to be active, faithful and holy in our contemporary culture, is to dig down into our own deep resources.[53]

What is important about deep church is that it is neither about 'syncretism' nor 'absorbing the next fad in the endless search for liturgical novelty' but rather a marriage between the ancient things that God has said and done in history and the new thing He is doing now.[54] In many ways, Walker's understanding is akin to Hanson's idea of the church's doctrinal continuity being like a ship tied to an anchor; while the wind and waves of contemporary culture may influence the church both for good and for ill, it is the anchor that prevents the ship from ever straying off course.[55]

> Emerging churches, for all their resourcefulness, vigour and imaginative drive, will not succeed unless they heed the lessons from their charismatic precursors in the renewal and drop anchors in the deep waters of a church that goes all the way down to the hidden reservoirs of the life-giving Spirit that, like the water that Jesus gives, gushes up like a spring to eternal life.[56]

This raises an important question as to what, if anything, functions as the anchor for the vessel of emerging ecclesiology. There is much in emerging church rhetoric that signifies a retrieval of historical and traditional practices which have been marginalized in the modern church. In many ways, the emerging church is highly critical of the modernist tendency, particularly among the mega-church movement, to create services free from liturgy and outdated practices that would be considered irrelevant by spiritual seekers. Therefore, it would be fair to suggest that the emerging church has a healthier attitude to history than the church from which it has emerged. Nonetheless there remain serious flaws in its relationship to history. Daniel Williams is highly critical of evangelicalism's lack of continuity with its historical past and suggests that even the few historical elements that some evangelical churches do cherish, such as the Nicene creed or the trinitarian baptismal formula, are little more than 'footprints . . . of a doctrinal and confessional past which has been peripheral for so many evangelicals that it has ceased to guide the direction of many present day congregations and in some cases, it is forgotten'.[57] Williams argues that this problem of discontinuity stems from a misunderstanding of the nature of the Christian tradition and confusing it with traditionalism. Thus tradition becomes understood as tired and static methods of meaningless repetition, illustrated by Brewin's stereotyping of liturgy as a 'nagging widow'. However, Williams regards the New Testament understanding of tradition as being an active and living process (2 Thess. 2.15) transmitted from one party to another:

> The Tradition denotes the acceptance and the handing over of God's word, Jesus Christ (tradere Christum) and how this took concrete forms in the apostles' preaching (kerygma), in the Christ-centred reading of the Old Testament, in the celebration of baptism and the Lord's supper, and in the doxological, doctrinal, hymnological and credal forms by which the declaration of the mystery of God Incarnate was revealed for our salvation.[58]

For Williams it is this living tradition which provides a 'bond which defines the way of faithfulness through the passing ages of the world'.[59] In other words, this living tradition functions as the anchor ensuring that the vessel never strays too far in unchartered waters. Williams makes the further point that to remove scripture from the tradition out of which it emerged was an alien concept to the early church and that evangelicalism's tendency to pitch these as two opposing authority sources is largely responsible for its *ahistorical* approach.

The concept of apostolicity is pertinent here since it provides a potential way of linking the current creative missionary initiative of the church – in this case a commitment to church in all its forms – with its historic foundations. The term apostolicity carries with it both aspects of the current church's 'sentness' and its relationship to its theological and doctrinal foundation.

McLaren comments directly and appreciatively on the four marks of oneness, holiness, catholicity and apostolicity, in *A Generous Orthodoxy*. When addressing the subject of apostolicity, McLaren is keen to point out that there are two contrasting ways of understanding apostolicity. The first is concerned with preservation of tradition, and establishing the 'rightness' of any given church's theological position on the basis of its lineage to the Apostles. The alternative understanding McLaren prefers is that of missional, and the idea that followers are invited to 'join God in bringing blessing to our needy world'.[60] This echoes Anderson's pivotal idea in his book *An Emergent Theology for the Emerging Church*, described by Tony Jones as 'a go-to book for emerging leaders for years to come'. Anderson draws a distinction between the inward-focused 'Jerusalem' which was concerned primarily with maintaining historical precedent, and the outward-looking 'Antioch' model, which was more concerned with the renewing and extending work of the Holy Spirit.[61] Anderson also argues that when Paul writes about the church being built upon the foundation of the apostles and prophets in Ephesians 2.19–20, he understood this link not in terms of historical continuity with the Apostles but in eschatological terms: the resurrected Christ, now present by the Holy Spirit in the community. Anderson sees the link with pneumatology as critical to the apostolic identity of the church:

> As the risen and ascended Lord who is coming, Christ's apostolic authority reaches toward us into the present time as the creative power for the church's apostolic ministry in every generation. Paul viewed the coming of Christ as his apostolic authority who, by virtue of his Holy Spirit, was already at work in transforming the old into the new.[62]

This understanding of the term leads Anderson to conclude that emerging churches can be seen as apostolic when they 'seek to define and make clear the apostolic work of Christ in the present century rather than the first century'.[63] It is in this way that, for the emerging radicals, apostolicity means that theology be understood primarily in terms of a forward motion rather than a retrospective exercise.

However, once again, the danger of pitting binary opposites against one another is apparent. It is the very concept of apostolicity that prevents us from setting missionary models of the church in opposition to the idea of the church as the guardian or preserver of truth, since the apostolicity of the church requires that both aspects have a significant role to play in developing ecclesiology. Torrance makes this past–present–future link apparent:

In its simplest sense the apostolicity of the Church refers back to the original foundation of the Church once for all laid by Christ upon the apostles, but it also refers to the interpenetration of the existence and mission of the Church in its unswerving fidelity to that apostolic foundation.[64]

A commitment to Apostolicity does not force the church to make a choice between its past and its future. By contrast, it provides the means of linking the two. As such, it provides an informative way of critiquing how emerging ecclesiology is formed both in relation to its historical past and its missionary future. The Apostles functioned as a link between Christ and his church, ensuring this connection by their teaching and embodiment of the truth of the Gospel as the foundation upon which the historical church is built (Eph. 2.20). In a similar way to Daniel Williams' explanation of the living nature of the tradition, Torrance is persuasive in his insistence that the apostolic deposit be understood not merely as the content of the Gospel in Apostolic writings, but as 'the life-giving reality of Christ himself' to which it points:

> It is only in Christ and not out of itself, and only through union and communion with Christ in its faith and mission and not through its own piety, that the Church is continuously sustained [. . .] That the Church is *apostolic* as well as one, holy and catholic, signifies, therefore, that it is ever one and the same with the Church once for all founded by Christ in the apostolate [. . .] That is to say, apostolicity has to do with the continuing *identity* of the Church as the authentic Body of Christ in space and time.[65]

Cray stresses the importance of apostolicity for understanding how the church relates to is cultural surroundings in the mission-shaped church report. It is both the mark that drives the church to constantly seek to relate its historical message to its present context, but is also the 'safeguard that prevents inculturation becoming syncretism'.[66] Torrance's understanding of apostolicity emphasized the importance of both Christology and also the exposition and application of Scripture in discerning the apostolic calling and witness of the church. These two aspects are key in the process of discernment about how the church should be shaped in relation to its cultural context:

> For it is through faithful transmission of the preaching and teaching of the apostles that the Church is itself constantly renewed and reconstituted as Christ's Church.[67]

Torrance cites the development of the church's creeds, such as Nicea, as examples of how scripture has been paramount in the development of the church's identity and mission and that, while leaders and theologians were not afraid of coining new phrases to explain the Christian faith adequately, such deliberations were always worked through in connection with a deep exposition of scripture. However, Tony Jones suggests that for those in the emerging church theology is 'local, conversational and temporary'.[68] The emphasis is upon continuing theological dialogue rather than preserving or passing on timeless truths. Therefore, apostolicity raises some serious questions about whether the emerging radical's desire to speak the language of faith in postmodern idiom is done in connection with a deep exposition of scripture, an issue which we will address in the final section of this chapter.

Marks of a deep church: Baptism and Eucharist

Apostolicity raises the question of the marks of the church, a subject upon which traditional definitions of ecclesiology have been founded and yet this is not a subject that the emerging radicals specifically refer to. For the purposes of simplicity I will consider the sacramental practices of the Eucharist and baptism as the bare essentials in any ecclesial expression that wishes to identify itself within the broader Protestant or evangelical tradition. Jones observes that the eight emerging churches he visited for his research celebrated communion far more readily than their mainstream counterparts. In emerging account of communion, the communitarian aspect is emphasized:

We seek to live reconciled lives to one another, so it's important to us that we serve the bread and the drink of communion to one another, offering ourselves to one another as expressions of peace and wholeness.[69]

This raises an important question about whether the Eucharist, or sacraments more generally, are considered marks of the emerging church.

For Volf the sacraments are essential to the *esse* of the church although they are not what ultimately comprise ecclesiology. It is through the confession of faith in Jesus Christ that the church is both constituted and manifested, and it is within this framework that the sacraments of Eucharist and baptism take their place:

There is no church without sacraments; but there are no sacraments without the confession of faith and without faith itself.[70]

Clapp regards the Eucharist as of paramount importance in ecclesiology, not purely in terms of an act of remembrance but in its culture-creating capabilities. The Eucharistic act is crucial in the establishment and ongoing sustainability of the church's identity in four noteworthy ways: based upon the Lordship of Christ, radical egalitarianism, people prepared to face conflict and failure, and people of peace and non-violence. Thus Clapp implies that the Eucharist is crucial in ecclesiology, serving as an impetus to mission and service.

In many ways the emerging radicals are seeking to redress the non-sacramental bias of the seeker movement, which sought to strip services of elements deemed inaccessible to those outside. The emerging radicals' re-emphasis on communion, therefore, is to be welcomed as one of the positive retrievals of the movement, yet further needs to be offered by way of theological and ecclesiological engagement with it.

The Eucharist has a significant role to play in churches that are seeking to be authentic, contextual and missional. Lindsay

Urwin argues for the rediscovery of the sacraments as essential to the mission of the church, an argument that would appeal to the emerging radicals, especially his insistence that the church 'chill out' about the rules that govern them. Urwin suggests that we understand the sacraments not as institutional events but as something that Christ does in and through his people and that their potency within postmodernity should not be underestimated:

> In a culture saturated with trivial, unmemorable and unreliable words Christ-filled symbol and action might have more chance of breaking through.[71]

Ian Stackhouse similarly affirms the missional potency of the sacraments, citing Wesley's affirmation of them as not merely a 'confirming ordinance' but a 'converting ordinance'.[72]

Chris Cocksworth suggests that, historically, the early evangelicals laid significant emphasis upon the Eucharist, regarding it as a celebration of the presence of Christ and the performance of the gospel. Cocksworth also identifies the missing liturgical framework from the emerging radicals' Eucharistic revival that links contemporary expressions of the Eucharist within a broader historical context. This framework preserves the fidelity of such contemporary expressions. In addition, Stackhouse considers that the re-enactment of the gospel through the Eucharist is of great missional significance, ensuring that the mission of the church is 'energized by the gospel itself' and not by other competing or conflicting agendas.[73]

Baptism is similarly foundational in fresh or emerging expressions of church, yet it is often not emphasized as readily as the Eucharist, the pragmatic reason being obvious; it is easier to share communion in a community space such as a coffee shop than it is to baptize someone there. Theologically, its absence is perhaps more significant and stems, in part, from a less conversion-oriented approach to evangelism. When conversion is no longer the goal of mission and belonging is prioritized above believing, baptism's necessity fades. Furthermore, an ecclesiological approach that resists boundaries can render baptism as a sign of membership oxymoronic.

Stackhouse suggests that while a commitment to 'belonging before believing' is attractive in the postmodern milieu, it ultimately circumvents the scandal of the cross that baptism demonstrates. Moreover, Stackhouse believes baptism challenges the homogeneity of many contemporary expressions of mission. The emerging church does not explicitly affirm the homogenous unit principle characteristic of the church growth methodology, yet some crossover is evident. The notion of homogeneity within church planting is largely attributed to Donald A. McGavran, a third-generation missionary to India in the mid 1990s. McGavran grew increasingly frustrated by the lack of conversions he and other missionaries were seeing in India, despite the large investment of people and money. His exploration of the factors that led to church growth was hugely influential in what later became called the Church Growth Movement. McGavran observed that western missionaries were preoccupied with individual conversion rather than whole groups and that historically a 'habit of independent decision' had been encouraged by revivalist gatherings. By contrast, McGavran became more concerned with the transformation of whole people groups in such a way that their indigenous identity was preserved rather than the existing expectation that, in order to follow Christ, an individual must step out from his or her pre-existing social community. McGavran summarizes this shift in missiological thinking in the following way:

> To Christianize a whole people, the first thing not to do is to snatch individuals out of it into a different society. Peoples become Christians where a Christward movement occurs within that society.[74]

McGavran called this experience of a 'Christward movement' within any given societal group a 'people movement' and he cited Paul's missionary experiences as following such a pattern in the New Testament. On one level McGavran's appeal is simply for a missionary enterprise which respects the communal nature of human society and cherishes an indigenous approach to church planting and discipleship – an approach not unlike that pioneered by Roland Allen in China. However, McGavran's approach, which later became known, through the Church Growth Movement, as 'the homogenous unit principle', goes a step further than an indigenous approach to missionary praxis. McGavran's observations led him to conclude that people converted most quickly when there was the least change to their racial or social grouping.

> People like to become Christians without crossing racial, linguistic, or class barriers.[75]

This belief led to the conviction, espoused in the homogenous unit principle, that churches grow fastest when its members are from a similar social, cultural or ethical background. Bosch observes that for McGavran, numerical growth was believed to be the ultimate driving force in a world where 3 billion people were not Christians.

The emerging church's commitment to the church in all its forms makes homogeneity of this kind pragmatically alluring; when advocating small informal groupings, the ease of doing so around pre-existing social networks is palpable. Chester comments that while McGavran's analysis was based largely upon rural communities that were broadly culturally homogenous, urban contexts are not culturally homogenous and thus the principle of homogeneity within church planting becomes more problematic.[76] Costas has been particularly critical of a homogenous approach to establishing new church communities, which he believes does violence to the reconciliatory message of the Gospel that the Christian community demonstrates and of which it provides a foretaste:

> The fellowship of faith (the church) is [. . .] a sign of the coming kingdom. If the kingdom of God represents the definitive reconciliation between God and humanity, between individuals, peoples, sexes, generations, and races, and between humanity and the rest of creation – a promise that will be fulfilled in the second coming of Christ – then the community of God's people is an overriding necessity, in order that the world might understand what the salvation that God offers in the gospel really is.[77]

The emerging church may have no 'official' commitment to the homogenous unit principle, and may, in many ways, reject core tenets of the Church Growth Movement; nevertheless, there is some acknowledgement about its homogeneity and even Tony Jones admits that by and large they are 'younger, more white, better educated and wealthier than the average American church goer'.[78] His research also identifies the average age as 32 with over 38% of its members holding degrees and 22% having postgraduate academic qualifications.

There is a strong pragmatic missiological argument for the homogenous unit principle and it is influential in many contemporary church-planting initiatives aside from the emerging church. As such it is not without its merits in its ability to attract people who are not currently engaged with church; however, there are limitations to its approach. Allowing homogeneity to govern ecclesiology permits the church to retreat into cultural fragmentation and seclusion, where the divisions of society go unchallenged. The ultimate surrender to postmodern fragmentation is individual congregations of like-minded people with age, hobbies or social groupings as the defining criteria rather than cross-boundary fellowship. While such an expression of church may have all the practical elements of a church, it can never be its fullest possible expression. Succumbing to homogeneity has two serious flaws. The first is that 'Christianizing' the networks that already exist in society robs the gospel of its unifying power. One could argue that the prophetic calling of the church is to demonstrate the truth that 'all are one in Christ Jesus' by rejecting the fragmentation of postmodern society and seeking community which crosses societal boundaries (Gal. 3.28). The church that Paul planted in Philippi spanned social and economic barriers, including a wealthy businesswoman, a slave girl and a Roman jailer and his family (Acts 16.11–40). This is the church Paul exhorted to 'be like-minded having the same love, being one in spirit and purpose' (Phil. 2.2).

The second is that where churches operate primarily within existing social networks, the vital discipleship that comes from learning to relate to people from a different background, age or race is lost. In Ephesians, Paul sets out that the gospel breaks down such barriers and in so doing declares the manifold wisdom of God in both its earthly and cosmic dimensions. He thus urges this mixed group to 'keep the unity of the Spirit in the bond of peace' (Eph. 4:39). The community that unites across societal and prejudicial boundaries is not an easy one but is one that testifies to the unifying power of the gospel both on earth and in heaven. Suggesting that the diversity inherent within multicultural society of the twenty-first century necessitates a homogenous approach to church planting appears to ignore the diversity evident in the first Christian communities. Volf argues that by functioning as 'homogenous units', the church commodifies the gospel and ultimately concedes to consumerism.

While homogeneity may make pragmatic sense, we must question whether this practice sacrifices distinctiveness for expediency. In addition, though homogeneity may also make evangelistic sense, providing fertile ground for the easy building of community, its resemblance to the culture of the world ultimately damages the integrity of its witness. Volf concludes that if the church is to make any missional contribution to the world then it must first be healed of its homogeneity. The sacrament of baptism enacts both this communal unity in diversity and also its trinitarian correspondence.

> Churches do not emerge from baptism simply as images of the triune God fashioned by human beings, but rather as concrete, anticipatory experiences, rendered possible by the Spirit, of the one communion of the triune God and God's glorified people.[79]

The sacrament of baptism ensures that homogeneity cannot flourish unchecked since it is into one body that all are baptized (1 Cor. 12.13). Baptism reminds us of the imperative of the deeper commitment to authentic relationships beyond pre-existing social networks.

Constantinian paradigm

The central thrust of the emerging church's bid for a new ecclesiology is built upon the premise that through the era of Constantine the church lost its way, aligning itself with the state-adopted practices and beliefs that were antithetical to the core of the Christian faith. Thus the end of the Christendom era is welcomed as an opportunity to free the church of its modernist influences and restore some of its pre-Constantinian values and practices. However, relying upon this Constantinian paradigm can be detrimental in at least two ways. First, this paradigm thinking is reluctant to see the vitality and continuity of the worshipping and confessing church throughout its history. Thus, it relies upon a one-dimensional understanding of church history as being about political-conciliar authority and fails to see the creative and innovative ways that individual churches and leaders in the past sought to keep the faith alive. This approach seems particularly ironic since the emerging church regards itself as playing a similar role, seeking renewal in the face of perceived mainstream inactivity and inflexibility. Second, an approach which is dismissive of nearly 1,500 years of Christian witness neglects what Williams describes as 'Christ's establishing the church in holiness', as if the Christendom paradigm somehow outsmarted God.[80] Generous orthodoxy can hardly be so selective.

For Williams, paradigm thinking has severe consequences for ecclesiology, particularly with regard to the emerging church's preference for small, local, non-denominational communities. He regards the autonomy of the local church as providing an artificial sense of doctrinal security, and its failure to connect with the wider historical tradition 'will eclipse the congregation's ability to know itself within the larger Christian story'.[81] There is arguably a strong synthesis between being rooted and grounded in tradition and the fidelity and credibility of the church. When the church fails to sufficiently anchor itself in the wider tradition then it will become less and less able to discern theological truth from passing fads:

> An absence of the church's theological past will produce believers who are not sure how to interpret their Bibles, apart from relative or fashionable opinion, or who are not able to position their interpretations within the wider framework of competing claims of new theologies.[82]

The relativization of church

Jones regards Moltmann as the influence par excellence upon emerging ecclesiology. Exploring how Jones understands Moltmann's ecclesiology reveals the theological shift that 'a commitment to the church in all its forms' requires. For Jones, the most influential aspect of Moltmann's ecclesiology is his rejection of the notion that the church is *the* vehicle of salvation. This relativizes the church as just one of the objects of Christ's mission in the world. In many ways, this conviction is exemplified in the emerging shift from institutional church to missional church, in that there is no longer one main model of ecclesiology but rather multiple models. Pagitt understands relativized ecclesiology to mean that 'the church is not necessarily the centre of God's intentions'.[83] In pragmatic terms, this means seeking smaller, more adaptable communities instead of larger institutional forms and leaving behind the trappings of institutionalism such as infant baptism and priest-led Holy Communion. Jones considers Moltmann a prophetic voice, championing a version of ecclesiology that suits the future generation more than it did his own. Jones summarizes Moltmann's teaching in this way:

> The church is relativised – its role in society is only known in its relationship to other societal forces and institutions and to its subsumption to the mission of God.[84]

Jones regards Moltmann's 'relativizing' of ecclesiology as relating not only to its multiplicity of forms but also its relationship to other societal forms. Thus the particularity of the church is preserved by its relationship to the many other forces present within culture.

There is no denying Moltmann's influence upon emerging theology. Moltmann's theology was forged in the brutal crucible of World War II and, while the emerging radicals do not share that same experience, collectively they seek a theological expression that relates to the stark realities of human existence, rejecting safe palatable versions of faith that have no place for suffering. In a similar way, their quest for a new ecclesiology is driven by a sense of disconnect rather than abstract theology.

While Moltmann's impact on the emerging radicals cannot be explored in depth, we will consider two crucial aspects: first, Moltmann's concept of the relativization of the church and second, an aspect of Moltmann's theology that has much to contribute to emerging ecclesiology:pneumatology.

Moltmann relocates the church from the centre of God's purposes for the world into the broader schemata of the kingdom of God; the church is simply one of the ways in which God fulfils his missionary purposes:

> As a call to freedom the gospel is an event of missionary calling. Its aim is not to spread the Christian religion or to implant the church; it is to liberate the people for the exodus in the name of the coming kingdom.[85]

Gibbs and Bolger identify the centrality of the kingdom as important to the ecclesial deconstruction project of the emerging church. However, Jones takes Moltmann to mean that the removal of the church from the centre of God's soteriological purposes 'relativizes' the church, as his description of the church as 'a non-exclusive vehicle of God's grace' indicates, making its role in society 'known in its relationship to other societal forces'.[86] Thomas Oden suggests that the emerging church ultimately de-emphasizes ecclesiology, by its preferential emphasis on God's kingdom in which the church has no right to exclusivity.[87] By contrast, Rowan Williams maintains that it is precisely because of the church's *difference* from all other human and relational institutions that it can be seen as applicable to all:

> Its relevance to all depends on its difference from existing patterns of human relation and power; if it 'fulfils' anything it is a buried capacity for communion between human beings as such – as flesh and spirit, as mortal and sinful and walled off from each other, in need of a relation God alone can provide.[88]

Thus the unique identity of the church can be seen to reside in its difference from all other institutions and relations rather than in its connection with them. This is the prophetic challenge of the church, which is absent when incarnation is understood purely in terms of identification and immersion as we have already seen. Williams also highlights the importance of Christ's resurrection to our thinking about ecclesiology:

> The Church . . . proclaims and struggles to realize a 'belonging together' of persons in community in virtue of nothing but a shared belonging with or to the risen Jesus.[89]

For Williams it is the presence of the risen Christ that provides the basis for the creation of a community transcending the normal boundaries of social and human interaction and which ultimately prevents the cultural captivity of the church:

> A human community different from what we ordinarily think of as 'natural communities', a community whose limits are at the same time the ultimate natural 'limits' – 'the ends of the earth'.[90]

It is when we are perceived in our relation to the risen Christ rather than to our background, race or education that the new creation is realized. This relatedness to Christ brings the familiarity and intimacy of family connection, yet it is not based upon any of the usual social connections. Ecclesiology is then about the creation of this 'new world' community, which can be neither tamed nor controlled by the other communities of the world. Thus, in antithesis to what the emerging radicals suggest, it is not the church that becomes relative in its relationship to other institutions but rather the other way round:

> The Church's good news is that human community is possible; the Church's challenge is in its insistence that this possibility is realised only in that giving away of power in order to nurture authority in others that is learned in the giving away of God in Jesus, and its further insistence that the relations constituting Christ's Body, neither compete with nor vindicate others, but simply stand in their own right as the context which relativises all others.[91]

In this way, the church, as the community gathered around the risen Christ, is empowered not to dominate or coerce but to provide a prophetic voice that both critiques and speaks hope into the world:

> The relations of human beings in the Body of Christ, relations based simply on a shared commitment to and promise to be with the risen Jesus, provide the context and the critique for other systems, the irritant that can prevent the human world from simply settling down with mutually exclusive and competing tribalisms.[92]

In a similar way, Hauerwas' understanding of the Christian community as 'resident aliens' contrasts strongly with Moltmann's relativized ecclesiology by incorporating a church/world dynamic that Moltmann neglects:

> The church is a colony, an island of one culture in the middle of another. In baptism, our citizenship is transferred from one dominion to another and we become, in whatever culture we find ourselves, resident aliens.[93]

For Hauerwas, baptism is the formative sign marking the distinctiveness of the Christian community and so it can be regarded as the antithesis of the relativization of the church.

However, I would argue that despite the emerging radicals' penchant for Moltmann's theology there is one aspect that they neglect to their detriment. The subject of pneumatology appears to have taken prominence in Moltmann's later writings and in some ways perhaps elevated his thinking about ecclesiology to greater prominence than his aforementioned understanding. Moltmann defines the three main eras of the church as being firstly the age of the Father, secondly the age of the Son where ecclesiology was determined by the person and work of Christ, and lastly the current age of the charismatic church of the Spirit. While Jones rejects Moltmann's taxonomy for being too neat and 'anthropologically naïve', he nevertheless admits that the inception of the emerging church did in fact coincide with 'a global awakening to the power of the Holy Spirit'.[94] However, Jones' reading of church history is problematic since chronologically the birth of Pentecostalism, which is generally located at the Asuza Street revival in the early 1900s, far precedes this current expression of emerging Christianity. In addition, while the emerging church may stylistically have common ground with what Kakkainen calls Pentecostalism's 'ad hoc nature which leaves much room for improvisation' and a less hierarchical approach, their ecclesiology nevertheless seems a significant diversion from a charismatic model.[95] Many of the emerging radicals were brought up in a charismatic expression of the Christian faith through the mega-church movement. Thus, in their rejection of this background, are they in danger of neglecting a feature which lies at the heart of any charismatic ecclesiology – a contribution of the gifts of the spirit from every member to the church community?

Simon Chan's work on Pentecostal ecclesiology, despite addressing more directly the Pentecostal tradition, is pertinent to the discussion surrounding emerging pneumatology. In contrast to Pentecostalism, which Chan believes has over-emphasized a personal Pentecost experience, he maintains that the Pentecost event is nevertheless paradigmatic for the church. Chan goes so far as to say that pneumatology cannot be understood apart from ecclesiology. In drawing attention to the inextricable link between the Spirit and the church, Chan identifies three features of Pentecostal ecclesiology, each of which can contribute something to the development of an emerging ecclesiology. The first is that the church is the place of the personal indwelling of the Holy Spirit. This indwelling of the Spirit means that holiness is properly a characteristic of the church and that sometimes it must 'stand out in sharp contrast to the world'.[96] Thus a properly formulated pneumatology can act as a rebuke to any ecclesiology that seeks to diminish the distinction between the church and the world. The second is that the Holy Spirit unites the church ontologically to its head, Christ. This ontological linking brings together pneumatology, Christology and ecclesiology. In this way, Chan argues, the church becomes the living tradition:

The church that holds the precious deposit of faith, the truth of the Gospel of Jesus Christ, is so united with it that it is constantly being rejuvenated by the Spirit.[97]

Chan suggests that the Pentecostal emphasis on freedom in the Spirit has often severed it from its historical roots, yet the doctrine of the Holy Spirit does the very opposite:

The Spirit comes to indwell the church and also to indwell each believer; he works *in* history to establish the institution and yet he comes from *beyond* history to renew the institution with his charisms [. . .] He reminds the church of what has been and also shows the church things to come. He illumines the church with an ever-growing understanding of the faith which is once delivered to the saints.[98]

The church that does not pay attention to the past cannot, Chan observes, navigate its way into the future without becoming in 'bondage to the reigning ideologies'. It can therefore be argued that a more adequately developed pneumatology could help the emerging church navigate its way more faithfully through cultural change. Lastly, the church that is indwelt by the Holy Spirit must also be seen as the temple of the Holy Spirit and, as such, the means of communion between God and humanity. This final aspect demonstrates the importance of pneumatology in establishing a missional ecclesiology.

The story of the Spirit is about his coming to the church making the church an inextricable part of the Spirit-event. The story of the church is part of the story of the Spirit and therefore part of the Trinitarian narrative. The church is thus more than an agent to carry out the mission of the Trinity; she is part of the Trinitarian mission itself. Mission is more than what the church does but what the church is.[99]

It can be argued that, in this regard, those who are seeking the shape of the church for a postmodern world have much to learn from a Pentecostal ecclesiology which is fuelled by its missiological foundations.

Moltmann concurs that pneumatology is crucial in formulating an understanding of Christian community since it is 'the goal of God's life-giving Spirit in the world of nature and human beings'.[100] Furthermore, it is the Spirit that enables the unity within diversity that must be characteristic of all Christian ecclesiology:

> When they take this diversity and variety seriously, people experience fellowship with God not as 'the power above them' or as 'the ground beneath them' but as the bond between them. Consequently, the Holy Spirit has been described from time immemorial in terms of sociality. It binds different people together and distinguishes between people who are thus bound.[101]

Patrick Oden has argued that Moltmann's pneumatology has significantly influenced emerging ecclesiology and cites Gibbs and Bolger's nine characteristics as relating to Moltmann's pneumatology. However, my belief is that this link is more implicit than it is explicit. For example, Gibbs and Bolger offer 'welcoming the stranger' as one of the nine characteristics, something which they regard as motivated by the Spirit who brings unity within diversity. However, the commitment to inclusion in emerging ecclesiology appears driven by a rejection of the exclusivity of modernity and a desire to embrace the outsider, rather than a charismatic vision of the church made up of many gifts. While the inclusivity of the emerging church is to be welcomed, it could be more deeply grounded in an understanding of the Spirit's animating, invigorating and unifying life within the Christian community.

One further example Oden offers is the characteristic of 'connecting with ancient spiritualities', which he believes to be a demonstration of the movement of the Spirit in both creating and reviving forms of worship in each generation. However, the emerging radicals do not understand their commitment to ancient liturgical forms in pneumatological terms. Brewin's spiritual cartography is driven by the temporality of ecclesiology, a process he details without reference to the ministry of the Spirit. Oden's conclusion that the emerging church can be understood as 'a form of neo-Pentecostalism in which a holistic pneumatology is embraced through a new, liberating, freedom for living' circumnavigates the problematic issue that the emerging church does not appear to regard itself as continuing in the Pentecostal tradition.[102]

The commitment to the church in all its forms seems to be appropriated pragmatically by the emerging radicals in their experimentation with multiple and varied expressions of church. However, it is my opinion that Moltmann's pneumatology should lead us not primarily to a multiplicity of forms of church operating independently but rather to multiplicity within a single context. The outworking of Paul's teaching in 1 Corinthians 12 is that the Spirit is the sign and seal of unity between those who, outside the church, would normally be disunited. It is to this diverse and yet gathered community that the charismata are imparted so that Paul can say 'there are different kinds of gifts, but the same Spirit' (1 Cor. 12:4). The pneumatological drive to multiplicity is primarily in terms of the diverse yet gathered and unified congregation rather than a licence for a scatter-gun approach to ecclesiology.

Thus a richer understanding of pneumatology leads us to conclude that a commitment to multiplicity is primarily to be understood as a call to unity and diversity within the gathered congregation, marked by the sign of baptism. Such multiplicity is both a witness to the gospel of Christ, which transcends human barriers, and an anticipation of the eschaton to come. Since no Christian community alone can reflect the full scope of the diversity of the people of God, a commitment to a deep church must also be sought. Volf writes that 'openness to all other churches is the interecclesial minimum of the concrete ecclesial proleptic experience of the eschatological gathering of the whole people of God'.[103]

Nevertheless, while acknowledging that the Spirit's commitment to multiplicity is primarily meant in terms of a diverse gathered congregation, the emerging radicals' commitment to creativity and ingenuity in ecclesiology should not be overlooked.

> In the new life we experience the Spirit as the 'broad place', as the free space for our freedom, as the living space for our lives, as the horizon inviting us to discover life.[104]

Moltmann here understands the freedom of the Spirit as the invitation to creativity and discovery, and these are crucial aspects that must not be ignored in the development of ecclesiology. Volf similarly reminds us that the Spirit is essential to a participative model, ensuring that we do not become captive to hierarchical sterility. However, does a commitment to the freedom and creativity of the Spirit mean that in ecclesial terms 'anything goes'? The weakness of experimenting with varied forms of church is that it becomes easier to reflect the connections that already exist within society, missing the discipleship call to extend bonds of community beyond what is natural and, in so doing, to miss the call of the Spirit. However, the call to diversity within unity must not be read as a call to inactivity but rather as an awareness that in experimenting with new forms of church the goal must ultimately be the fullest vision of unity in diversity that represents the heart of the gospel. Rowan Williams' words are pertinent here:

> If 'church' is what happens when people encounter the Risen Jesus and commit themselves to sustaining and deepening that encounter in their encounter with each other, there is plenty of theological room for diversity of rhythm and style, so long as we have ways of identifying the same living Christ at the heart of every Christian life in common.[105]

Perhaps then the core ecclesiological conviction that the church in the postmodern age needs not *a commitment to the church in all its forms* but rather *a commitment to Christ in many ways and places*. This does not and cannot mean that there is one fixed expression of church for all times and places. However, a commitment to varied expressions requires a unifying anchoring in the deep church of which Lewis spoke. A deep church is one rooted in and seated under the lordship of the risen Christ, uniquely and definitively marked by baptism in his name and a shared meal in his remembrance. While prizing freedom of expression and creativity of form, these Christological marks ensure that any expression of church strives towards the unity within diversity that those marks embody, and that the course chosen is a deep one, anchored in a vision of the risen and exalted Christ, rather than the often shallow waters of a fluctuating culture.

The community as shapers of truth

If one word were to describe emerging ecclesiology then 'community' would stand in strong contention. This high commitment to community is partly a reaction against modern forms of worship where the service was regarded as a performance. Thus emerging ecclesiology's emphasis on participation and collaboration is engineered in antithesis to the idea of congregation members as passive observers. In pragmatic terms, this commitment is often reflected in the design and format of emerging gatherings:

> People expecting to find rows of folded chairs find instead groupings of couches, chairs and tables, recliners, and the like arranged in the round with an open centre area.[106]

While this is a welcome corrective to patterns of church that devalue community, the emerging emphasis is not merely about reasserting *koinonia*, but is in some cases about elevating the role of the community to that of shaper and definer of truth. At the heart of this is the idea that truth is not external to the community, imposing its authority from above or outside, but rather intrinsic, emerging through the community's social interaction and relationships. As Ben Edson states:

> Truth gradually emerges through involvement in an authentic life-changing hermeneutic community.[107]

The idea that truth emerges as part of a social process is found in a number of emerging writings, not least in the following by Leonard Sweet:

> Postmoderns don't know what they think until they hear themselves say it in discourse. Thinking is a group process, and truth emerges from the give-and-take dialogue and discussion with input from as many angles as possible.[108]

Jones proposes that 'truth cannot be definitively articulated' in contrary to modern understandings of ecclesiology which regard the church as the guardian of definitively articulated truth.[109] This echoes Pagitt's desire to move beyond belief-based faith to 'life-lived holistic faith'.[110] For Rollins, what is important is not *what* we believe but *the way in which we believe*; the basis of unity does not lie in the content of belief but in the event of revelation itself:

> The revelation of God will speak in multiple ways depending on the context in which we read it and into which it speaks.[111]

Understanding community in this way necessarily entails the rejection of the notion that the church is the herald or witness of truth, or the place where answers can be found:

> The church has for too long been seen as an oasis in the desert – offering water to the thirsty. The emerging communion appears more as a desert in the oasis of life, offering silence, space and desolation amidst the 'sickly nourishment of Western capitalism'. It is in wandering as nomads in this desert that God is found.[112]

This is not to say that the issue of truth is not important to the emerging radicals but rather that a shift has taken place in terms of understanding how that truth is mediated and received.

The idea of truth as a social construct is central to postmodern thinking, elevating the community above the individual, and is arguably influential to emerging ecclesiology, where an excessive emphasis upon personal salvation is considered a 'vestige' of modernity. Franke demonstrates the impact of the social construct of truth in the role that the community plays in the creation of theology. While acknowledging that the authority of the Spirit speaking through scripture is crucial, Franke is critical of how this approach can lead to subjectivism, in which our individual reception of the transcendent word of God becomes paramount. As an alternative, Franke proposes a fluid understanding of the relationship between the actual text and the revelation of God, citing the canonization of scripture as an example of this approach which conjoins collaboration between the written text, the guidance of the Holy Spirit and the faith community's endeavour to 'understand the ongoing work of God in the world in the light of God's earlier activity as described in the oral and written traditions of the community'. In this pneumatological and community-oriented understanding of theology, the key word for Franke is that the spirit 'appropriates' the word of God into the contemporary embodiment of the age-old Christian community:

> We read knowing that the Spirit speaks through scripture, appropriating the text so as to create our communal world through it. While the world the spirit fashions is so specific to our situation and hence not merely a transplanting of the world of the text into the present, the spirit-constructed world we are to inhabit is nevertheless shaped by the world disclosed in the text.[113]

For Franke, pneumatology is vital in the interpretation of scripture; its concern is not to explicate the original or fixed meaning of the text but to allow it to take on a life of its own, shaped by the reader and trusting that 'the text has its own intention, which has its genesis in the author's intention but is not exhausted by it'.[114]

This position has significant implications for hermeneutics, but it is the emphasis upon the interpretative role of the Christian community that is of most interest to our discussion on ecclesiology. Franke does not envisage the Spirit as the one who interprets God's word to the believer but as 'world creating'. Franke maintains that as the Spirit appropriates the text, its goal is to create the eschatologically intended world at the heart of the Bible: the new creation of Jesus Christ.

However, before evaluating this new perspective on the community as shapers of truth, we must acknowledge that the prominence of communitarian thinking is part of a more general emphasis that writers such as Gunton and Volf made asserting the centrality and relevance of the Trinity. In many ways emerging ecclesiology is to be praised for emphasizing the community aspect of ecclesiology again. However, it appears that in so doing, the emerging radicals have not merely reaffirmed the importance of community but have elevated the status of the community to shaper and creator of truth. The epistemic humility of the emerging radicals relies upon a false association of truth with arrogance. An ecclesiological approach which seeks not to impose dogmatically what is universally true for all times and cultures, may appear humble, but ends up elevating the role of the church to that of creator rather than guardian of truth. Elevating ecclesiology in this way moves away from the trajectory of church history, which has sought to define ecclesiology in terms of holiness, catholicity, apostolicity and unity. Ecclesiology must always be secondary to Christology and cannot be defined other than in direct relationship and correlation to Christ. The church exists only because Christ has risen and it stands inextricably linked to the person of Christ and his gospel. Moltmann identifies the priority of this relationship:

> The church's first word is not 'church' but Christ. The church's final word is not 'church' but the glory of the Father and the Son in the Spirit of Liberty. Because of this the church, as Ambrose said, is like the moon, which has no light of its own or for itself.[115]

It is only as a servant of Christ and as the guardian of Christ's gospel that the church can forge its identity. It can bathe only in the reflected glory of Christ and not that of its own making.

We must ensure that a constructivist agenda does not propel ecclesiology to emphasize the community above Christ. While an understanding of the dynamic work of the Spirit within the Christian community is much needed, we must also safeguard the connectedness to Christ that is inherent in so many of the New Testament images of the church, such as the Pauline 'body of Christ' or the Petrine 'temple' or 'building' (1 Cor. 12.27; 1 Peter 2.5). There is the possibility that emerging ecclesiology is not dependent on objective connectedness to Christ nor progression towards God's intended future, but on the assumption that the Spirit will enable us to correctly read the times. This reading of pneumatology can allow culture a disproportionate role in defining ecclesiology.

The problematic implications of this approach towards ecclesiology are pluriform. First, ecclesiology is in danger of being so flexible that it can be started from scratch, at the Spirit's behest, in every generation. While Franke maintains the trajectory of biblical narrative from the inception of the church to God's eschatological future, he never provides any fixed markers from these reference points to indicate how ecclesiology might be shaped in the present. One further problem with the constructivist ecclesiology is that, despite its humble protestations, the impression is given that the emerging radicals consider themselves to have a unique vantage point from which they observe the rest of the church's faltering and blundering attempts, as the following statement by Rollins illustrates:

> The emerging church is able to leave aside the need for clarity and open up the way for us to accept the fact that what is important is that we are embraced by the beloved rather than finding agreement concerning how we ought to understand this beloved.[116]

How then does ecclesiology relate to truth? Carson's critique of the emerging church has focused primarily on the issue of epistemology, which he regards as central to the postmodern turn. While Carson has been vehemently criticized by many sympathetic to the emerging church for wrongly assuming that the emerging church is primarily about epistemology, in this particular aspect of its theology the epistemological question is an important one. It is easy to see how Franke's non-foundational approach appeals to the emerging radicals because he stresses the importance of context in the development of theology, something the modern church was reluctant to do. His non-foundational approach means all beliefs are open to scrutiny and there exists the possibility of revision and rejection through interaction between God's revelation in Christ, the church community and the cultural context. On the one hand we should not dismiss Franke's dynamic approach or deny the contextual nature of theology. On the other hand, his refusal to allow one voice to take primacy over another prevents the church from developing its distinctive missional identity. Without the primacy of revelation over context, the church has no legitimacy with which to regard itself as the herald of the kerygma, which Stott affirms as one of the primary roles of the Christian community:

> The herald of God comes with an urgent proclamation of peace through the blood of the cross, and with a summons to men to repent, to lay down their arms and to humbly accept the pardon.[117]

One further weakness is the false antithesis drawn between personal and propositional truth. Sweet argues that 'truth is not a principle of a proposition but a person. Truth is not rules and regulators but a relationship. God did not send us a principle but a presence.'[118]

In many ways the emerging radicals at this point echo the neo-orthodoxy of Brunner, who asserted the Christ-centric nature of revelation as God himself in a personal encounter.

> In this event of revelation, in the person of Christ, the divine thou addresses me, in love. God imparts himself to me in the life of Him who alone was able to say 'I came not to be ministered unto but to minister, and to give my life a ransom for many.'[119]

While the emerging radicals' affirmation of the personal nature of truth is to be welcomed, as Brunner's was, as a counter to excessively rationalistic understandings of revelation, the dichotomy that is forged between personal and propositional is not justifiable. Propositional understandings of Christian revelation must always be understood as personal because they do not exist as detached statements but as calls to faith that engender personal and communitarian response. As Paul Helm states:

> The personal directness of the propositional view of special revelation can be saved if it is borne in mind that the propositions may be 'response-invoking', not just reporting the fact but calling for a response.[120]

This dichotomy between personal and propositional truth is another example of the emerging radicals' reliance upon false antithesis, which drives them to more extreme theological positions. Associating knowledge with power means that in a desire to be humble and inclusive, they lose the central core of ecclesial identity – the revelation of God in Christ. It is my contention that it is in response to this personal and propositional revelation that the Christian community can find the basis upon which it can establish its ecclesiological identity and its missiological mandate.

The impact of constructivist thinking is evidenced most clearly in the emerging radicals' attitude towards preaching and teaching which, for Pagitt and Jones, is governed by what they call their 'relational hermeneutic'. In this, the role of the community is privileged above everything in the pursuit of truth and so dialogue becomes the defining characteristic of this relational hermeneutic. Pagitt regards the traditional sermon monologue, or 'speaching' as he calls it, as a product of Enlightenment rationality, and harmful to community development. The idea that truth is fixed or in some way already defined is unappealing to Pagitt, who assumes that for truth to be dynamic it must also be changeable, involving a multiplicity of views:

The living Bible invites us to step into the stories, not as observers, but as participants in the faith that is alive and well and still being created.[121]

In contrast to the idea that a leader has hermeneutical authority within the Christian community, the emerging radicals assert the 'hermeneutical authority' of every member. Tony Jones calls this 'hermeneutical enrichment', when the preacher or leader shifts position from 'primary hermeneut to one of a facilitator of conversations'.[122] Pagitt coined the phrase 'progressional dialogue' to describe his position that context establishes the content, an approach which ensures that there is an 'intentional interplay of multiple view points' which guarantees that 'the message will change depending on who is present and who says what'.[123]

What then are we to make of the emerging radicals' preference for *progressional* dialogue? In many ways a heuristic approach to learning that involves the whole community is desirable. However, Grenz suggests that a distinction must be drawn between constructive theological conversations and open-ended conversations.[124] The first of these is done in dialogue with scripture and has the potential to yield constructive and positive insights; he cites the formation of the Apostles' Creed as one such example. By contrast, the open-ended approach may also yield interesting insights but the indefinite nature of its dialogue means that it may ultimately lead anywhere. This distinction is one that the emerging church must pay heed to, for while its open-ended approach to theological 'conversations' enables everyone's voice to be heard, there can be no guarantee that its final destination will be within the margins of orthodoxy.

For Luther, public preaching was a principal mark of the church and answered the question of how the authentic church could be identified. However, possession of the word was not seen as merely holding onto scripture but allowing it to take hold of the church both corporately and individually. For Luther, preaching was a word rooted in history but which, through the present spirit-invigorated proclamation, becomes a living and active experience of participation in the story of

God and self-abandonment to his will. It is 'the announcement, the declaration in the living present, indeed the opening of the eschatological future or at least the foretaste thereof, that creates faith'.[125] It is done in such a way that the word is no longer addressed to a particular group in history but becomes a living and real word to the church community in its present life.

In rejecting Christendom-style preaching it can be argued that Murray, Pagitt and others are not rejecting preaching per se, but a narrowly defined version that is lifeless, dull, overly cerebral and non-transformative for the listener. Once again the accusation of having created a straw man is warranted. Although such preaching certainly exists, and is perhaps more commonplace in some churches than we would like to admit, there is the possibility of a form of preaching that is engaging, thoughtful, challenging and invokes the listeners' full attention and participation. Stackhouse regards the rejection of preaching as a 'lack of nerve'. Since the true nature of preaching is not a burdensome didactic but revelatory and the means by which the church can celebrate and sustain its story:

> At the heart of classical preaching is an appreciation of the gospel's own power in the act of preaching to create its own space – an awareness that regular celebration of the gospel itself, and our co-option into it, is essential for the sustenance of the church, including its witness to the world.[126]

While attention must be given to the creativity of preaching in a postmodern context, Stackhouse is justified in his debunking of the assumption that sermons should be short and simple, since relevance is a false criterion upon which to base evangelism. Jesus' teaching was rarely simplistic and his form of rhetoric often served to confuse as well as clarify (Mark 4.11–12). If the emerging church is moving towards an ecclesial account of the community as shapers and definers of truth, then progressional dialogue leads to community consensus defining what is palatable and acceptable. The elevation of the community to definers of truth potentially denigrates the vital and engaging role that scripture could play within the emerging church context.

This also raises the question of whether the biblical world is interpretative of our world or vice versa: the image of the 'double-edged sword' positions the word as the judge rather than our cultural sensibilities (Hebrews 4.12). Thus the relevancy of the living word is not determined by our perception of it but our reception of it as we allow it to do the often painful work of sifting and dividing within the human heart. The word of God contains a relevancy de facto of itself, bringing us into connection with the one story the world needs to hear, the story of the gospel of God in Christ. We must also consider what the implications will be for discipleship and catechism if progressional dialogue is adopted. Duncan MacLaren argues that some form of adult education is crucial to sustain the church in the West, bridging the plausibility gap between people's experience in church gatherings and the rest of their working week. He states that 'mature thinking is important for restoring credibility to the church, because it acts like an anchor able to resist the pressures of winds and tides'.[127] MacLaren argues that such credibility can be safeguarded when there is anchoring within the Christian tradition and ecclesial experience.

The prophetic calling of the church requires it to think both biblically and culturally. Brueggemann presents a case for prophetic preaching which compels the listener to choose between the dominant worldview and the alternative kingdom offered by God through scripture. Though the emerging radicals resist accounts of faith that polarize in this manner, there is much in Brueggemann's approach that is relevant to them. He advocates creativity and a powerful use of imagination in creating an image of the alternative way of life. However, he stresses the importance of a competition between the worldview of our surrounding context and that of God's kingdom as expressed in scripture:

> Prophetic proclamation is the staging and performance of a contest between two narrative accounts of the world and an effort to show that the YHWH account of reality is more adequate and finally more reliable than the dominant narrative account that is cast among us as though it were true and beyond critique.[128]

By contrast, emerging constructivist ecclesiology has little of the sense of contest of which Brueggemann speaks. There is much to be embraced in the emerging radicals' rejection of a model of preaching that is perhaps tired and outdated, reliant upon congregation members as consumers rather than participants. The call to discussion and engagement with God's word should indeed be part of what sustains and envisions the life of any Christian community. While it is arguably the case that dull and irrelevant preaching, or preaching intended to merely entertain will have little impact on the discipleship of a church community, it is my conviction that preaching has not yet had its day. One of the challenges that faces the church of tomorrow is that of training and equipping the next generation of women and men who are gifted in this area. Preaching that is bold and courageous, creative and insightful, deeply engaging with Scripture and offers Christ in a compelling and humble way will always serve the church in its service and mission. It is through such creative and prophetic preaching that the church is enabled to understand the alternative narrative in which it is invited to take part and through which the church can discover its missional and ecclesiological identity.

Notes

1 Hauerwas, *In Good Company*, p. 58.
2 Grenz, *Renewing the Center*, p. 299.
3 McLaren, *A New Kind of Christianity*, p. 41.
4 Laarman, 'Toward a Non-Malignant Faith: an Interview with Brian McLaren'.
5 McLaren, *The Church on the Other Side*, p. 204.
6 Bauman, 'Postmodern Religion?', p. 69.
7 Quoted in Noll, *The Rise of Evangelicalism*, p. 89.
8 Williams, *Retrieving the Tradition and Renewing Evangelicalism*, p. 10.
9 Clapp, *A Peculiar People*, p. 89.
10 Healy, *Church, World and the Christian Life*, p. 163.
11 McLaren, *A New Kind of Christianity*, p. 22.
12 McLaren, *The Church on the Other Side*, p. 95.
13 Webber, *The Younger Evangelicals*, pp. 36–47.
14 Murray, *Church After Christendom*, p. 74.

15 Brewin, *Other*, p. 146.

16 Bey, *T. A. Z.*, p. 92.

17 Brewin, *In Defence of Pirates*.

18 Bey, *T. A. Z.*, p. 67.

19 Brewin, *Mutiny!*, p. 8.

20 Brewin, *Pancake and Carnivals: Fools and Dirty Revolutions*.

21 Bey, *T. A. Z.*, p. 78.

22 Brewin, *Other*, pp. 147–8.

23 Ibid., p. 159.

24 Sellars, *Hakim Bey: Repopulating the Temporary Autonomous Zone*.

25 McCracken, *Pirates and Prodigals – with Kester Brewin, Pete Rollins and Barry Taylor*.

26 De Groot, 'Three Types of Liquid Religion'.

27 Bey, *Part 3 – T. A. Z.*

28 Wells, *Above All Earthly Pow'rs*, p. 68.

29 Brewin, *Other*, pp. 191–3.

30 Church of England, *Authorization, Preface, and Declaration of Assent*.

31 Zahl et al., *Exploring the Worship Spectrum*.

32 Cocksworth, 'Holding Together', p. 138.

33 Williams, *Retrieving the Tradition and Renewing Evangelicalism*, p. 11.

34 Walker, 'Recovering Deep Church', p. 17.

35 Donnelly, *The Confetti Generation*.

36 Newbigin, *The Household of God*, p. 22.

37 Volf, *After Our Likeness*, pp. 129, 141.

38 Stackhouse, *Gospel-Driven Church*, p. 28.

39 McLaren, *More Ready Than You Realize*, p. 86.

40 McLaren, *Finding Our Way Again*.

41 Lyotard describes such eclecticism as the 'degree zero of contemporary general culture'. Lyotard, *The Postmodern Condition*, p. 76.

42 Carson, *Becoming Conversant with the Emerging Church*, p. 141.

43 http://www.vaux.net/about-vaux

44 McCaughan, *Alternative Worship 'pops up' in Portland, Oregon, for Advent*.

45 Jones, *The New Christians*, p. 8.

46 Ibid., p. 224.

47 Pagitt, *Reimagining Spiritual Formation*, p. 39.

48 Jones, *The Church Is Flat*, p. 179.

49 Sweet, *Post-Modern Pilgrims*, p. 127.

50 Pagitt, *Reimagining Spiritual Formation*, p. 133.

51 Walker and Bretherton, 'Introduction: Why Deep Church?', p. xvii.

52 Ibid., p. xviii.

53 Ibid., p. 11.

54 Ibid., p. 20.

55 Williams, *Retrieving the Tradition*, p. 138.

56 Walker, *Recovering Deep Church*, p. 20.

57 Williams, *Retrieving the Tradition*, p. 11.

58 Ibid., p. 36.

59 Ibid., p. 206.

60 McLaren, *A Generous Orthodoxy*, p. 225.

61 Anderson, *An Emergent Theology for Emerging Churches*, pp. 19–42.

62 Ibid., p. 209.

63 Ibid., p. 211.

64 Torrance, *The Trinitarian Faith*, p. 285.

65 Ibid., p. 287.

66 Cray, *Mission-shaped Church*, p. 98.

67 Torrance, *The Trinitarian Faith*, p. 287.

68 Jones, *The New Christians*, p. 111.

69 Pagitt, *Reimagining Spiritual Formation*, p. 73.

70 Volf, *After Our Likeness*, p. 154.

71 Urwin, *What Is the Role of Sacramental Ministry in Fresh Expressions of Church?*, p. 31.

72 Stackhouse, 'God's Transforming Presence: Spirit Empowered Worship', p. 152.

73 Ibid., p. 134.

74 McGavran, *The Bridges of God*, pp. 9–10.

75 McGavaran, *Understanding Church Growth*, p. 163.

76 Chester, *The Homogenous Unit Principle*.

77 Costas, *Christ Outside the Gate*, p. 31.

78 Jones, *The Church Is Flat*, p. 162.

79 Volf, *After Our Likeness*, p. 195.

80 Williams, *Retrieving the Tradition*, p. 131.

81 Ibid., p. 204.

82 Ibid., p. 217.

83 Gibbs and Bolger, *Emerging Churches*, p. 42.

84 Jones, *The Church Is Flat*, p. 135.

85 Moltmann, *The Church in the Power of the Spirit*, p. 84.

86 Jones, *The Church Is Flat*, p. 135.

87 Oden, *An Emerging Pneumatology*.

88 Williams, *On Christian Theology*, p. 230.

89 Ibid., p. 231.

90 Ibid.

91 Ibid., p. 233.

92 Ibid., p. 237.

93 Hauerwas, *Resident Aliens*, p. 12.

94 Jones, *The Church Is Flat*, p. 145.

95 Kärkkäinen, *An Introduction to Ecclesiology*, p. 73.

96 Chan, *Pentecostal Ecclesiology*, p. 87.

97 Ibid., p. 65.

98 Ibid., p. 92.

99 Ibid.

100 Moltmann, *The Spirit of Life*, p. 219.

101 Moltmann, *Sun of Righteousness, Arise!*, p. 25.

102 Oden, *An Emerging Pneumatology*.

103 Volf, *After Our Likeness*, p. 157.

104 Moltmann, *The Spirit of Life*, p. 178.

105 In Cray, *Mission-Shaped Church*, p. vii.

106 Pagitt, *Church Re-imagined*, p. 59.

107 Edson, *An Exploration into the Missiology of the Emerging Church in the UK through the Narrative of Sanctus1*.

108 Sweet, McLaren and Haselmayer, *A Is for Abductive*, p. 99.

109 Jones, *The New Christians*, p. 153.

110 Pagitt, *Church Re-imagined*, p. 23.

111 Rollins, *How (Not) to Speak of God*, p. 18.

112 Ibid., p. 42.

113 Grenz and Franke, *Beyond Foundationalism*, p. 85.

114 Ibid., p. 74.

115 Moltmann, *The Church in the Power of the Spirit*, p. 19.

116 Rollins, *How (Not) to Speak of God*, p. 18.

117 Stott, *The Preacher's Portrait*, p. 36.

118 Sweet, *Soul Tsunami*, p. 385.

119 Brunner, *Revelation and Reason*, p. 9.

120 Helm, *The Divine Revelation*, p. 27.

121 Pagitt, *A Christianity Worth Believing*, p. 67.

122 Jones, *The Church Is Flat*, p. 170.

123 Pagitt, *Preaching in the Inventive Age*, p. 45.

124 Grenz, 'Articulating the Christian Belief-Mosaic', p. 108.

125 Forde, *The Word that Kills and Makes Alive*, p. 6.

126 Stackhouse, *The Gospel-Driven Church*, p. 83.

127 MacLaren, *Mission Implausible*, p. 150.

128 Brueggemann, *The Practice of Prophetic Imagination*, p. 3.

6

The Church of Tomorrow

At the beginning of this book I raised the question of where the emerging church now sits within evangelicalism: in many ways the emerging church continues in the trajectory of a movement that has always sought to respond to the cultural world in which it finds itself. However, I have also suggested that it is in the three areas of eschatology, missiology and ecclesiology that the emerging church is both reacting against evangelicalism and diverging from it, seeking to forge new theological expression within these areas. It seems to me that these three themes are of critical importance in the emerging church's endeavour to create a new church for a new world. These three themes are interrelated, driving and feeding one another. They are not hermetically sealed, water-tight compartments, but they are interconnected realities. Thus, theological revision in one of these areas alone will have consequences for the other two. Most importantly, eschatology, missiology and ecclesiology ultimately determine how the church is to relate to its cultural surroundings, how it addresses the question 'what should our role be in challenging times?'. When cultural values are allowed to overly direct this quest, then the resulting expression of church can easily become immersed within its environment to such an extent that its prophetic critique of its context is blunted; a factor which is critical to both its ecclesiological and missiological identity.

It must also be acknowledged that it is not easy to draw definite conclusions about the emerging church since it is a broad and diverse phenomenon, and there is still plenty of debate as to who or what constitutes the emerging church movement – and indeed whether it can be called a movement at all. One further challenge is the evolutionary nature of the theological conversation within the emerging church over its recent history. Theological revision that is hinted at in some of its earlier publications become more explicitly acknowledged later on, as evidenced in the fact that while Rob Bell's earlier publications such as *Sex God* and *Velvet Elvis* were accepted without debate as part of mainstream evangelical literature, his later publication, *Love Wins*, propelled him to the centre of a Christian media frenzy that has resulted in him being ostracized by the more conservative wing of evangelicalism. Brewin makes this theological evolution explicit in his preface to the e-edition of his 2004 publication *The Complex Christ*, acknowledging that ten years 'has also been a huge amount of time theologically'. He recognizes that this time period has seen his thinking evolve from an evangelical approach to that which now may not even be considered orthodox:

> Where I speak here about church growth and renewing our view of God, the current location of these tentative first moves away from a fairly traditional evangelicalism is now outside of what would be taken for orthodox belief.[1]

While the emerging radicals' theological progression over a short time period renders the task of distilling the theological core of the emerging church even more challenging, it nevertheless remains informative. This evolution reveals the adapting nature of the emerging church and demonstrates the extent to which cultural change impacts its theological revision. This theological progression indicates that the emerging church may indeed have started out as a movement for renewal within traditional evangelicalism, but that the content of its theological discourse is now leading it beyond the boundaries of a traditional understanding of evangelicalism.

However, debating whether the emerging church is 'in' or 'out' of evangelicalism may not be that profitable a pursuit and is, ironically, a particularly 'un-emerging' way to approach its impact. Instead, I hope in this chapter to offer an exploration of what positive insights the emerging church has to contribute to the ongoing discussion taking place within evangelicalism about the future shape and direction of the church in the twenty-first century. I also hope to consider four theological areas which I believe are critical and essential to the emerging church as it embarks upon its pursuit of building a new church for a new world.

1. Holistic Mission

The discussion that the concept of *Missio Dei* received at the Tambaran Missionary Conference in 1952 revolutionized the way evangelicals, among others, understood mission. In many ways, the emerging church continues down this path in seeking a more holistic understanding of mission, focused less on the church and more directly upon the presence of God in the world. The emerging church's holistic approach to mission is one of the strengths of the movement, as is the intention of individuals such as Brian McLaren to engage with the issues of global poverty and economic imbalance. While other evangelical movements and organizations are also seeking to redress the balance of evangelical mission to a more holistic approach, the emerging church's contribution to the nature of mission should be welcomed as part of this process.

A tension between Mission as social action and mission as evangelism, has been a recurring debate within the history of evangelicalism. Early evangelical activism was rooted in a dual allegiance to preaching the Gospel along with a commitment to the alleviation of poverty and slavery, demonstrated in the ministry of Wesley and Wilberforce, to name but two. This relationship is beautifully illustrated by Wesley's deathbed letter to Wilberforce, urging him on in his abolitionist fight. Evangelicalism's tendency in the early twentieth century to prioritize personal piety over social engagement is a reminder of the need to maintain an integrated approach in our thinking about mission, an approach exemplified in Stott's statement that 'authentic mission is a comprehensive activity which embraces evangelism and social action, and refuses to let them be divorced'.[2] This dual emphasis he believed to be rooted in the character of God, the teaching ministry of Jesus and the communication of the Gospel itself.

The emerging radicals appeal to a more holistic approach towards mission, and thus helpfully illustrate the importance of eschatology to this critical task of defining mission. In their reaction against the theology of the *Left Behind* novels, they demonstrate how this particular eschatological scenario allows little need for the renewal or care of creation, and mission becomes preoccupied purely with soul-winning evangelism.

In the same way, the emerging church's preference for a more collaborative approach to eschatology, in terms of the church's call to be part of God's renewal and restoration of creation, can lead to a more generous expression of mission that can encompass all aspects of our human life. Within a church context, a renewed sense of participatory eschatology can be deeply motivating and liberating as we encourage those in our Christian communities to participate in God's plans and purpose for creation, so that those who serve in healthcare, in the arts, in finance, in education and in the home are encouraged to see their contribution as playing a part in God's restorative purposes for the world and to live with the expectation of Christ's return.

However, we must ensure that the pendulum does not swing too far to the other extreme whereby conversion becomes so tainted by its *'left behind'* connotations that the simple call of Jesus to 'come follow me' becomes lost from our missionary dialectic. Individuals may be uneasy with some of the language with which evangelism is articulated, but the church in the twenty-first century needs to keep the simple commitment to 'talk to people about Jesus' at the heart of its missionary calling. In Colossians 1.15–20 Paul reminds us that the whole of creation is created by Christ, sustained by Christ, belongs to Christ and is redeemed by Christ through the cross. To put our faith and hope in Jesus is to recognize his creating, sustaining and redeeming work in all aspect of human life. The challenge of articulating a deeper and more courageous expression of what it means to 'come and follow Jesus' in our world today is one the church needs to hear.

2. Critique of the modern church

A second area in which the emerging church makes a positive contribution is in its critique of the modern church. While we must be aware of the sometimes caricaturized nature of this critique, such stereotyping should not prevent us from hearing the validity of its protest. As much as the emerging church can be accused of an absence of critique of the postmodern culture it inhabits, so evangelicalism can be accused of an absence of critique of its own practices, both missiological and ecclesiological. McLaren must be lauded for his courage in acknowledging that many of evangelicalism's cherished evangelistic formulae have become obsolete in a changing cultural milieu. Mainstream evangelicalism can learn much from the emerging radicals' willingness to think creatively about ecclesial life and to evaluate and reject cherished forms and practices if they no longer serve their purpose.

In addition, the emerging church also draws attention to those who find the current evangelical culture stifling and inhibitive. We must acknowledge the increasing number of people disillusioned by certain established expressions of church. The research of Alan Jamieson and Steve Aisthorpe similarly highlight the growing number of those who still identify with the Christian faith without being part of a fixed worshipping community.[3] In addition, the popularity of the emerging church reveals that there are those who have experienced evangelicalism to be a place where doubts and questions cannot be freely expressed. The emerging church stands as a stark reminder that when questioning is deemed unacceptable, people are simply driven outside the community of the church to seek answers elsewhere. There is much to be learned from the emerging church in terms of the importance of allowing questions and doubts to be raised without stigmatization. Evangelicalism must hear the challenge that when such conversations are not permitted an airing they are driven outside the Christian community and so lose the connection with the deep well of Christian tradition and scriptural engagement that provides the resources to attend to those very questions. Furthermore, the emerging church's conviction that God is already at work outside the confines of the church means that nothing and no one is beyond the reach of God's presence. Such an approach can act as a timely rebuke to an all-too-frequent preoccupation with our own ecclesiastic interests. While I have already sought to stress the need to critique the emerging church's lack of emphasis on evangelism and the proclamation of the gospel, we must not neglect the insights the emerging church brings from those outside the church who are put off by some of the more modernistic approaches.

3. The possibility of change

The title of Brian McLaren's bestselling book *Everything Must Change* is, in many ways, the battle-cry of the emerging church movement. It is a movement about change and, most importantly, it believes that change can happen quickly and effectually. It does not seek to be hierarchical, which means that change is not dependent upon the lengthy process of blessing by an ecclesiastical committee, a process that has dampened many an innovative idea. The emerging church's faith in its own ability to create something new, appealing and authentic in the postmodern world is one of its greatest strengths – as is its encouragement of creative and innovative individuals and communities who wish to implement that change. This is a challenge to an often overly centralized approach that relies on the expectation that change within the church happens only at the behest of its leaders. The history of evangelicalism's development has frequently been the story of individuals or small groups of women and men who have sought ecclesial and societal change, often pioneered by those who have not held positions of central authority. History bears witness to the impact of courageous individuals such as the Wesleys, Hannah Moore and the Clapham sect whose critique of both the church and society have led to innovative and enduring legacies. To their credit, the emerging radicals show some of these characteristics in their innovation and fervour. However, they must also learn the lessons from history of those whose frustration with the current state of the church also spurred them to action, but whose lack of anchorage to the church's doctrinal core ensured that that impact was short-lived.

The emerging church's belief in the possibility of change is one of its greatest appeals, but it also belies one of its greatest weaknesses. Its desire to resist institutional stultification and implement change means that it is quick to accept the insights of postmodern culture without offering sufficient critique of them. The question of what serves as the anchor rooting the emerging church within the Christian tradition remains a significant question. While many renewal movements have emerged within evangelicalism, each seeking to seize the *kairos* moment of change, those without a sufficiently deep theological foundation have not stayed the course. It can be argued that a lack of developed ecclesiology is a frequent cause of decline of such movements for renewal. It is my firm conviction that if the emerging church is to exist as a movement which champions lasting change and offers a distinctive voice, then it must give attention to its theological development in the following areas.

1. Prophetic Imagination

It is my supposition that if the emerging church is to survive as a credible and persuasive force for positive ecclesiological change, it must develop the ability to critique as well as to reflect postmodern culture. In order to ensure that a deference to culture is not the Achilles heel of the emerging church, greater critical appraisal of the postmodern ideology that individuals such as Rollins adopt needs to be offered.

Brueggemann's concept of prophetic imagination, which blends eschatological, missiological and ecclesiological themes is pertinent here. Brueggemann imagines the church to be a community that offers both a critique of its present context and a prophetic view of God's future, of which the church is to be a part. In so doing, Brueggemann demonstrates the significance of eschatological perspective in defining missiology and ecclesiology. For Brueggemann, prophetic imagination has two central components: the criticism of the surrounding culture and the energizing of the present context with a hope-filled vision of God's alternative future. He believes that it is in the dialectic of these two tasks that the church can be faithful to God and develop its missional and ecclesiological identity.

> The task of prophetic ministry is to nurture, nourish, and evoke a consciousness and perception alternative to the consciousness and perception of the dominant culture around us.[4]

However, as we have seen, an incarnational approach to mission that elevates immersion and identification as its central theological themes contains little sense of a prophetic critique of the current culture. Instead, by directing its critique at the modern church and its ills, not much is offered by way of appraisal of the dominant culture of postmodernity, which therefore creates little sense of the contrast between two opposing narratives. Once again we become aware of the importance of eschatology to the endeavour to create a new church for a new world. However, understanding eschatology primarily in terms of a progressive move towards full integration with God downplays the way in which the vision of God's future world is regarded as an alternative to the present dominant culture. This vision of an alternative community is also of huge significance in ecclesiology, since hope is 'sealed in baptism' and 'dramatized in eucharist'.[5] The eschatological agenda is crucial in ensuring that the church is shaped primarily by God's future for it and so is able to contribute prophetically and compassionately within the current context without being subsumed by it.

It is my conviction that the development of prophetic imagination is critical for the church as it continues its journey into the unknown territory of the twenty-first century. It emboldens the church to challenge and contradict culture, both within its walls and outside of them, when it does not reflect the values and principles of God's character and kingdom. In many ways this is a call to rekindle Stott's discerning art of 'double-listening' as the church seeks to engage in a humble yet bold critique of the context in which it exists. This is a process that needs to be continual, prayerful and relentless in order to engage appropriately and maintain pace with the changing cultural climate. There can be no monolithic response to the relationship between church and culture, rather an ongoing dedication to a perpetual process of discernment and critique.

Vincent Donovan is often quoted by Brian McLaren as an example of the primacy of praxis in missionary engagement. *Christianity Rediscovered* records Donovan's experiences as he sought to evangelize the Masai people in East Africa. Donovan found that traditional missionary strategies failed to impact a community that was entirely self-sufficient and required nothing from western development. Through a lifetime of living alongside the Masai people, Donovan discovered how to bring the gospel message to them in a way that they could not only understand intellectually but also inhabit as a community. His belief that praxis must be considered before theology reflects his conviction that soteriology cannot be the starting place for missiology and that theology must have a dialogical relationship with both previous missionary experience and the culture into which it seeks to bring the gospel.

However, while Donovan espouses the dynamic nature of missionary praxis and theological reflection, he remains committed to the uniqueness of the gospel:

> The gospel, the secret hidden from the beginning of the world – is outside every culture, is supracultural. It comes from outside our cultures and yet is destined for all of them – a supracultural, unchanging message of good news.[6]

Thus, for Donovan, the praxis of mission is fluid and adaptable, but the message is not subject to the same flexibility – a principle he demonstrates through tireless attempts to communicate the 'unchanging message of good news' to people with no monotheistic preconceptions. Second, Donovan adhered to the conviction that the gospel will not always be accepted by a community, no matter how much praxis is rethought:

Christianity by its very essence is a message that can be accepted – or rejected – that somewhere close to the heart of Christianity lies that terrible and mysterious possibility of rejection; that no Christianity has any meaning or value if there is not the freedom to accept it or reject it.[7]

This conviction that the Christian gospel will not always be palatable is one of the starker contrasts between Donovan's approach and that of the emerging radicals where the priority of praxis in theology can lead to doctrinal revision. Developing a stronger sense of prophetic critique as part of our missionary engagement enables the church to identify those aspects of culture which do not sit easily alongside the Gospel and in which followers of Jesus need to be bold and fearless in their discipleship of Him.

We need to rekindle this sense of theology as a discipline borne in missionary engagement. At the forefront of our doctrinal and biblical debates must be this emphasis on the church community living out the good news of Jesus in the contemporary world. Cray reminds us of the importance of the study of theology within a missional mindset:

It is called into being in response to the questions raised by the church's engagement with new cultures and contexts . . . True Christian theology is missionary thinking for missionary action, or missionary reflection on missionary engagement.[8]

Exploring prophetic critique as part of our missional and theological engagement enables us to discern which aspects of our practice need to change and be reimagined in order better to reflect and serve the 'supracultural unchanging message' of Jesus. Such critique can prevent us from allowing acceptability to be the criterion for determining truth and reminds us of the propensity of the Gospel to cause disruption as well as garner acceptance. Missiology that ultimately permits the triumph of praxis over theology will easily lose the more confrontational element. Historically, the witness of the church has been most potent and distinctive where Christian communities have refused to accommodate themselves to that which is deemed culturally acceptable, often facing persecution for so doing, be that in the Roman empire, under communism in China, or in western secularism. In the face of the statistics of decline, maybe one of the challenges facing the church is that of presenting not a more palatable gospel, but a more radical one.

In addition, prophetic imagination reminds the church of the power of eschatological vision to shape how it relates to its surrounding culture. In the letter to the Philippians, the Apostle Paul reminds the church in Philippi of their dual citizenship. They are both God's holy people in Philippi (Phil. 1.1) and citizens of Heaven (Phil. 3.20). This reminder of citizenship in heaven is, as we have seen, not a call to world-escapism but an energizing vision of an alternative future. This alternative future is glimpsed partially in our present reality, inaugurated by Christ, but its fulfilment is that which the church seeks and towards which it strives. Furthermore, this vision of God's alternative future provides the church with a narrative that is more dominant than its cultural context. And it is this narrative which must shape and direct its mission. This does not mean that the church should be isolated from its cultural context, nor that it should ignore the ways in which culture is changing, but that by means of a prophetic critique it can confront those aspects of culture that make false promises, while also channelling signs and moments of God's activity both within and outside the church.

The call here in our missionary engagement is to live both incarnationally and prophetically. One without the other simply will not do. Where incarnational mission is expressed without prophetic imagination as its accompaniment it faces the temptation merely to accommodate to the dominant culture and thus lose the potency of the gospel and its ability to signpost to God's alternative future. The call to engage both prophetically and incarnationally will be costly and uncomfortable. However, it is what missional living needs to entail if the church wants to engage faithfully and effectively in the changing world of the twenty-first century.

2. *Christology*

The second area which I believe is of critical importance is the development of a deeper and broader Christology. The tendency to focus on the Incarnation in missiological praxis means that other aspects of Christology such as Christ's pre-existence, his deity, death, resurrection, ascension and return do not receive equal treatment. In particular, the notion of Christ as resurrected and ascended Lord does not seem to be a much-explored motif in the incarnational Christology of the emerging church.

We have already explored how the oft-quoted statistics of institutional church decline in the West can arouse a 'panic mentality' with regards to the future of the church: the church must change in order to survive. A properly developed Christology, however, means that while creativity and innovation are to be welcomed, the western church need not be lured into thinking that the future of Christianity rests upon its shoulders. Understanding that Christ is the head of a new community awaiting future resurrection enables the church to trust that the future of Christianity rests primarily in his hands. Matthew's Gospel reminds us of the promise of Jesus to build his church no matter what might stand against it (Matt. 16.18).

Furthermore, the church's unique connection to the risen Christ drives an ecclesiology that is both present and participative within culture but also radically different:

> For the sake of its mission, the church must risk being genuinely alternative in our culture. This alternativeness does not mean a withdrawal of the church from society, but rather an intentional demonstration in the actions of our connecting structures of this basic fact: Christ is Lord, and we are his witnesses and the firstfruits of his in-breaking rule.[9]

The temptation to prioritize the incarnation over other aspects of Christology can result in an overly deferential approach to culture in ecclesiology, weakening the church's prophetic impact, since it prioritizes standing as one with culture rather than offering a radical alternative. It is in harnessing an understanding of Jesus as one of us but also as Lord over us that a genuinely missional ecclesiology can be formed: one in which the church is engaged within the culture but which also points anticipatorily to God's eschatological future.

For Nicholas Healy, Christology has been important in the development of his practical-prophetic ecclesiology. While he acknowledges that the constantly changing and evolving nature of culture is amenable to the formation of a distinctive ecclesiology, for him it is a proper account of Christology that provides the anchor for this development:

> Ecclesial cultural identity is constructed as a struggle, not to preserve some cultural identity, but to construct and reconstruct that identity in light of an orientation to what it alone seeks, the truth revealed in the person and work of Jesus Christ. That identity is constructed by experimentation, by bricolage and by retrieval of earlier forms.[10]

There is much in Healy's ecclesiological formation that resonates with the emerging radicals, not least its creative emphasis on experimentation and retrieval of ancient forms. However, for Healy the central point of orientation is the person and work of Christ. While the emerging radicals seek to 'identify with Jesus', their failure to embrace a sufficiently broad understanding of Christology results in emerging ecclesiology being oriented towards culture rather than the person and work of Christ. To pit the incarnational Christ against the resurrected Christ is perhaps a crass distinction to make; however, any Christological approach that stresses one at the expense of the other potentially leads to an imbalance in ecclesiology. To express it somewhat crudely, churches emphasizing incarnation at the expense of resurrection are in danger of cultural assimilation whereas those emphasizing resurrection over incarnation are in danger of a non-contextualized approach to missionary engagement. These two imbalanced approaches have often been responsible for weaknesses in evangelical engagement with mission.

I have already sought to draw attention to the lack of developed doctrine of the resurrection within the emerging conversation and Rollins' preference to talk about it as part of his 'world-affirming' theology. However, it is my conviction that a failure to develop a theology of resurrection not only results in a weakened Christology but also downplays the sense of discontinuity between this world and the next. While there are elements of continuity between the kingdom inaugurated by Jesus and the life of the age to come, the completion of the future age requires God's dynamic and future intervention in transformation of those who will be raised to life in Christ (1 Cor. 15.52). Christology here is of critical importance to our ecclesiology since it is its connection to Christ as risen and ascended Lord of this new community that the church is charged with a mandate for mission and service. It is primarily in its connection to the risen Christ that the church, as the first-fruits of that new age, is marked out as distinct from the rest of the world. The doctrine of the ascension is the paradigm through which the church currently lives out its community life. When the church understands Christ as risen and ascended lord, its attention is then drawn to those aspects of culture that challenge and reject his lordship and against which its prophetic voice ought to be heard. By contrast, the emerging church's prophetic voice is largely heard in disapproval of the modern church. Colin Buchanan regards the resurrection as critical to the missionary engagement of the church; it is through its 'sentness' that the church extends the salvation work of the resurrected Christ into the world.

> The infant Church is not just the agent of an absent landlord, but is corporately the working presence of Christ on earth in respect of his communicating with the unbelieving world, and of his purifying his people to serve his purposes better. They are the em-bodi-ment of Jesus.[11]

Christology further reveals itself as critical to the pursuit of missiology as well as ecclesiology. An understanding of Christ as both 'God with us' and also 'God above us' has vast implications for the church's mission and praxis. Christian mission gives expression to the dynamic relationship between God and the world, and therefore it can never be considered apart from the story of Jesus Christ, his birth, life, death and resurrection. However, an insufficiently 'high Christology' will inevitably lead to a lessening of missiological conviction. The church that seeks to be missional must ensure it seeks to develop a fully formed Christology, allowing every aspect of the identity, person and work of Christ to shape its engagement and praxis within the world. A limited Christology will arguably lead to a limited missiology also. Newbigin's reflection on the significance of a full understanding of Christology, both for his own personal spiritual growth and for the wider church, are pertinent here:

> This acknowledgement and confession means that I acknowledge and confess in Jesus Christ, in his life and teaching, his death and passion, his resurrection and exaltation, the decisive turning point in human history, the centre from which alone the meaning of my own personal life, and the meaning of the public life of mankind, is disclosed.[12]

As unremarkable as it may seem, the key to the future mission and direction of the church, as Newbigin hints, lies not in newfangled theories of how to resonate culturally but in the development and proclamation of a full Christology. It is in grasping this full Christology that the church is charged once again with its missionary mandate to be 'sent into the world' in the way that Jesus was sent (John 17:20). It is in developing its incarnational theology that the church is invited to be present within society, living in costly, sacrificial and authentic patterns of life. However, it is in developing its fuller approach to Christology that it is emboldened to present the radical and transformative gospel of Jesus Christ which cannot be tamed or weakened by the dominant cultural mood of any age.

3. Deep Church

The third area which I believe is critical to the discussion around the shape of church for the twenty-first-century world is that of 'deep church' to which I have already referred. While this necessarily entails a call to a church that engages deeply in discipleship, encouraging its members to behave not as consumers but contributors, it is in its connection to the common orthodox tradition, as envisaged by Lewis, that is particularly relevant. The image of a ship dropping its anchors down into the deep and living tradition was used earlier in this context. However, perhaps the anchor is a somewhat static and restrictive image for a church seeking to be dynamic and responsive within a cultural context. A preferable image might be the roots of a tree, digging deep into the nourishing and life-giving soil, ensuring that future growth and development is resourced and directed by them.

It is this connection to the source of tradition that is critical for both missiological and ecclesiological development, ensuring that any fresh or emerging expression of church life is a demonstration of what gospel community looks like; rooted in the faith expressed in the creeds, celebrated in a shared meal in remembrance and symbolized in the water of baptism. Such marks of our ecclesial life are not tick boxes by which we can define 'church' but rather they act as both signs of our rootedness in the wonderful Gospel of Jesus and imperatives of the faithfulness, love and hope with which we are called to live.

These deep roots in the living tradition through the word and spirit also aid us in our task of critical prophetic discernment, enabling those who would be pioneers of new and culturally savvy expressions of church to determine which aspects of the dominant culture conflict and which can co-exist. It is through its roots in the living tradition of the Gospel that the church is reminded of the kerygmatic nature of its life and witness. Those who seek to be bold and courageous with the form and style of church need to be similarly bold and courageous in allowing the good news of Jesus Christ that cannot be fettered

by human sensibilities to be the message of life-changing transformation that it is.

This is the apostolic nature and calling of the church, to be
the church that is both then and now – the church that makes
manifest in its present forms and shared life a commitment to
the good news in the person of Jesus Christ – his life, death, resurrection and future return. It is also the calling which emboldens its witness and the future hope towards which it strives.
The apostolic church is the church faithful in its creeds but also
courageous in its proclamation of them.

This is one of the weaknesses with the reliance upon the
Constantinian paradigm which can all too easily create a rup-
ture in this sense of the apostolic tradition passed up from generation to generation. Understanding the church as the 'pilgrim
people of God' requires that we observe the church throughout
history as part of that apostolic continuation in which, despite its
many and often devastating failings, God's spirit has remained
presently active. Being 'the pilgrim people of God' reminds us that
we are always part of something bigger than our own particular
ecclesiological preferences. Furthermore, it is the apostolic foundation that invites us to seek creativity and resourcefulness in a
missiological approach to ecclesiology. This does not require us
to retreat into cultural fragmentation which mirrors the divisions
already existing within society but rather calls us to cross-boundary
fellowship, which is central to the life of deep church.

Commitment to Deep Church also frees us from our preoccupation with denominational boundaries and releases the church
to be committed to that task of being a faithful expression of
the church in the world today, in which both the challenges
and opportunities for the Christian faith are great indeed. I am
grateful for the emerging church's contribution to what that
expression of faith might look like in the western world, but
the Deep Church connection is a much need reminder that the
answer does not lie in second-guessing the future but in remembering the past and seeking to walk together in the life-giving
and deeply arresting Gospel of Jesus.

Deep Church also reminds us of the interrelation of these three
crucial doctrines: eschatology, missiology and ecclesiology. It is

the future vision of what the church will be that inspires the church in the present to walk in the conviction and courage of that hope, welcoming signs and manifestations of God's work in her present life. It is this future vision that prevents the church from giving in to the prophets of gloom who tell us the future prospects of Christianity in the West are bleak indeed. It is the missiological identity of the church that compels the church to address the kerygmatic question, since the good news of Jesus is both the foundation of apostolic faith and the source of conversion. The missional church, therefore, seeks to reflect in both her life and witness the transformative and salvific work of Christ in his death and resurrection. Kerygmatic conviction thus drives the church into missiological engagement in which both loving service and spoken witness have a vital part to play. In this way, the church is aided in its often perilous journey between the two extremes of cultural irrelevance on the one hand and cultural assimilation on the other, neither of which can effectively partner the church in its witness and mission.

Seeking to be part of a Deep Church ensures that the question of the primacy of the gospel is attended to, ensuring that the message of the Gospel that the church is called to live and proclaim is neither tamed nor watered down. It is confidence in the transformative power of the Gospel of Jesus Christ alone that will embolden and encourage the witnessing life of the church in the contemporary world.

Pneumatology

The final area which I believe is of critical importance in theological development for the emerging church in the world of the twenty-first century is that of pneumatology. While this doctrine was not included as one of my three core areas, I have sought to demonstrate how integral it is to them all.

In terms of eschatology, the Holy Spirit as the one who links the present age with God's future age to come is strongly attested to in the New Testament as the means by which the believer can call God 'Father' (Romans 8.15), serve (1 Cor. 12.11) and witness (Act 1.8). It seems, then, that the development of pneumatology is critical to an understanding of discipleship in our present context.

With regards to missiology, pneumatology also enables us to develop a fuller understanding of the scope and breadth of mission. Newbigin asserted the importance of the doctrine of the Trinity for missiological thinking, stating that it was worked out by the church at the interface with paganism as the means by which the church defended its uniqueness as against any other religion. Thus, the Trinity must be integral to forging the contemporary church's understanding of mission also.

> It is significant that the Church found itself driven to articulate the Christian message in this situation in terms of trinitarian doctrine, and that, during the period in which the intellectual struggle took place to state the gospel in terms of Graeco-Roman culture without thereby compromising its central affirmation, it was the doctrine of the Trinity which was the key to the whole theological debate.[13]

In many ways a trinitarian doctrine of mission enables the church to discern its correct place within *Missio Dei* and relieves it from the misapprehension that the responsibility for the future of Christianity rests upon its shoulders. The church is invited to participate in the Trinity's mission in the world but is not the creator of its own destiny. The church is the community of those who follow Jesus, are indwelt by the Spirit and seek to live out the calling of Jesus to make disciples of all nations. The Spirit is fundamental to this missiological task as the one who is the invigorating and equipping power of mission. Without the Spirit's work in mission, the church is left with the impossible task of changing lives through human effort alone.

It is the Spirit who enables the church to witness not only to all nations and peoples but through all time to the end of the ages. Mission has a pneumatological and also an eschatological perspective based on the very nature and action of the triune God.[14]

A deeper understanding of the Spirit's active role in mission also encourages emerging leaders and pioneers who seek innovation and creativity to welcome the role of the miraculous and the prophetic – issues that are not often mentioned in an earthy incarnational missional practice. Developing a deeper pneumatological theology means that mission cannot be understood purely in terms of social transformation and relational discourse but would also allow room for the miraculous, along with a deep conviction of the Spirit's work in conversion.

Pneumatology also holds great significance for the development of ecclesiology. The identity of the church is rooted definitively in the purpose of the Father to reconcile all things to himself through the Son and in the Spirit. In this sense, the church is the community of the 'last days', which exists in the time in which God is at work in the world by his Spirit to bring new life and restoration. The church is, therefore, an eschatological community, a community in which the Spirit is actively at work in its discipleship, growth and mission.

> There is no timeless Church; only a Church then and now and to be, as the spirit ever and again incorporates people into Christ and in the same action brings them into and maintains them in community with each other.[15]

In this way pneumatology can provide a solution to the problems posed by an emerging emphasis on temporary ecclesiology. The church may change and adapt in form but the thread of continuity is provided by the work of the Spirit who is continually adding people into the body of Christ and sustaining and resourcing the church community. It is the Spirit who brings diversity and multiplicity within the Christian community and enables the church to live in unity rather than reflecting the divisions and fragmentation of our contemporary context.

For Volf, pneumatology is essential to the development of a model of church that is truly participative and does not rely on an overly hierarchical and institutional structure:

> The church needs the vivifying presence of the Spirit, and without this presence, even a church with a decentralized participative structure and culture will become sterile, and perhaps more sterile than a hierarchical church.[16]

Volf's strong pneumatological emphasis allows him to link his ecclesial model with an eschatological vision of God's people before the throne of God; it incorporates a sense of progression and movement without falling into hierarchy. Volf's concept of the church as an image of the trinity, vivified by the active presence of the Spirit means that there can be both continuity and flexibility in our ecclesiology.

Pneumatology is also necessary to the development of prophetic engagement of culture. The presence of the Holy Spirit ensures that our critique of our context is not based merely on majority opinion within the Christian community but through prayer and discernment. A fuller understanding of the person and work of the Holy Spirit is indispensable to the vital task of developing a missiological and ecclesiological identity that responds and relates to its cultural context as well as being rooted in the life-giving gospel of Jesus Christ.

Conclusion

I have sought in this final chapter to draw attention to four areas that I believe are important to those in the emerging church seeking to create a 'new church for a new world'. Contrary to the opinion of those who have already written its obituary, I do not believe that the emerging church's impact will dissipate in the immediate future. While there may, in the UK at least, be little sense of it as a quantifiable movement, the popularity of its protagonists' speaking tours and publications ensures that this is a conversation which will continue both inside and outside the evangelical church. The increasing number of those reported as leaving institutional churches and disengaging from church life cannot be ignored. Evangelicalism must therefore not disregard the uncomfortable challenges that the emerging church presents. It must hear the emerging church's critique of the church's captivity to modernity and the questions raised by those who find its culture stifling and confining. In this sense, there is much to be welcomed in the emerging church's desire for a more authentic experience of church, not least in its boldness in questioning some of the shibboleths of evangelical religion. Such questions are to be welcomed, even when they cause unease, since in our attempts to communicate the gospel simply and accessibly we always run the risk of losing something of its wonder and complexity.

Where the emerging radicals seek genuine and authentic missional engagement, the evangelical church must discover ways in which it can work in collaboration and formulate a missiological approach that is truly holistic, attending to both social action and evangelism without relying on reactionary theological formation. Evangelicalism must be spurred on by the emerging church's desire to see change and must ensure that evangelicalism's own future development does not quash creativity and innovation where it can also be rooted deeply.

However, the emerging church also raises a warning to those of us who seek to be creative and innovative in mission and cultural engagement, that we do not neglect the ancient biblical wisdom of prophetic discernment, which calls us to affirm the new movement of God's spirit in each age but also causes us to discern what needs challenging and rejecting since it is antithetical to the very nature of the gospel. The issues raised by the emerging church remind us that while we need creativity and innovation we need this alongside a courageous and deep confidence in the good news of Jesus Christ.

We need the prophets and dreamers who call us to imagine a better future, a bolder and more courageous way of being church, who challenge us to leave behind comfortable patterns that have become tired and worn, to journey into unchartered territory. But we also need the sages who remind us that the answer to the new challenges of each age lies not necessarily in pursuing the latest novelty or new fad, but in digging deeper into that which we already know to be true and enduring. We need the sages who remind us that the answers to the future lie in the past, in God's unique revelation in Christ which, by the ongoing work of the Spirit, we can proclaim and live afresh in the present.

In all this, we are not nomads, wandering without direction, but pilgrims on a journey – a journey which is towards God's future when Jesus will return to judge and restore all creation. It is for this great day that we wait and towards which we journey, seeking in each new generation to proclaim this hope afresh with boldness, compassion and faith. We must be brave, creative and prepared to take risks, to allow ourselves to hear the voices from those on the margins who hear and see things in a different way, but we must be ever convinced that it is Christ who builds his church and we must not yield too readily to the pursuit of the novel and the instant, presuming that they will provide us with the answer to change. The hope of the church in the twenty-first century lies not primarily in our ability to create, innovate and pioneer but in the faithful and dynamic working of the Spirit of God. And so our starting place for this grand adventure is on our knees in humble gratitude, worship and expectant hope that God will build his church, in us, through us and with us.

Notes

1 Brewin, e-Edition of *The Complex Christ*.
2 Stott, *The Contemporary Christian*, p. 337.
3 Jamieson, *A Churchless Faith*; Aisthorpe, *The Invisible Church*.
4 Brueggemann, *The Prophetic Imagination*, p. 13.
5 Ibid., p. 68.
6 Donovan, *Christianity Rediscovered*, p. 47.
7 Ibid., p. 108.
8 Cray, *Focussing Church Life on a Theology of Mission*, p. 62.
9 Guder and Barrett, *Missional Church*, p. 259.
10 Healy, *Church, World and the Christian Life*, p. 175.
11 Buchanan, *Is the Church of England Biblical?*, p. 151.
12 Newbigin, *Missionary Theologian: A Reader*, p. 164.
13 Newbigin, *Trinitarian Doctrine for Today's Mission*, p. 34.
14 Thompson, *Modern Trinitarian Perspectives*, p. 73.
15 Gunton and Hardy, *On Being the Church*, p. 79.
16 Volf, *After Our Likeness*, p. 257.

Bibliography

Printed Sources

Abraham, William. 'A Theology of Evangelism; The Heart of the Matter', in *The Study of Evangelism: Exploring a Missional Practice of the Church*, ed. P. Chilcote and L. Warner. Grand Rapids and Cambridge: Eerdmans, 2008.

Abraham, William. *The Logic of Evangelism*. London: Hodder & Stoughton, 1989.

Aisthorpe, Steve. *Invisible Church; Learning from the Experiences of Churchless Christians*. Edinburgh: Saint Andrew Press, 2016.

Allen, Roland. *Missionary Methods: St. Paul's or Ours?* Grand Rapids: Eerdmans, 1962.

Anderson, Allan. *Spreading Fires: The Missionary Nature of Pentecostalism*. London: SPCK, 2002.

Anderson, Ray. *An Emergent Theology for Emerging Churches*. Downers Grove, IL: InterVarsity Press, 2006.

Anderson, Walter Truett. *Reality Isn't What It Used to Be: Theatrical Politics, Ready-to-Wear Religion, Global Myths, and Other Wonders of the Postmodern World*. San Francisco: Harper & Row, 1990.

Baker, Jonny. *Alternative Worship*. London: SPCK, 2003.

Balleine, G. R. *A History of the Evangelical Party in the Church of England*. London: Longmans Green & Co, 1908.

Balmer, Randall. *The Making of Evangelicalism: From Revivalism to Politics and Beyond*. Waco: Baylor University Press, 2010.

Barclay, Oliver. *Evangelicalism in Britain 1935–1995: A Personal Sketch*. Leicester: InterVarsity Press, 1997.

Bauman, Zygmunt. 'Postmodern Religion?' in *Religion, Modernity and Postmodernity*, ed. Paul Heelas. Oxford: Blackwell Publishing, 1998.

Bebbington, D. W. 'Eschatology in Evangelical History', in *What are We Waiting For? Christian Hope and Contemporary Culture*, ed. S. Holmes and R. Rook. Milton Keynes: Paternoster, 2008, pp. 75–86.

Bebbington, D. W. *Evangelicalism in Modern Britain: a History from the 1730s to the 1980s*. London: Routledge, 1989.

Bebbington, D. W. 'Towards an Evangelical Identity' in *For Such a Time As This: Perspectives on Evangelicalism, Past, Present and Future*, ed. S. Brady and H. Rowdon. London: Scripture Union, 1996.

Bebbington, D. W. *The Dominance of Evangelicalism: The Age of Spurgeon and Moody*. Leicester: InterVarsity Press, 2005.

Bell, Rob. *Velvet Elvis: Repainting the Christian Faith*. Grand Rapids: Zondervan, 2006.

Bell, Rob. *Love Wins: At the Heart of Life's Big Questions*. London: Collins, 2011.

Bennett, David M. *The Origins of Left Behind Eschatology*. Maitland, FL: Xulon Press, 2010.

Bennett, Dennis. *Nine O'Clock in the Morning*. London: Coverdale House, 1974.

Bevans, Stephen. *Models of Contextual Theology*. New York: Orbis Books, 2002.

Bey, Hakim. *T. A. Z.: The Temporary Autonomous Zone*. Seattle: Pacific Publishing Studio, 2011.

Bosch, David. *Transforming Mission: Paradigm Shifts in Theology of Mission*. Maryknoll, NY: Orbis Books, 1993.

Bosch, David. *Believing in the Future: Toward a Missiology of Western Culture*. Valley Forge, PA: Trinity Press International, 1995.

Brantely, Richard E. *Locke, Wesley and The Method of English Romanticism*. Gainsville, FL: Florida University Press, 1984.

Bretherton, Luke. 'Beyond the Emerging Church?' in *Remembering Our Future: Explorations in Deep Church*, ed. A. Walker and L. Bretherton. London: Paternoster Press, 2007.

Brewin, Kester. *The Complex Christ: Signs of Emergence in the Urban Church*. London: SPCK, 2004.

Brewin, Kester. *Other: Loving Self, God and Neighbour in a World of Fractures*. London: Hodder & Stoughton, 2010.

Brewin, Kester. *Mutiny! Why We Love Pirates, And How They Can Save Us*. London: Vaux, 2012.

Bridge, Donald. *Power Evangelism and the Word of God*. Eastbourne: Kingsway Publications, 1987.

Bridger, Francis. *The Diana Phenomenon*. grovepastoral, P75. Cambridge: Grove Books, 1998.

Bruce, Steve. *God Is Dead: Secularization in the West*. Oxford: Blackwell, 2002.

Bruce, Steve. 'The Demise of Christianity in Britain', in *Predicting Religion: Christian, Secular and Alternative Futures*, ed. G. Davie et al. Farnham: Ashgate, 2003.

Brueggemann, Walter. *The Prophetic Imagination*. London: SCM Press, 1992.

Brueggemann, Walter. *The Practice of Prophetic Imagination: Preaching an Emancipating Word*. Minneapolis: Fortress Press, 2012.

Brown, Callum. *The Death of Christian Britain*. London: Routledge, 2000.

Brunner, Emil. *Revelation and Reason: the Christian Doctrine of Faith and Knowledge*, trans. O. Wyon. London: SCM Press, 1947.

Buchanan, Colin. *Is the Church of England Biblical?: An Anglican Ecclesiology*. London: Darton Longman & Todd, 1998.

Campolo, Tony and Brian McLaren. *Adventures in Missing the Point: How the Culture-controlled Church Neutered the Gospel*. Grand Rapids and Cambridge: Zondervan, 2006.

Carson, Donald. *The Gagging of God: Christianity Confronts Pluralism*. Leicester: InterVarsity Press, 1996.

Carson, Donald. *Becoming Conversant with the Emerging Church: Understanding a Movement and its Implications*. Grand Rapids and Cambridge: Zondervan, 2005.

Carson, Donald. *Christ and Culture Revisited*. Grand Rapids and Cambridge: Eerdmans, 2012.

Carter, Grayson. *Anglican Evangelicals: Protestant Secessions from the via Media, c. 1800–1850*. Oxford: Oxford University Press, 2001.

Chapman, Alister. 'Secularisation and the Ministry of John R. W. Stott at All Souls, Langham Place, 1950–1970'. *The Journal of Ecclesiastical History* 56/03 (2005): 496–513.

Clapp, Rodney. *A Peculiar People: the Church as Culture in a Post-Christian Society*. Downers Grove, IL: InterVarsity, 1996.

Cocksworth, Christopher. 'Holding Together: Catholic Evangelical Worship in the Spirit', in *Remembering Our Future: Explorations in Deep Church*, ed. A. Walker and L. Bretherton, London: Paternoster Press, 2007.

Costas, Orlando E. *Christ Outside the Gate*. Maryknoll, NY: Orbis Books, 1984.

Cray, Graham (ed.). *Mission-Shaped Church*. London: Church House Publishing, 2004.

Cray, Graham. 'Focussing Church Life on a Theology of Mission', in *Future of the Parish System: Shaping the Church of England in the 21st Century*, ed. S. Croft, London: Church House Publishing, 2010.

Cray, Graham, Ian Mobsby and Aaron Kennedy (eds). *New Monasticism as Fresh Expression of Church*. Norwich: Canterbury Press, 2011.

Croft, Steven. *Transforming Communities: Re-imagining the Church for the 21st Century*. London: Darton Longman & Todd Ltd, 2002.

Daley, Brian. *The Hope of the Early Church: A Handbook of Patristic Eschatology*. Cambridge: Cambridge University Press, 1991.

De Groot, Kees. 'Three Types of Liquid Religion'. *Implicit Religion* 11/3 (2008): 277–296.

Derrida, Jacques. *Of Grammatology*, trans. G. C. Spivak. Baltimore, MD: Johns Hopkins University Press, 1976.

Devine, Mark. 'The Emerging Church: One Movement – Two Streams', in *Evangelicals Engaging Emergent: A Discussion of the Emergent Church Movement*, ed. W. Henard et al. Nashville: B&H Publishing Group, 2009.

DeYoung, Kevin. 'God is Still Holy and What You Learnt in Sunday School is Still True: A Review of *Love Wins*'. *The Master's Seminary Journal* 23/1 (Spring 2012): 113–131.

Dickens, Charles. *A Tale of Two Cities*. London: Chapman & Hall, 1859.

Doerksen, Paul. 'The Air Is Not Quite Fresh: Emerging Church Ecclesiology'. *Direction: a Mennonite Brethren Forum* 39/1 (Spring 2010): 3–18.

Donovan, Vincent J. *Christianity Rediscovered: An Epistle from the Masai*. London: SCM Press, 1982.

Donnelly, William J. *The Confetti Generation: How the New Communications Technology is Fragmenting America*. New York: Henry Holt, 1986.

Dudley-Smith, Timothy. *John Stott: A Global Ministry*. London: InterVarsity Press, 2001.

Eagleton, Terry. *The Illusions of Postmodernism*. Oxford: Blackwell Publishing, 1996.

Edson, Ben. 'An Exploration into the Missiology of the Emerging Church in the UK through the Narrative of Sanctus1'. *International Journal for the Study of the Christian Church* 6/1 (2006): 24–37.

Effa, Alan. 'Missional Voices Down Under A Canadian Response to the Missiology of Michael Frost and Alan Hirsch'. *Missiology: An International Review* 38/1 (January 2010): 61–73.

Epperly, Bruce G. *Emerging Process*. Cleveland, TN: Parson's Porch Books, 2012. (Kindle Edition)

Epperly, Bruce G. *Process Theology: A Guide for the Perplexed*. London: T&T Clark, 2011.

Erdozain, Dominic. 'Emerging Church: a Victorian Prequel', in *A Great Tradition – A Great Labor: Studies in Ancient-Future Faith*, ed. P. Harrold and D. Williams. Eugene, OR: Wipf & Stock, 2011.

Erickson, Millard J. *Contemporary Options in Eschatology: A Study of the Millenium*. Grand Rapids: Baker Book House, 1977.

Farrow, Douglas. *Ascension Theology*. London: T&T Clark Ltd, 2011.

Fergusson, David and Marcel Sarot (eds). *The Future as God's Gift: Explorations in Christian Eschatology*. London: T&T Clark Ltd, 2000.

Fielder, Geraint. *Lord of the Years*. Leicester: InterVarsity Press, 1988.

Finstuen, Andrew. *Original Sin and Everyday Protestants: the Theology of Reinhold Niebuhr, Billy Graham, and Paul Tillich in an Age of Anxiety*. Chapel Hill: University of North Carolina Press, 2009.

Fitch, David. *The Great Giveaway: Reclaiming the Mission of the Church from Big Business, Parachurch Organizations, Psychotherapy, Consumer Capitalism, and Other Modern Maladies*. Grand Rapids: Baker Books, 2005.

Flett, John G. *The Witness of God: The Trinity Karl Barth, Missio Dei and The Nature of Christian Community*. Grand Rapids: Eerdmans, 2010.

Forde, Gerhard O. 'The Word That Kills and Makes Alive', in *Marks of the Body of Christ*, ed. C. Braaeten and R. Jenson. Grand Rapids and Cambridge: Eerdmans, 1999.

Franke, John. 'Christian Faith and Postmodern Theory', in *Christianity and the Postmodern Turn: Six Views*, ed. M. Penner. Grand Rapids: Brazos, 2005.

Franke, John. *The Character of Theology: An Introduction to Its Nature, Task, and Purpose*. Grand Rapids: Baker Academic, 2005.

Frost, Michael and Alan Hirsch. *The Shaping of Things to Come: Innovation and Mission for the 21st-century Church*. Peabody, MA: Hendrickson Publishers, 2003.

Frykholm, Amy Johnson. *Rapture Culture: Left Behind in Evangelical America*. Oxford and New York: Oxford University Press, 2004.

Gabriel, Ralph H. 'Evangelical Religion and Popular Romanticism and early Nineteenth Century America'. *Church History* 19/1 (1950): 34–47.

Galli, Mark. *God Wins: Heaven, Hell, and Why the Good News Is Better Than Love Wins*. Carol Stream, IL: Tyndale House Publishers, 2011.

Geisler, Norman and William D.Watkins. 'Process Theology: A survey and an Appraisal'. *Themelios* 12/1 (September 1986): 5–15.

Gibbs, Eddie and Ryan Bolger. *Emerging Churches: Creating Christian Communities in Postmodern Cultures*. London: SPCK, 2006.

Green, Michael. *The Message of Matthew: The Kingdom of Heaven*. Downers Grove, IL: InterVarsity Press, 2000.

Green, Michael. *Adventures of Faith: Reflections on Fifty Years of Christian Service*. Harrow: Zondervan, 2002.

Grenz, Stanley J. *A Primer on Postmodernism*. Grand Rapids: Eerdmans, 1996.

Grenz, Stanley J. *Renewing the Center: Evangelical Theology in a Post-Theological Era*. Grand Rapids: Revell, Baker Publishing Group, 2000.

Grenz, Stanley J. 'Articulating the Christian Belief-Mosaic: Theological Method after the Demise of Foundationalism', in *Evangelical Futures: a Conversation on Theological Method*, ed. J. Stackhouse. Grand Rapids: Baker Books, 2000.

Grenz, Stanley J. and John R. Franke. *Beyond Foundationalism: Shaping Theology in a Postmodern Context*. Louisville, KY: Westminster John Knox Press, 2001.

Grenz, Stanley J. *Reason for Hope: The Systematic Theology of Wolfhart Pannenberg*. Maryknoll, NY and Edinburgh: Orbis Books, 2006.

Gribben, Crawford. *Rapture Fiction and the Evangelical Crisis*. Webster, NY: Evangelical Press, 2005.

Gribben, Crawford. *Writing the Rapture: Prophecy Fiction in Evangelical America*. Oxford and New York: Oxford University Press, 2009.

Grudem, Wayne. *Systematic Theology: An Introduction to Biblical Doctrine*. Leicester: InterVarsity Press, 1994.

Guder, Darrell. *The Continuing Conversion of the Church*. Grand Rapids: Eerdmans, 2000.

Guder, Darrell and Lois Barrett. *Missional Church: A Vision for the Sending of the Church in North America*. Grand Rapids: Eerdmans, 1998.

Guder, Darrell. 'Incarnation and the Church's Evangelistic Mission', in *The Study of Evangelism: Exploring a Missional Practice of the Church*, ed. P. Chilcote and L. Warner. Grand Rapids and Cambridge: Eerdmans, 2008.

Guest, Matthew et al. (eds). *Evangelical Identity and Contemporary Culture: A Congregational Study in Innovation*. Milton Keynes: Paternoster, 2007.

Guest, Matthew and Steve Taylor. 'The Post-evangelical Emerging Church; Innovations in New Zealand and the UK'. *International Journal for the Study of the Christian Church* 6/1 (2006): 49–64.

Guinness, O. 'Mission Modernity; Seven Checkpoints on Mission in the Modern World', in *Faith and Modernity*, ed. P. Samson, V. Samuel and C. Sugden. Oxford: Regnum Books International, 1994.

Gunton, Colin and Daniel Hardy (eds). *On Being the Church*. London: T&T Clark, 1989.

Hart, Darryl. *Deconstructing Evangelicalism: Conservative Protestantism in the Age of Billy Graham*. Grand Rapids: Baker Academic, 2004.

Hart, Kevin. *The Trespass of the Sign: Deconstruction, Theology, and Philosophy*. New York: Fordham University Press, 2000.

Hart, T. 'Eschatology and Imagination', *What are We Waiting For? Christian Hope and Contemporary Culture*, ed. S. Holmes and R. Rook. Milton Keynes: Paternoster, 2008.

Hartshorne, Charles. *The Divine Relativity: A Social Conception of God*. New Haven, CT: Yale University Press, 1976.

Harvey, David. *The Condition of Postmodernity: An Enquiry into the Origin of Cultural Change*. Oxford: Blackwells, 1989.

Hatch, Nathan. *The Democratization of American Christianity*. New Haven, CT: Yale University Press, 1989.

Hauerwas, Stanley. *In Good Company: the Church as Polis*. Notre Dame, IN and London: University of Notre Dame Press, 1995.

Hauerwas, Stanley and William Willimon. *Resident Aliens: Life in the Christian Colony*. Nashville: Abingdon Press, 1989.

Healy, Nicholas. *Church, World and the Christian Life: Practical-prophetic Ecclesiology*. Cambridge: Cambridge University Press, 2000.

Helm, Paul. *The Divine Revelation*. London: Marshall Morgan and Scott, 1982.

Hennell, Michael. *John Venn and the Clapham Sect*. Cambridge: Lutterworth Press, 1958.

Hennell, Michael. *William Wilberforce*. Cambridge: Lutterworth Press, 1947.

Hilborn, David, *Picking Up the Pieces: Can Evangelicals Adapt to Contemporary Culture?* London: Hodder & Stoughton, 1997.

Hill, Craig. *In God's Time: The Bible and the Future*. Grand Rapids: Eerdmans, 2002.

Hill, Harriet. 'Incarnational Ministry; A Critical Examination'. *Evangelical Missions Quarterly* 26/2 (April 1990): 196–201.

Hilton, Boyd. *The Age of Atonement*. Oxford: Oxford University Press, 1986.

Hindmarsh, Bruce. 'Is Evangelical Ecclesiology an Oxymoron?', in *Evangelical Ecclesiology: Reality or Illusion*, ed. J. Stackhouse. Grand Rapids: Baker Books, 2003.

Hoedemaker, L. A. 'Hoekendijk's American Years'. *Occasional Bulletin of Missionary Research* (April 1977): 7–10.

Hoekendijk, Hans. 'The Church in Missionary Thinking', *International Review of Missions* 41/3 (July 1952): 324–336.

Holmes, Stephen and Russell Rook (eds). *What Are We Waiting For? Christian Hope and Contemporary Culture*. London: Paternoster, 2008.

Hunsberger, George R. 'Is There Biblical Warrant for Evangelism?', in *Evangelism: Exploring a Missional Practice of the Church*, ed. P. Chilcote and L. Warner. Grand Rapids: Eerdmans, 2008.

Hunsberger, George R. 'Proposals for a missional hermeneutic: mapping a conversation', *Missiology* 39/3 (July 2011): 309–321.

Hunt, Stephen. 'The Emerging Church and its Discontents', *Journal of Beliefs and Values: Studies in Religion and Education* 29/3 (2008): 287–296.

Hunt, Stephen. 'Inhabiting a Space on the Outer Edges of Religious Life; the Radical Emergent Christian Community of Ikon'. *Marburg Journal of Religion* 15 (2010): 1–20.

Hunter, James Davidson. *To Change the World: The Irony, Tragedy and Possibility of Christianity in the Late Modern World*. New York: Oxford University Press, 2010.

Jamieson, Alan. *A Churchless Faith*. London: SPCK, 2002.

Jones, Tony. *Postmodern Youth Ministry: Exploring Cultural Shift, Creating Holistic Connections, Cultivating Authentic Community*. Grand Rapids: Zondervan, 2001.

Jones, Tony. *The New Christians: Dispatches from the Emergent Frontier*. San Francisco: Jossey-Bass, 2008.

Jones, Tony. 'A Hopeful Faith', in *An Emergent Manifesto of Hope*, ed. T. Jones and D. Pagitt. Grand Rapids: Baker Books, 2008.

Jones, Tony. *The Church Is Flat: The Relational Ecclesiology of the Emerging Church Movement*. Minneapolis: The JoPa Group, 2011.

Kimball, Dan. *The Emerging Church: Vintage Christianity for New Generations*. Grand Rapids: Zondervan, 2003.

LaHaye, Tim F. and Jerry Jenkins. *Left Behind: A Novel of the Earth's Last Days*. Carol Stream, IL: Tyndale House Publishers, 1996.

LaHaye, Tim F. and Jerry Jenkins. *Desecration: Antichrist Takes the Throne*. Carol Stream, IL: Tyndale House Publishers, 2002.

LaHaye, Tim F. and Jerry Jenkins. *Kingdom Come: The Final Victory*. Carol Stream, IL: Tyndale House Publishers, 2007.

Langmead, Ross. *The Word Made Flesh: Towards an Incarnational Missiology*. Dallas and Oxford: University Press of America, 2004.

Lewis, C. S. *The Problem of Pain*. London: Harper Collins, 1978.

Lints, Richard. *Renewing the Evangelical Mission*. Grand Rapids: Eerdmans, 2013.

Lloyd, Trevor. *Evangelicals, Obedience and Change*. Bramcote: Grove Books, 1977.

Lohfink, Gerhard. *Jesus and Community: Social Dimension of Christian Faith*. Minneapolis: Augsburg Fortress Publishers, 1984.

Lynch, Gordon. *Understanding Theology and Popular Culture*. Oxford: Blackwell, 2005.

Lyotard, Jean-François. *The Postmodern Condition: A Report on Knowledge*. Minneapolis: University of Minnesota Press, 2010.

MacLaren, Duncan. *Mission Implausible: Restoring Credibility to the Church*. Bletchley: Paternoster, 2004.

Martin, Hugh (ed.). *Christian Social Reformers of the Nineteenth Century*. London: SCM Press, 1927.

McElhannon, Kevin. 'Don't Give up on the Incarnational Model'. *Evangelical Missions Quarterly* 27/4 (October 1991): 390–393.

McGavran, Donald. *The Bridges of God; a Study in the Strategy of Missions*. New York: Friendship Press, 1955.

McGavran, Donald. *How Churches Grow*. New York: Friendship Press, 1966.

McGavran, Donald. *Understanding Church Growth*. Grand Rapids: Eerdmans, 1970.

McGrath, Alister. *Evangelicalism and the Future of Christianity*. London: Hodder & Stoughton, 1994.

McGrath, Alister. *A Passion for Truth: The Intellectual Coherence of Evangelicalism*. Nottingham: Apollos, 1996.

McGrath, Alister. *Christianity's Dangerous Idea: The Protestant Revolution – a History from the Sixteenth Century to the Twenty-first*. New York: Harper One, 2007.

McKnight, Scot. *A Community called Atonement*. Nashville: Abingdon Press, 2007.

McLaren, Brian. *Reinventing Your Church*. Grand Rapids: Zondervan, 1998.

McLaren, Brian. *A New Kind of Christian: A Tale of Two Friends on a Spiritual Journey*. San Francisco: Jossey Bass, 2001.

McLaren, Brian. *The Church on the Other Side: Doing Ministry in the Postmodern Matrix*. Grand Rapids: Zondervan, 2002.

McLaren, Brian. *A Generous Orthodoxy: Why I Am a Missional, Evangelical, Post/Protestant, Liberal/Conservative, Mystical/Poetic, Biblical, Charismatic/Contemplative . . . Emergent, Unfinished Christian*. Grand Rapids: Zondervan, 2006.

McLaren, Brian. *A Search for What Is Real*. Grand Rapids: Zondervan, 2007.

McLaren, Brian. *Everything Must Change: Jesus, Global Crises, and a Revolution of Hope*. Nashville: Thomas Nelson Inc, 2008.

McLaren, Brian. *The Last Word and the Word After That: A Tale of Faith, Doubt, and a New Kind of Christianity*. New York: John Wiley & Sons, 2008.

McLaren, Brian. *Finding Our Way Again: The Return of the Ancient Practices*. Nashville: Thomas Nelson Inc, 2008.

McLaren, Brian. *More Ready Than You Realize: The Power of Everyday Conversations*. Grand Rapids: Zondervan, 2009.

McLaren, Brian. *The Secret Message of Jesus: Uncovering the Truth That Could Change Everything.* Nashville: Thomas Nelson, 2012.

McLaren, Brian. *A New Kind of Christianity: Ten Questions That Are Transforming the Faith.* London: Hodder & Stoughton, 2010.

McLaren, Brian. *The Word of the Lord to Evangelicals.* (Kindle edition). Brentwood TN: Creative Trust Digital, 2012.

Moltmann, Jürgen. *The Spirit of Life: A Universal Affirmation.* London: SCM, 1992.

Moltmann, Jürgen. *The Church in the Power of the Spirit: A Contribution to Messianic Ecclesiology.* London: SCM, 1981.

Moltmann, Jürgen. *Sun of Righteousness, Arise!: God's Future for Humanity and the Earth.* London: SCM Press, 2010.

Moluf, Robert. *The Whiteheadean Foundation of Process Theology: A Philosophical Critique.* Washington DC: Open Source Faith, 2013.

Morris, Leon. *The Gospel According to Matthew.* Leicester: Inter-Varsity Press, 1992.

Murray, Iain H. *Evangelicalism Divided: A Record of Crucial Change in the Years 1950 to 2000.* Edinburgh: The Banner of Truth Trust, 2000.

Murray, Stuart. *Post-Christendom.* Carlisle: Paternoster, 2004.

Murray, Stuart. *Church After Christendom.* London: Paternoster Press, 2005.

Newbigin, Lesslie. 'Cross Currents in Ecumenical and Evangelical Understandings of Mission'. *International Bulletin of Missionary Research* 6/4 (October 1982): 146–152.

Newbigin, Lesslie. *The Gospel in a Pluralist Society.* London: SPCK, 1989.

Newbigin, Lesslie. *The Household of God.* London: Paternoster Press, 1998.

Newbigin, Lesslie. *The Open Secret: Sketches for a Missionary Theology.* London: SPCK, 1978.

Newbigin, Lesslie. *Trinitarian Doctrine for Today's Mission.* Carlisle: Paternoster Press, 1998.

Newbigin, Lesslie. *Truth and Authority in Modernity.* Valley Forge PA: Trinity Press International, 1996.

Niebuhr, Richard. *Christ and Culture.* London: Harper Collins, 2002.

Noll, Mark. *A History of Christianity in the United States and Canada*. Grand Rapids and Cambridge: Eerdmans, 1992.

Noll, Mark. *Turning Points: Decisive Moments in the History of Christianity*. Leicester: InterVarsity Press, 1998.

Noll, Mark. *The Rise of Evangelicalism: the Age of Edwards, Whitefield and the Wesleys*. Nottingham: InterVarsity Press, 2004.

Oden, Patrick. 'An Emerging Pneumatology: Jurgen Moltmann and the Emerging Church in Conversation'. *Journal of Pentecostal Theology* 18/2 (2009): 263–284.

Oden, Thomas. *Two Worlds: Notes on the Death of Modernity in Russia and America*. Downers Grove IL: InterVarsity Press, 1992.

Overton, John. *The English Church in the Nineteenth Century (1800–1833)*. London: Longmans, Green & Co., 1894.

Pagitt, Doug. *Reimagining Spiritual Formation: A Week in the Life of an Experimental Church*. Grand Rapids and Cambridge: Zondervan, 2004.

Pagitt, Doug. *Church Re-imagined: The Spiritual Formation of People in Communities of Faith*. Grand Rapids: Zondervan, 2005.

Pagitt, Doug. 'The Emerging Church and Embodied Theology', in *Listening to the Beliefs of Emerging Churches: Five Perspectives*, ed. R. Webber. Grand Rapids: Zondervan, 2007.

Pagitt, Doug. *A Christianity Worth Believing: Hope-filled, Open-armed, Alive-and-well Faith for the Left Out, Left Behind, and let Down in Us All*. New York: John Wiley & Sons, 2008.

Pagitt, Doug. *Preaching in the Inventive Age*. Minneapolis: Sparkhouse Press, 2011.

Pagitt, Doug. 'Response to John Burke', in *Listening to the Beliefs of Emerging Churches: Five Perspectives*, ed. R. Webber. Grand Rapids: Zondervan, 2009.

Pederson, S. G. 'Hannah More meets Simple Simon: Tracts, chapbooks and popular culture in late eighteenth-century England'. *The Journal of British Studies* 1/25 (January 1986): 84–113.

Percy, Martin. 'A Place at High Table? Assessing the Future of Charismatic Christianity', in *Predicting Religion: Christian, Secular and Alternative Futures* ed. G. Davie et al. Farnham: Ashgate, 2003.

Perriman, Andrew. *The Coming of the Son of Man: New Testament Eschatology for an Emerging Church*. London: Paternoster Press, 2005.

Perriman, Andrew. *Re:Mission Biblical Mission for a Postbiblical Church*. London: Paternoster Press, 2007.

Perriman, Andrew. *Hell and Heaven in Narrative Perspective*. Perriman: Postost, 2011. (Kindle Edition)

Philipps, Timothy R. and Dennis L. Okholm (eds), *Christian Apologetics in the Postmodern World*. Downers Grove, IL: InterVarsity Press, 1995.

Pittenger, Norman. *The Lure of Divine Love. Human Experience and Christian Faith in a Process Perspective*. New York: The Pilgrim Press, 1979.

Pollock, John. *The Cambridge Seven: A Fire in China*. London: InterVarsity Press, 1996.

Price, Lucien (ed.). *Dialogues of Alfred North Whitehead*. New York: Mentor Books, 1956.

Rah, Soong-Chan. *The Next Evangelicalism: Releasing the Church from Western Cultural Captivity*. Leicester: InterVarsity Press, 2009.

Rauschenbusch, Walter. *Christianity and The Social Crisis in the Twenty First Century* (100th Anniversary Edition). New York: Harper Collins, 2007.

Richardson, Rick. 'Emerging Missional Movements: An Overview and Assessment of Some Implications for Mission(s)'. *International Bulletin of Mission Research* 37/3 (2013): 131–136.

Roberts, Kyle B. 'Locating Popular Religion in the Evangelical Tract: The Roots and Routes of The Dairyman's Daughter', *Early American Studies: An Interdisciplinary Journal* 4.1 (2006): 233–270.

Rollins, Peter. *How (Not) to Speak of God*. London: SPCK, 2006.

Rollins, Peter. 'Biting the hand that feeds: an apology for encouraging tension between the established church and emerging collectives', in *Evaluating Fresh Expressions: Explorations in Emerging Church*, ed. L. Nelstrop and M. Percy. Norwich: Canterbury Press, 2008.

Rollins, Peter. *Insurrection: To Believe Is Human; to Doubt, Divine*. London: Hodder & Stoughton, 2011.

Rollins, Peter. *The Idolatry of God: Breaking Our Addiction to Certainty and Satisfaction*. London: Hodder & Stoughton, 2013.

Ross, Cathy and Andrew Walls. *Mission in the 21st Century: Exploring the Five Marks of Mission*. London: Darton Longman & Todd, 2008.

Russell, G. W. E. *The Household of Faith*. London: A. R. Mowbray & Co., 1913.

Russell, G. W. E. *A Short History of the Evangelical Movement*. London: A. R. Mowbray & Co., 1915.

Sanneh, Lamin. *Translating the Message: The Missionary Impact on Culture*. Maryknoll, NY: Orbis Books, 1992.

Saunders, Martin. 'Profile: Graham Cray'. *Christianity Magazine*, November 2009.

Stackhouse, Ian. *The Gospel-driven Church: Retrieving Classical Ministry for Contemporary Revivalism*. Carlisle: Paternoster Press, 2004.

Stackhouse, Ian. 'God's Transforming Presence: Spirit Empowered Worship', in *Mission-shaped Questions: Defining Issues for Today's Church*, ed. S. Croft. London: Church House Publishing, 2008.

Stackhouse, John (ed.). *Evangelical Ecclesiology: Reality or Illusion?* Grand Rapids: Baker Academic, 2003.

Smith, David. *Transforming the World? The Social Impact of British Evangelicalism*. Carlisle: Paternoster, 1998.

Smith, James K. A. *Who's Afraid of Postmodernism?: Taking Derrida, Lyotard, and Foucault to Church*. Grand Rapids: Baker Academic, 2006.

Sproul, R. C., John Gerstner and Arthur Lindsley. *Classical Apologetics: A Rational Defense of the Christian Faith and a Critique of Presuppositional Apologetics*. Grand Rapids: Zondervan, 1984.

Stetzer, Ed. 'A Missiological Perspective', in *Evangelicals Engaging Emergent: A Discussion of the Emergent Church Movement*, ed. W. Henard et al. Grand Rapids and Cambridge: B&H Publishing Group, 2009.

Stewart, Robert (ed.). *The Resurrection of Jesus: John Dominic Crossan and N. T. Wright in Dialogue*. Minneapolis: Augsburg Fortress, 2005.

Stott, John. *The Preacher's Portrait*. London: Tyndale Press, 1961.

Stott, John. *The Lausanne Covenant: an Exposition and Commentary*. London: Scripture Union for the Lausanne Committee for World Evangelization, 1979.

Stott, John. *Issues Facing Christians Today*. Basingstoke: Marshalls, 1984.

Stott, John. *The Cross of Christ*. Leicester: InterVarsity Press, 1986.

Stott, John. *The Contemporary Christian*. Leicester: InterVarsity Press, 1992.

Sweet, Leonard. *Post-Modern Pilgrims: First Century Passion for the 21st Century World*. Nashville: Broadman & Holman Publishers, 2000.

Sweet, Leonard. *Soul Tsunami: Sink or Swim in New Millennium Culture*. Grand Rapid: Zondervan, 2001.

Sweet, Leonard, Brian McLaren and Jerry Haselmayer. *A Is for Abductive: The Language of the Emerging Church*. Grand Rapids and Cambridge: Zondervan, 2003.

Tate, A. W. 'Evangelical Certainty: Charles Spurgeon's "Calls to the Unconverted"', in *Reinventing Christianity: Nineteenth-century Contexts*, ed. Linda Woodhead. Farnham: Ashgate, 2001.

Thompson, John. *Modern Trinitarian Perspectives*. New York and Oxford: Oxford University Press, 1994.

Tickle, Phyllis. *The Great Emergence: How Christianity Is Changing and Why*. Grand Rapids: Baker Books, 2008.

Tickle, Phyllis. *Emergence Christianity: What It Is, Where It Is Going, and Why It Matters*. Grand Rapids: Baker Books, 2012.

Tilby, Angela. 'What Questions Does Catholic Ecclesiology Pose for Contemporary Mission and Fresh Expression?', in *Mission-shaped Questions: Defining Issues for Today's Church*. ed. S. Croft. London: Church House Publishing, 2008.

Till, Rupert. 'The Nine O'clock Service: Mixing Club Culture And Postmodern Christianity'. *Culture and Religion* 7/1 (2006): 93–110.

Tomlin, Graham. 'Can We Develop Churches That Can Transform the Culture?' In *Mission-shaped Questions: Defining Issues for Today's Church*, ed. S. Croft. London: Church House Publishing, 2008.

Tomlinson, Dave. *The Post-evangelical*. London: Triangle, 1995.

Tomlinson, Dave. *Re-enchanting Christianity*. Norwich: Canterbury Press, 2008.

Torrance, Thomas Forsyth. *The Trinitarian Faith*. London; New York: Continuum, 1993.

Torrance, Thomas Forsyth. *The Christian Doctrine of God, One Being Three Persons*. Edinburgh: T&T Clark, 1996.

Torrance, Thomas Forsyth and Robert Walker (eds). *Incarnation: The Person and Life of Christ*. Nottingham: InterVarsity Press, 2008.

Torrance, Thomas Forsyth and Robert Walker (eds). *Atonement: The Person and Work of Christ*. London: Paternoster, 2010.

Travis, Stephen. *I Believe in the Second Coming of Jesus*. London: Hodder & Stoughton, 1988.

Urwin, Lindsay. 'What Is the Role of Sacramental Ministry in Fresh Expressions of Church?', in *Mission-shaped Questions: Defining Issues for Today's Church*, ed. S. Croft's. London: Church House Publishing, 2008.

Vanhoozer, Kevin. *Is There a Meaning in This Text?: the Bible, the Reader, and the Morality of Literary Knowledge*. Leicester: Apollos, 1998.

Vanhoozer, Kevin. 'Pilgrim's Digress: Christian Thinking on and About the Post/Modern Way', in *Christianity and the Postmodern Turn: Six Views*, ed. M. Penner. Grand Rapids: Brazos, 2005.

Vanhoozer, Kevin (ed.). *The Cambridge Companion to Postmodern Theology*. Cambridge: Cambridge University Press, 2003.

Volf, Miroslav. *After Our Likeness: Church as the Image of the Trinity*. Grand Rapids and Cambridge: Eerdmans, 1998.

Walker, Andrew. 'Recovering Deep Church: Theological and Spiritual Renewal' in *Remembering Our Future: Explorations in Deep Church*, ed. A. Walker and L. Bretherton. London: Paternoster Press, 2007.

Walker, Andrew. *Restoring the Kingdom: The Radical Christianity of the House Church Movement*. Guildford: Eagle, 1998.

Walker, Andrew and Luke Bretherton (eds). *Remembering Our Future: Explorations in Deep Church*. London: Paternoster Press, 2007.

Walls, Andrew. 'The Gospel as Prisoner and Liberator of Culture', in *Landmark Essays in Mission and World Christianity*, ed. R. Gallagher and P. Hertig. Maryknoll, NY: Orbis Books, 2009.

Ward, Pete. *Selling Worship: How What We Sing has Changed the Church*. London: Paternoster Press, 2006.

Warner, Rob. *Reinventing English Evangelicalism, 1966–2001: A Theological and Sociological Study*. Milton Keynes: Paternoster, 2007.

Warren, Rick. *The Purpose Driven Life: What on Earth Am I Here For?* Grand Rapids: Zondervan, 2002.

Webber, Robert E. *Ancient-future Faith: Rethinking Evangelicalism for a Postmodern World*. Grand Rapids: Baker Academic, 1999.

Webber, Robert E. *The Younger Evangelicals: Facing the Challenges of the New World*. Grand Rapids: Baker Books, 2002.

Webber, Robert E. *Ancient-future Evangelism: Making Your Church a Faith-forming Community*. Grand Rapids: Baker Books, 2003.

Webber, Robert E. (ed.) *Listening to the Beliefs of Emerging Churches: Five Perspectives*. Grand Rapids: Zondervan, 2007.

Wells, David F. *Above All Earthly Pow'rs: Christ in a Postmodern World*. Grand Rapids and Cambridge: Eerdmans, 2005.

Wells, David F. *God in the Wasteland: Reality of Truth in a World of Fading Dreams*. Leicester: InterVarsity Press, 1994.

Wells, David F. *No Place for Truth, or, Whatever Happened to Evangelical Theology?* Grand Rapids: Eerdmans, 1993.

Wells, David F. *The Courage to Be Protestant: Truth-lovers, Marketers, and Emergents in the Postmodern World*. Grand Rapids and Cambridge: Eerdmans, 2008.

Wells, David F. *The Person of Christ: A Biblical and Historical Analysis of the Incarnation*. Westchester, IL: Crossway Books, 1984.

Whitehead, Alfred North. *Process and Reality: An Essay in Cosmology: Gifford lectures delivered in the University of Edinburgh during the session 1927–28*, ed. David Ray Griffin and Donald W. Sherburne. (Corrected edition). New York: The Free Press, 1978.

Wilberforce, William. *A Practical View of the Prevailing Religious System of Professed Christians in the Higher and Middle Classes in this Country, Contrasted with Real Christianity*. London: T. Cadell, 1830.

Williams, Daniel Day. *Retrieving the Tradition and Renewing Evangelicalism*. Grand Rapids and Cambridge: Eerdmans, 1999.

Williams, Rowan. *On Christian Theology*. Oxford: Blackwell Publishers, 1999.

Wolffe, John. *The Expansion of Evangelicalism; The Age of Wilberforce, More, Chalmers and Finney*. Leicester: InterVarsity Press, 2006.

Wright, Christopher J. *Knowing Jesus through the Old Testament*. Oxford: Monarch Books, 2005.

Wright, N. T. *Jesus and the Victory of God*. London: SPCK, 1996.

Wright, N. T. *The Challenge of Jesus*. London: SPCK, 2000.

Wright, N. T. *Surprised by Hope*. London: SPCK, 2011.

Yates, Timothy Edward. *Christian Mission in the Twentieth Century*. Cambridge: Cambridge University Press, 1994.

Yoder, John Howard. 'How H. Richard Niebuhr Reasoned: a Critique of "Christ and Culture"', in *Authentic Transformation: a New Vision of Christ and Culture*, ed. G. Stassen et al. Nashville: Abingdon Press, 1996.

Zahl et al., *Exploring the Worship Spectrum*, ed. P. A. Basden. Grand Rapids: Zondervan, 2004.

Web sources

Bashir, Martin. *Bishop's Heaven: Is there life after the Afterlife?* http://abcnews.go.com/Nightline/FaithMatters/story?id=4330823&page=1

Benedict XVI, Pope. *Westminster Hall Address*, http://www.telegraph.co.uk/news/religion/the-pope/8009884/Pope-visit-Pope-Benedict-XVI-rails-against-marginalisation-of-religion.html

Bey, Hakim. *Part 3 – T. A. Z.: The Temporary Autonomous Zone, Ontological Anarchy, Poetic Terrorism*. Hermetic Library. http://hermetic.com/bey/taz3.html#labelTAZ

Billings, Todd. 'The Problem with 'Incarnational Ministry': What If Our Mission Is Not to 'Be Jesus' to Other Cultures, but to Join with the Holy Spirit?' *Christianity Today*. July 2012. http://www.christianitytoday.com/ct/2012/july-august/the-problem-with-incarnational-ministry.html

Brewin, Kester. *In Defence of Pirates*. http://www.kesterbrewin.com /wordpress/wp-content/uploads/2010/08/In-Defence-of-Pirates.pdf

Brewin, Kester. *Pancake and Carnivals: Fools and Dirty Revolutions*. http://www.kesterbrewin.com/2013/02/06/pancakes-and -carnivals-fools-and-dirty-revolutions/

Brewin, Kester. *The Complex Christ / Signs of Emergence*. e-Edition http://www.kesterbrewin.com/2013/07/01/e-edition-of-the -complex-christ-signs-of-emergence

Buckeridge, John. 'Profile: Brian McLaren'. *Christianity Magazine*, April 2009. https://www.premierchristianity.com/Past-Issues /2009/April-2009/Profile-Brian-McLaren

Chandler, Russell. 'Customer Poll Shapes a Church: A Minister Discovered Why People Don't Attend'. *Los Angeles Times*. 11 December 1989. http://articles.latimes.com/1989-12-11/news/mn -126_1_willow-creek

Chester, Tim. *Why I Don't Believe in Incarnational Mission*. http:// timchester.wordpress.com/2008/07/19/why-i-dont-believe-in -incarnational-mission

Chester, Tim. *The Homogenous Unit Principle*. http://timchester. wordpress.com/2006/12/08/the-homogeneous-unit-principle/

Church of England, *Authorization, Preface, and Declaration of Assent*. http://www.churchofengland.org/prayer-worship/worship /texts/mvcontents/preface.aspx

Clark, Jason. *Reflection*. http://www.emergingchurch.info/reflection /jasonclark/index.htm

Clark, Jason. *Beyond the Emerging Church*. http://deepchurch .org.uk/2008/09/24/beyond-the-emerging-church/

Graham, Billy. 'The 2005 Time 100. Heroes and Icons: John Stott'. *Time Magazine*, 18 April 2005. http://www.time.com/time/specials /packages/article.html

Jones, Tony. *Lonnie Frisbee and the Non Demise of the Emerging Church*. http://blog.tonyj.net/2009/12/lonnie-frisbee-and-the-non -demise-of-the-emerging-church/

Keller Tim. *In Defense of Apologetics*. http://thegospelcoalition. org/blogs/tgc/2012/08/05/in-defense-of-apologetics/

Keller Tim. *Late Modern or Post Modern?* http://www.thegospelco- alition.org/blogs/tgc/2010/10/06/late-modern-or-postmodern/

Keller, Tim. *The Missional Church*. http://download.redeemer. com/pdf/learn/resources/Missional_Church-Keller.pdf

Kimball, Dan. *Out of Ur: Dan Kimball's Missional Misgivings*. http:// www.outofur.com/archives/2008/12/dan_kimballs_mi.html

Kimball, Dan. *The Emerging Church*. http://www.dankimball. com/vintage_faith/2008/09/the-emerging-ch.html

Kwon, Lillian. 'Willow Creek Sets Record Straight on Mission Focus'. *Christian Today*. http://www.christiantoday.com/article /willow.creek.sets.record.straight.on.mission.focus/

Laarman, Peter. 'Towards a Non-Malignant Faith: An Interview with Brian McLaren'. *Religion Dispatches*. http://religiondispatches.org /toward-a-non-malignant-faith-an-interview-with-brian-mclaren/

Marrapodi, Eric. *Christian Author's Book Sparks Charges of Heresy*. CNN Belief blog. March 1st 2011. http://religion.blogs.cnn.com /2011/03/01/what-is-a-heretic-exactly-in-the-evangelical-church/

McCaughan, Pat. *Alternative Worship 'pops up' in Portland, Oregon, for Advent*. http://episcopaldigitalnetwork.com/ens/2011/12/12/ alternative-worship-pops-up-in-portland-oregon-for-advent/

McCracken, Matthew. *Pirates and Prodigals – with Kester Brewin, Pete Rollins and Barry Taylor*. http://matthewgmccracken.word press.com/2012/11/27/pirates-and-prodigals-a-conversation -in-radical-theology-from-kester-brewin-peter-rollins-and-barry -taylor/

McKnight, Scot. 'Five Streams of the Emerging Church'. *Christianity Today*. http://www.christianitytoday.com/ct/2007/ february/11.35.html

McKnight, Scot. 'The Ironic Faith of Emergents: McLaren Shows Us Not Only Where 'Post-evangelicals' are Going, but Also How They Get There.' *Christianity Today*. September 2008. http:// www.christianitytoday.com/ct/2008/september/39.62.html

McLaren, Brian. *Making Eschatology Personal*. http://www.pres- ence.tv/making-eschatology-personal-what-is-judgment-bri- an-mclaren/

McLaren, Brian. *Q & R: Really, Resurrection?* http://brianmc- laren.net/q-r-really-resurrection/ McLaren, Brian. *Extended Interview*. http://www.pbs.org/wnet/religionandethics/episodes/ july-15-2005/brian-McLaren-extended-interview/11774/

McLaren, Brian. *A Good Man has Walked Among Us*. http://brian mclaren.net/a-good-man-has-walked-among-us/

Olsen, Roger E. 'Is the emerging/emergent church movement (ECM) a real movement?' *Patheos*. http://www.patheos.com/blogs/rogereolson/2011/08/is-the-emergingemergent-church-movement-ecm-a-real-movement

Perriman, Andrew. 'An Incarnational Missiology for the Emerging Church'. *Collaborative Theology for the Emerging Church*. http://www.opensourcetheology.net/node/1116

Perriman, Andrew. 'NT Imminence of Parousia'. *Collaborative Theology for the Emerging Church*. http://www.opensource-theology.net/node/493

Piper, John. *Farewell Rob Bell*. 26th February 2011. https://twitter.com/JohnPiper/status/

Sellars, Simon. *Hakim Bey: Repopulating the Temporary Autonomous Zone*. http://www.simonsellars.com/hakim-bey-repopulating-the-temporary-autonomous-zone

Tuama, Padraig O. 'Take a Second to Unravel'. *Ikon*. http://ikon-belfast.wordpress.com/2007/09/01/take-a-second-to-unravel/

Wardrop, Murray. *Michael Jackson*. http://www.telegraph.co.uk/culture/music/michael-jackson/5656181/Michael-Jackson-the-best-of-the-tributes.html

Wright, N. T. 'Farewell to the Rapture'. *Bible Review*, August 2001. http://ntwrightpage.com/2016/07/12/farewell-to-the-rapture/

Subject and Name Index